M000306464

# Making Foreigners

This book reconceptualizes the history of U.S. immigration and citizenship law from the colonial period to the beginning of the twenty-first century by joining the histories of immigrants to those of Native Americans, blacks, women, Asian Americans, Latino Americans, and the poor. Kunal Parker argues that during the earliest stages of American history, being legally constructed as a foreigner, along with being subjected to restrictions on presence and movement, was not confined to those who sought to enter the country from the outside, but was also used against those on the inside. Insiders thus shared important legal disabilities with outsiders. It is only over the course of four centuries, with the spread of formal and substantive citizenship among the domestic population, a hardening distinction between citizen and alien, and the rise of a powerful centralized state, that the uniquely disabled legal subject we recognize today as the immigrant has emerged. This book advances new ways of understanding the relationship between foreignness and subordination over the long span of American history.

Kunal M. Parker is a Professor of Law and Dean's Distinguished Scholar at the University of Miami School of Law. His first book, *Common Law, History, and Democracy in America, 1790–1900: Legal Thought before Modernism*, was published by Cambridge University Press in 2011.

# Making Foreigners

## Immigration and Citizenship Law in America, 1600–2000

**KUNAL M. PARKER**

*Professor of Law*
*University of Miami School of Law*

CAMBRIDGE
UNIVERSITY PRESS

# CAMBRIDGE
## UNIVERSITY PRESS

University Printing House, Cambridge CB2 8BS, United Kingdom

One Liberty Plaza, 20th Floor, New York, NY 10006, USA

477 Williamstown Road, Port Melbourne, VIC 3207, Australia

4843/24, 2nd Floor, Ansari Road, Daryaganj, Delhi - 110002, India

79 Anson Road, #06-04/06, Singapore 079906

Cambridge University Press is part of the University of Cambridge.

It furthers the University's mission by disseminating knowledge in the pursuit of education, learning and research at the highest international levels of excellence.

www.cambridge.org
Information on this title: www.cambridge.org/9781107698512

First published 2015

*A catalogue record for this publication is available from the British Library*

*Library of Congress Cataloging in Publication data*
Kunal M. Parker, 1968–
Making foreigners : immigration and citizenship law in America,
1600–2000 / Kunal M. Parker, Professor of Law, University of
Miami School of Law.
pages   cm. – (New histories of american law)
Includes bibliographical references and index.
ISBN 978-1-107-03021-3 (hardback) –
ISBN 978-1-107-69851-2 (pbk.)
1. Citizenship – United States – History.   2. Emigration and immigration
law – United States – History.   I. Title.
KF4700.P39   2015
342.7308′2–dc23          2015005349

ISBN 978-1-107-03021-3 Hardback
ISBN 978-1-107-69851-2 Paperback

# Contents

# Preface and Acknowledgments

The special powerlessness of the immigrant has its source, we are wont to think, in the fact that the foreigner comes from elsewhere. The foreigner's origins outside the community supposedly make it possible and permissible for the community to deny his or her claims upon it. An entrenched constitutional tradition in the United States undergirds this view. Political theorists have offered elaborate arguments defending it.

My own particular experience of the powerlessness of the immigrant seeking admission led me to wonder exactly what it is about an individual's coming from elsewhere that makes it possible to deny his or her claims on the community. I turned to the archives, if not for definitive answers, then at least for ways to transcend my own experience by learning about the experiences of others. What I discovered was that the experience of foreignness – and of the powerlessness associated with it – has never been unique to those coming from outside the United States. Over the centuries, Americans have named and treated like foreigners not only immigrants from outside the country, but also Native Americans, blacks, Latino Americans, Asian Americans, women, the poor, and political minorities. Designation as foreign is not a function of coming from the territorial outside. It is a political strategy that has been used inside *and* outside the country and to multiple ends.

The *Making Foreigners* of the title of this book focuses attention on the multiple processes of rendering foreign that have been at work vis-à-vis outsiders *and* insiders over the long span of American history. On the one hand, it is an exhortation to immigrants to recognize the parallels between their experiences and the experiences of those "on the inside." On the other hand, it is an exhortation to those "on the inside" to recognize the foreigners they have once been (and might still be) so as to rethink their relationship to those "on the outside." In this vein, as I see it, the cover image – a stark photograph of a room at San Francisco's Angel Island immigration station – deconstructs notions of "inside" and "outside" insofar as the room likely served not only for the exclusion of outsiders, but also for the ejection of insiders. As I will argue in this book, if the former was the experience of Asian immigrants, the latter could be the experience of Asian Americans.

*Making Foreigners* is intended to be a *concise* work covering four centuries of U.S. immigration and citizenship law. Accordingly, even as it builds upon the work of multiple scholars, it is deliberately very lightly footnoted. The reader is urged to consult the bibliographic essay at the end of the book for a guide to the sources and literatures I have relied upon.

If the history recounted in *Making Foreigners* can be dark, my opportunity to thank those who have helped me in the writing of this book fills me with elation. First and foremost, I wish to thank an extraordinary (and extraordinarily generous) group of friends and scholars who took the time to read an earlier version of the manuscript in its entirety and to offer me extensive, engaged, and pointed comments. David Abraham, Linda Bosniak, Charlton Copeland, David Fitzgerald, Jon Goldberg-Hiller, Tracy Devine Guzmán, David Johnson, Anil Kalhan, Linda Kerber, Erika Lee, Renisa Mawani, Mae Ngai, Aziz Rana, Rebecca Sharpless, Stephen Siegel, and Barbara Welke all gave me written or oral comments that have made this a far stronger book than it was before they looked at it. Renisa Mawani, Charlton Copeland, Tracy Devine Guzmán, and Barbara Welke went even further: they had endless conversations about the manuscript with me, read earlier and later versions, helped with title and cover image choices, and talked me through the glitches. Tracy in particular devoted valuable time she could not possibly have had to helping me with a Spanish translation of a talk based on the book and ended up doing an entire translation of the talk herself. To Renisa, Charlton, Tracy, and Barbara: my most profound thanks. I recognize what you have done for me and hope to repay you in kind soon. Jim Caras also gets special thanks for hearing me out repeatedly as the book neared completion.

Other friends and colleagues with whom I discussed ideas in or about the book, or who looked at parts of the manuscript, or who served as commentators on presentations drawn from the book are Kathryn Abrams, David Ambaras, Susan Bandes, Al Brophy, Bettye Collier-Thomas, George Cozonis, Laura Edwards, Mary Anne Franks, Shannon Gayk, Stephen Halsey, Isabel Jaramillo, Daniel Kanstroom, Clayton Koppes, Sophia Lee, Lisa Levenstein, Patricia McCoy, Bernadette Meyler, Jessica Morris, Brenna Munro, Ileana Porras, Jedediah Purdy, Lucy Salyer, Christopher Schmidt, Camille Serchuk, Yasmin Solomonescu, Karen Tani, Allison Brownell Tirres, Lea Vandervelde, Leti Volpp, and Nan Woodruff.

I would also like to thank the editors of the *New Histories of American Law* series, Michael Grossberg and Christopher Tomlins, as well as the outside readers for Cambridge University Press, for their comments. Chris has been a good friend, supporter, and collaborator for many years. He has always been available to answer questions along the way and has done so with alacrity and insight. Debbie Gershenowitz, Dana Bricken, and Diane Aronson at Cambridge University Press in New York offered comments and shepherded the book through the production process. Mary Becker and the team at Newgen provided excellent copyediting and production services. I would also like to express my profound appreciation to Dean Patricia White and the University of Miami School of Law for valuable research support and significant funding for conferences, research assistants, and research and writing time. In Miami, my research assistants over the years (Zachary Hammond, Eamon Welch, Christina Margolles, and Adam Weiss), my assistant Tara Lora, and Barbara Cuadras and Nery Ruiz at the library provided essential help. This book was completed during a year's leave at the National Humanities Center in Research Triangle Park, North Carolina. I am grateful to the National Humanities Center for providing me a congenial environment in which to bring this project to a close. At the Center, Karen Carroll provided invaluable copyediting help, and Brooke Andrade and Sarah Harris accommodated my book and article requests unhesitatingly.

I have presented versions of this book at multiple venues: the University of Minnesota Law School, Duke Law School, the National Humanities Center, Wake Forest University, Cleveland-Marshall College of Law, Oberlin College, the American Legal History Annual Meeting, the University of Iowa College of Law, the Law and Society Annual Meeting, the Universidad de los Andes, the Chicago Legal History Roundtable, and Cornell Law School. I would like to thank audiences at each of these venues for their questions and comments.

Finally, I would like to thank my family. Special thanks to my mother, Nanda Parker, for telephonic and electronic support and occasional prodding to get this book done.

# I

# Introduction

## Introduction

Over the centuries, prominent American thinkers have joined America's self-image as a nation of immigrants to its self-image as a universal nation founded upon abstract values. In *Common Sense* (1776), just as Americans were beginning their struggle to break with Great Britain, Thomas Paine triumphantly declared America "an asylum for mankind," a refuge for the entire human species.[1] In his novel *Redburn* (1849), published during the years of mass migration from Northwestern Europe, Herman Melville made the link in even more grandiose terms, declaring that, as a result of immigration, "American blood" was "the blood of the whole world," even as Americans were "the heirs of all time."[2] In the late nineteenth and early twentieth centuries, as the country experienced even greater migration from all over Europe, as well as from Asia and the Americas, thinkers again emphasized the link between immigration and universalism. Emma Lazarus's widely celebrated poem, "The New Colossus" (1883), written to celebrate the Statue of Liberty, announced a "world-wide welcome" for "huddled masses yearning to breathe free."[3] Israel Zangwill's play

[1] Thomas Paine, "Common Sense" (1776), in Philip S. Foner, ed., *The Life and Major Writings of Thomas Paine* (New York: Citadel Press, 1945), p. 31.

[2] Herman Melville, *Redburn, His First Voyage* (Evanston, IL: Northwestern University Press, 1969) (1849), p. 169.

[3] Emma Lazarus, "The New Colossus" (1883), in *Emma Lazarus: Selections from Her Poetry and Prose* (New York: Book League, 1947), pp. 40–41.

*The Melting Pot* (1908) hailed America's ability to absorb immigrants effortlessly from many different nations, even as the play's title secured a permanent place in the everyday American lexicon.[4] In the post–World War II period, with a keen eye on Cold War politics, presidential hopeful John F. Kennedy wrote *A Nation of Immigrants* (1958), a book that struck the same note, joining immigration and universal values as the logic of American history.[5]

This powerful strand of American thinking that has linked immigration, openness, and universalism as the very ontology of the country finds confirmation in brute numbers. From the early nineteenth century to the early twentieth, the United States received three-fifths of all the world's immigrants. The country remained the world's largest immigrant-receiving country throughout the twentieth century. In the early decades of the twenty-first, the United States continues to admit over a million immigrants annually to permanent residence, more than the number admitted by any other country. In fiscal year 2011, for example, the United States admitted 1,062,040 non-citizens to legal permanent resident (LPR) status and granted asylum to 24,988.

The United States' openness to immigrants has not been restricted to opening its territory to them. Throughout its history as an independent nation, the country has adopted citizenship laws that have been liberal relative to those of most other countries. Since the early nineteenth century, immigrants have been able to apply to become citizens after only five years of residence. This has greatly facilitated their quick incorporation into the polity. In the nineteenth century, land policies and voting laws granted immigrants valuable economic and political privileges even before they became citizens. If in the early twenty-first century the United States no longer grants immigrants suffrage rights or lands, it continues to facilitate their access to citizenship. In fiscal year 2011, the country granted citizenship to 694,193 immigrants.

All of this testifies to the United States' unquestionably impressive record of receiving and absorbing immigrants. However, Americans' rather determined chorus of insistence upon the country's openness

---

[4] Israel Zangwill, *The Melting Pot* (1908), in Edna Nahshon, ed., *From the Ghetto to the Melting Pot: Israel Zangwill's Three Jewish Plays* (Detroit: Wayne State University Press, 2006).

[5] John F. Kennedy, *A Nation of Immigrants* (New York: Harper & Row, 1964) (1958).

to immigrants should itself suggest that realities have fallen short of rhetoric.

The United States has never welcomed all possible immigrants. Over the course of four centuries, Americans have written immigration laws to exclude individuals from their territory on grounds of religion, race, national origin, health, sexuality, poverty, political ideology, and criminal or terrorist background, to name only a few of the major legal grounds of exclusion. Over the same period, the image of the desirable immigrant has changed considerably: sturdy republican farmer, unskilled worker, agricultural laborer, refugee from Communism, highly skilled worker, high net worth investor. Each one of these images has had exclusionary effects. Americans have also made it difficult or impossible for resident immigrants to accede to citizenship. From the country's inception until the early 1950s – in short, for approximately three-fourths of its history as an independent nation – race was a barrier to naturalization. Resident immigrants who were not "white" were unable to become full participants in the affairs of the community regardless of how long they had lived in the country. In the twentieth century, political affiliation also prevented immigrants from naturalizing.

If the United States has never welcomed and absorbed all potential immigrants, it has also turned on those it has chosen to admit. Over the centuries, pursuant to a body of law that legal scholars call "alienage law," resident immigrants have been barred from exercising political rights, holding property, entering various professions and trades, and availing of public benefits. If many immigrants were able to overcome such legal disabilities by naturalizing, those barred from naturalizing on grounds of race would face them their entire lives. Legal disabilities have been visited with especial severity on undocumented immigrants, whose numbers escalated in the twentieth century as a result of the closure of borders, the institution of numerical limits on immigration, and the complicity of public and private actors. Millions of undocumented immigrants have lived – and continue to live – in the shadows of society, fearful of turning to public authorities for assistance and unable to resist exploitation and abuse at work, in the home, and in the community.

Equally serious, long-term resident immigrants have been punished through an often callous use of deportation. Notwithstanding long periods of residence in the United States, immigrants who have sought public benefits, espoused frowned-upon political views, or engaged in criminal acts have been shipped out of the country, often to homelands they barely know, with few of the legal protections accorded criminals. During the first half of the twentieth century, the government also employed denaturalization as a weapon, punishing naturalized immigrants who expressed unpopular views by setting aside their citizenship, converting them into aliens, and then deporting them. Since the immigration reforms of 1996, the country has shipped millions of resident immigrants to their home countries even when such immigrants, many of whom arrived in the United States as children, are in every sense the product of American society and have few if any connections to their countries of origin. In fiscal year 2011, the United States apprehended 641,633 non-citizens within the country and officially deported 391,953. That year, an additional 323,542 non-citizens accepted "voluntary departure," choosing to leave the country without having formal removal proceedings instituted against them.

The gap between rhetoric and reality when it comes to how Americans have received, treated, and expelled immigrants is, therefore, very real. However, it is only part of the story.

Over the course of American history, the impulse to regulate, reject, exclude, and remove undesirables on grounds of race, gender, poverty, and political opinion has ranged very widely indeed. Whether at the national, state, or local level, it has driven communities to target insiders as well as outsiders. In the process, Americans have named and treated as foreigners not only those from outside the country's borders, but also those in their very midst. The history of immigration and citizenship law thus encompasses two intimately conjoined histories: that of the country's absorption and rejection of those from *beyond* its limits and that of its simultaneous efforts to render foreign those *within* its limits.

Readers will readily understand the concept of the country's absorption and rejection of outsiders. They might find rather more unfamiliar the concept of rendering insiders foreign. It is important, therefore, to set it forth.

In my mind, insiders have been rendered foreign through a host of politico-legal strategies that the national, state, and local governments have deployed over the long span of American history vis-à-vis portions of the domestic population. These include formally designating portions of the domestic population alien; formally converting citizens into aliens for having committed specified acts; subjecting portions of the domestic population to extensive regimes of borders and restrictions on movement and residence; seeking to expel portions of the domestic population from the community; subjecting portions of the domestic population to legal disabilities comparable to those visited upon aliens; indiscriminately mingling citizens with aliens for bureaucratic purposes or in times of war; and refusing to recognize that long-term resident immigrants might, after a certain point, have become insiders despite the fortuity of their not having naturalized. Each of these different strategies of rendering insiders foreign has been deployed along axes of race, gender, class, and political opinion (to name only the most significant) to suppress, exploit, reject, exclude, expel, and refuse responsibility for portions of the domestic population. Different domestic groups have had vastly different experiences of being rendered foreign.[6]

Although Great Britain, and later the United States, claimed sovereignty over Native American lands, Native Americans were formally designated aliens from the very first English settlement of North America until the end of the nineteenth century. Formal designation as alien served various purposes. As the occasion demanded, it allowed whites to question Native Americans' ability to confer good title to property and to deny them the vote; placed Native Americans beyond the advancing frontier of white settlement; and facilitated their expulsion from their ancestral lands during the Jacksonian era. If Native Americans might from time to time have welcomed formal designation as aliens in support of their claims to sovereignty, lasting respect for a robust Native American sovereignty was not forthcoming. Formal designation as alien was more a gesture of exclusion than a recognition of parity. This is proved by the fact that, in the twentieth century,

---

[6] It is important to alert the reader to the fact that the terms "citizen" and "alien" – especially the former – have multiple usages. On the one hand, the terms designate *formal* legal membership or non-membership in a polity. On the other hand, in both scholarly and popular discourses, "citizenship" designates *substantive* membership within a polity, referring to the possession of civil, political, social, and other rights, as well as to subjective experiences of membership. Both usages are important for my purposes in this book. The context will make clear which usage is at work.

alienage followed Native Americans even *after* statutory extensions of formal citizenship to them in the late nineteenth century. Despite being formal citizens, Native Americans found themselves subjected to congressional "plenary power," a power grounded in sovereignty, unfettered by the U.S. Constitution, and surprisingly similar to the constitutional regime then extended to immigrants.

Blacks had a distinct experience being rendered foreign. In the aftermath of the American Revolution, although slaves were not considered citizens, in some states free black males came to possess important markers of citizenship such as the vote. As the slavery crisis heated up, however, free black males lost the vote all over the country except for the New England states. At the same time, free blacks became subject to an extensive regime of territorial borders. With the blessing of the U.S. Supreme Court, states in the North and the South sought to exclude and expel free blacks from their territories. After the U.S. Supreme Court declared in *Scott v. Sandford* that blacks could not be citizens of the United States, certain Southern courts formally labeled free blacks from other states aliens and subjected them to traditional common law alien legal disabilities such as the inability to inherit property.[7] The American Colonization Society sought to repatriate free blacks to Africa, where they allegedly "belonged" once they ceased to be slaves. After the ratification of the Fourteenth Amendment, which granted formal federal and state citizenship to individuals born in the United States, it became impossible to designate native-born blacks aliens or to push seriously for their repatriation to Africa. Other ways were found of regulating blacks' participation, movement, and presence. A host of measures stripped blacks of the vote. Discrimination in virtually every realm of life became rampant. Formal laws barring blacks from entering states' territories gave way to micro-borders of segregation that would endure into the post–World War II period. Segregation would touch not just blacks, of course, but every racial minority in the country. Although the Civil Rights movement brought an end to formal segregation, de facto segregation continues into the twenty-first century.

American women had yet another experience of being rendered foreign. The virtually complete occlusion of women's legal personalities

---

[7] *Scott v. Sandford*, 60 U.S. 393 (1857).

under the common law doctrine of coverture meant that their formal and substantive citizenship could be deemed derivative of those of their husbands. In the mid-nineteenth century, American men won the right to confer their nationality on their alien wives. American women, however, did not win such a right. In the view of prominent politicians, they had no nationality to confer. In 1907, Congress confirmed its dim view of women's citizenship by passing a law that stripped American women of their formal citizenship if they married alien men. Thousands of native-born American women married to aliens found themselves literally converted into aliens overnight. As aliens, they were unable to obtain certain kinds of employment, forfeited property in wartime, and even found themselves subject to exclusion and removal from the country. The occlusion of women's legal personalities would erode bit by bit, even as women's formal and substantive citizenship slowly came into being, over the course of the twentieth century.

America's poor were made foreign by being subjected to a centuries-old, complex, and extensive regime of territorial borders, one whose significance for questions of immigration has not sufficiently been recognized, but which is central to my account. Until the Civil War, immigration restriction was enacted at the state level. Antebellum state legislation built upon colonial poor laws that did not adequately distinguish between the native-born poor and the foreign-born poor. Both were equally undesirable from the perspective of states, counties, and towns that bore responsibility for policing borders: both were excluded and removed from communities. When the federal government took over the regulation of foreign immigration after the Civil War, state and local poor laws remained in effect to manage the movement and residence of poor Americans within the country. Only the recognition of a constitutional "right to travel" during the post–World War II rights revolution would definitively end this regime of territorial borders for the poor. Barriers to voting by the poor would last into the 1970s.

Asian Americans and Latino Americans would have the experience of repeatedly being assimilated with, and treated like, immigrants from Asia and Latin America. Beginning in the late nineteenth century and extending into the twenty-first, immigration raids and border patrol activities indiscriminately mingled citizens with aliens, disregarding the rights of the former by treating them like the latter. Mexican Americans would experience repatriation – literal expulsion from the country – in the state's mass removals of Mexican immigrants in the 1930s. Japanese Americans found themselves interned during World War II along with resident Japanese nationals. Those who espoused unpopular political views – from Loyalists at the time of the American Revolution to naturalized citizens with communist or anarchist leanings in the twentieth century – were vulnerable to legal proscription, involuntary expatriation or denaturalization, and expulsion from the country. For a significant stretch of the twentieth century, American citizens also found themselves converted into aliens against their will if they committed certain proscribed acts. Today, thousands of American citizens find themselves caught in the dragnet of the immigration enforcement regime. Some have even been deported against their will to other countries.

In considering these various forms of rendering insiders foreign, it is appropriate to anticipate and respond to an objection. It might legitimately be observed that there has always been a meaningful difference between being a second-class citizen, on the one hand, and a non-citizen or foreigner, on the other. For much of American history, white women were second-class citizens to the extent that they were denied political rights, barred access to various trades and professions, and subjected to legal coverture when they got married. They were not, it might be contended, considered non-citizens or foreigners. Indeed, white women were imagined – and often saw themselves – as being at the very heart of the nation as mothers, wives, and daughters. While I do not dismiss this objection, and indeed welcome it because it acts as an imprecise limit to the scope of my argument, I would invite the reader to attend to the following. Second-class citizenship can shade off, and all too frequently *has* shaded off, into formal non-citizenship, into genuine foreignness. One can observe this at various points in American history.

Thus, the legal subordination of free blacks in antebellum America, and the widespread acceptance of the practices of excluding them from states and repatriating them to Africa, easily slipped into formal assertions in certain slave states that free blacks were aliens vis-à-vis such states and subject to alien legal disabilities. The long tradition of regarding women's citizenship as subordinate to and derivative of their husbands' led seamlessly to the view, expressed in the United States' 1907 expatriation law, that American women who married non-citizens ceased to be U.S. citizens. The second-class citizenship of free blacks and women thus literally became non-citizenship.

More frequently, strategies of rendering insiders foreign had the effect of impressing upon those affected that they were foreigners vis-à-vis their own country even if they did not lose formal citizenship thereby. Feminists in the nineteenth century expressed the view that, as second-class citizens, American women were akin to aliens. In the post–Civil War years, blacks were formal citizens of the United States. However, their second-class citizenship convinced some that leaving the country and returning to Africa was their only option. Japanese American internees during World War II understood perfectly well that their formal citizenship had not prevented them from being treated like aliens. Many repudiated their U.S. citizenship and repatriated themselves to Japan. In other instances, subordinated groups might not express their sense of foreignness vis-à-vis the nation. But a cursory glance at the substantive legal deprivations they suffered points to far greater substantive similarities to aliens than it does to citizens.

Recognizing the ubiquity of processes of rendering insiders foreign across the long span of American history is a stepping-stone to understanding the history of U.S. immigration and citizenship law recounted in this book. Studying the country's absorption and rejection of foreigners from the outside alongside its practices of rendering insiders foreign reveals how terms and concepts such as "citizen" and "alien," "insider" and "outsider," "native" and "foreign" – and hence the very objects that immigration and citizenship law regulate – have been fluid and changeable and ranged inside and outside the United States' territorial borders.

During the colonial period, in both Great Britain and the North American colonies, the distinction between British subject and alien consisted of a range of alien legal disabilities: the inability to hold real property, to vote, and to enjoy offices to which real property qualifications were attached. But the overwhelming majority of British subjects – women and propertyless males – were slotted into legal statuses that subjected them to comparable disabilities when it came to holding property and voting. If aliens might be barred from entering and remaining within the kingdom, British subjects lacked rights to leave, remain within, or travel throughout the kingdom. In other words, borders were ubiquitous for British subjects and aliens alike. "Immigration restriction," such as it was, was a thoroughly local affair directed principally at regulating the movement and residence of the poor from neighboring towns, counties, provinces, and "beyond sea," regardless of whether they were British subjects or aliens. At the same time, however, there were a range of developments in the North American colonies: efforts to facilitate the migration and incorporation of desirable white settlers, formal designations of Native Americans as aliens, and efforts to render free blacks excludable and removable at the moment of passing from slavery to freedom.

How did we get from that world – a world of multiple legal statuses in which the distinction between British subject and alien was relatively weak and in which aliens existed at home and abroad – to the world of the early twenty-first century? Today, every individual born within the United States is a formal citizen thereof under the U.S. Constitution. Many of the formal legal disabilities that once subordinated women, the poor, and racial minorities – ranging from a lack of voting rights to a lack of rights to move and reside throughout national territory – have eroded. It has become extremely difficult for the state to strip citizens of their citizenship. At the same time, the gulf between citizen and alien yawns wide. Aliens are subjected to a range of formal legal disabilities (bars to voting, the inability to hold certain jobs) that citizens largely no longer suffer. Aliens are also subject to the ubiquitous experience of borders: they might be formally excluded and removed in ways that citizens no longer experience.

How we got from there to here is the narrative traced in this book. Briefly put, the narrative traces a gradual, albeit by no means unequivocal, separation over time of insiders from outsiders. Efforts to render insiders foreign have varied depending upon the group involved, the resistance such efforts have encountered, and the resolution of the struggles that have ensued. But it is fair to say that many – but, it must be emphasized, not all – forms of rendering insiders foreign have ebbed over the course of four centuries of American history. Over the same period, an increasingly powerful immigration regime has emerged and centered its activities more and more on the immigrant: the alien from another country seeking to enter and remain within the polity.

This book thus reveals the arc of a halting (and sometimes reversible) extension of formal and substantive citizenship among the native-born population, an intensifying substantive distinction between citizen and alien, and a centralization of governmental regulation of the alien under the auspices of an increasingly powerful state. This arc is paralleled by a transition from a highly decentralized polity in which towns, counties, and states enforced borders vis-à-vis those from other towns, counties, states, *and* foreign countries to a centralized polity in which towns, counties, and states are barred from wielding borders vis-à-vis those inside the country, while the federal government monopolizes the wielding of borders vis-à-vis aliens.

Various historical milestones and formations – ranging from the American Revolution to the post–World War II rights revolution, from entrenched legal structures controlling the movement of the poor to the legal structures of patriarchy and race – make up this historical arc. Along the way, one observes multiple intersections and parallels between ways of absorbing and rejecting outsiders and ways of rendering insiders foreign. Although they are too numerous to list in this introduction, one worthy of mention has to do with the intimate, and not often sufficiently highlighted, relationship between slavery and immigration. Before the Civil War, slave states anxious to preserve slavery were insistent on their right to exclude free blacks from their territories and fearful that conferring immigration powers upon the federal government would rob them of that right. Despite tensions during the antebellum period over the proper locus of authority to regulate immigration, therefore, a federal immigration regime focused on regulating aliens' access to and presence within national territory could not emerge until after the Civil War, when the problem of black citizenship was formally resolved.

At the end of four centuries of American history, as one traces the twisting path that has come to separate insiders from outsiders and given rise to a powerful immigration state, the immigrant has emerged as a lonely legal subject, one uniquely marked with a set of distinct legal and territorial disabilities that he or she once shared with many insiders and that now distinguish him or her from them. Today, immigrants are the only ones rejected in certain ways, because the rejection of insiders in such ways has been rendered more difficult or impossible. This is not a clean historical narrative. The older hierarchies through which insiders used to be rendered foreign have had a very long half-life. The threat of their reinstatement has necessitated constant vigilance. At the same time, immigrants have ceaselessly agitated to improve their lot. But the narrative holds.

Telling the story this way bespeaks a specific orientation toward the category of citizenship that is worth highlighting briefly. In many discourses, citizenship is represented as a *positive* good, bringing with it a sense of communal membership, the ability to participate in the affairs of the community, and so on. Citizenship can, no doubt, be understood that way. By contrast, my orientation toward questions of citizenship in this book is *negative*. The acquisition of citizenship over time is a story about being rendered *less* foreign. Over the centuries, insiders – women, racial minorities, the poor, political dissidents – have acquired legal statuses and rights that rendered them *less* like the aliens with whom they once shared much. There was nothing necessary or foreordained about this, just as there was nothing necessary or foreordained about the state forms that emerged over time to govern aliens. The processes of extending and enriching citizenship among and for the native-born – and the related processes of centralization and state-building that subjected aliens to ever greater state power – were always the subject of bitter, tense, and often violent contestation. The rendering foreign of America's insiders ebbed over centuries, even as the rendering foreign of America's outsiders grew, as a result of the *work* of revolution, war, endless litigation, and considerable protest and struggle.

Writing the history of U.S. immigration and citizenship law with a focus on processes of rendering insiders foreign compels a reimagining of U.S. immigration and citizenship history. Conventionally, the historiographies of U.S. citizenship, on the one hand, and U.S. immigration, on the other, have divided up the field based upon entrenched understandings of distinctions mapped onto one another: citizen and alien, native and foreigner, territorial inside and territorial outside. In recent years, scholars working on borderlands, Asian and Latino immigration, labor, and undocumented immigration have questioned these conventional approaches. Nevertheless, such approaches are still very much at work in both scholarly and popular understandings. It is worth setting them forth to distinguish what is attempted here.

Historians of U.S. citizenship have traditionally written about the changing formal and substantive meanings of citizenship, explored the history of its inclusions and exclusions, and discussed its role in major historical events. For the most part, however, they have tended to plot histories of U.S. citizenship from the "inside," from the perspective of a national territorial community projected backward in time. Given their interest in examining the career of citizenship on the "inside," they have not always been interested in interrogating the basic distinction between citizen and alien. For example, in Rogers Smith's monumental *Civic Ideals*, still the most comprehensive history of U.S. citizenship, citizenship is described as follows:

Citizenship laws – laws designating the criteria for membership in a political community and the key prerogatives that constitute membership – are among the most fundamental of political creations. They distribute power, assign status, and define political purposes. They create the most recognized political identity of the individuals they embrace, one displayed on passports scrutinized at every contested border. They also assign negative identities to the 'aliens' they fence out. The attention people give to national citizenship reflects the hard-boiled reality that governments are more likely to use their powers to aid those who are their citizens than those who are not ... Citizenship laws also literally constitute – they create with legal words – a collective civic identity. They proclaim the existence of a political "people" and designate who those persons are as a people, in ways that often become integral to individuals' senses of personal identity as well.[8]

Here, Smith reveals his recognition of citizenship's formal negative role (keeping out aliens). But this recognition never becomes central to his account. Indeed, his "inside" understanding of citizenship as "the most recognized political identity" of individuals and one that is "integral to individuals' senses of personal identity" – precisely the *positive* orientation toward citizenship that I eschew – rather takes this formal negative function as a given. This colors the way Smith writes the history of U.S. citizenship. Domestic groups – the propertyless, the indigent, women, and racial minorities – appear as citizens-in-the-making rather than as closer to aliens. They are *already* part of a given (albeit deeply inegalitarian and imperfectly realized) national community that

---

[8] Rogers M. Smith, *Civic Ideals: Conflicting Visions of Citizenship in U.S. History* (New Haven, CT: Yale University Press, 1997), pp. 30–31.

will slowly realize its liberal commitments toward them. What is missing here is adequate attention to how Americans actively rendered foreign those living in their midst.

Historians of U.S. immigration have traditionally shared the same bias but in the form of an "outside" approach. They choose as their preferred object of study those coming *to* America from its "outside" and pay less attention to the rendering foreign of those "inside" the country. The titles of some prominent immigration histories in the second half of the twentieth century – Oscar Handlin's *The Uprooted*, Ronald Takaki's *Strangers from Another Shore*, and Roger Daniels's *Coming to America* – suggest that their authors have subscribed to precisely such an understanding of immigration.[9] Even where historians of U.S. immigration recognize that Americans sought to render those inside the country foreign, they can pass this over in favor of cataloguing the country's efforts to regulate the influx and presence of those from the territorial outside. Thus, Aristide Zolberg's important *A Nation by Design* acknowledges at the very outset:

Long before what is conventionally regarded as the beginning of national immigration policy, the Americans undertook to violently eliminate most of the original dwellers, imported a mass of African workers whom they excluded from their nation altogether, actively recruited Europeans they considered suitable for settlement, intervened in the international arena to secure freedom of exit on their behalf, elaborated devices to deter those judged undesirable, and even attempted to engineer the self-removal of liberated slaves, deemed inherently unqualified for membership.[10]

But a few pages later, Zolberg indicates that he is interested principally in what he calls "international migration," which he defines as "the transfer of a person from the jurisdiction of one state to that of another and the eventuality of a change of membership in an inclusive political community."[11] The bulk of the book – albeit not all of

---

[9] Oscar Handlin, *The Uprooted: The Epic Story of the Great Migrations That Made the American People* (Boston: Little, Brown, 1951); Ronald K. Takaki, *Strangers from a Different Shore: A History of Asian Americans* (Boston: Little, Brown, 1989); Roger Daniels, *Coming to America: A History of Immigration and Ethnicity in American Life* (New York: Harper Collins, 1990).

[10] Aristide Zolberg, *A Nation by Design: Immigration Policy in the Fashioning of America* (New York: Russell Sage Foundation, 2006), pp. 1–2.

[11] Id., p. 11.

it – focuses on law and policy relating to "international migration"; its primary focus is not on Americans' related efforts to create foreigners inside the country.

Closely related to such conventional historiographical approaches, in my view, has been a powerful intellectual and popular tradition in American political thought that has made the case for closed borders vis-à-vis immigrants on the ground that our primary responsibility must be to citizens. Thus, decades ago, the liberal political thinker Michael Walzer famously argued: "Neighborhoods can be open only if countries are at least potentially closed."[12] The claim is that we can fulfill our commitments to our neighbors (citizens) only if we exclude strangers (aliens). This line of thinking maps perfectly onto a venerable positivist tradition in international law that authorizes states to close their territories to those from other states. This tradition has long been endorsed by the U.S. Supreme Court. For example, in *New York v. Miln* (1837), the Court approvingly cited the eighteenth-century Swiss international law theorist Emmerich de Vattel for the following proposition: "The sovereign may forbid the entrance of his territory, either to foreigners in general, or in particular cases, or to certain persons, or for certain particular purposes, according as he may think it advantageous to the state."[13]

Such approaches to questions of immigration and citizenship are seemingly confirmed by the activities of a contemporary national immigration regime that claims to focus exclusively on aliens, while leaving the regulation of citizens to other state authorities. The immigration controversies of the early twenty-first century – apprehensions at the U.S.-Mexico border, detention centers for apprehended aliens, mass deportation to countries in Latin America and the Caribbean – all concern aliens. This is indeed (one possible rendering of) the present situation. But instead of letting the present normalize how we look at the past, we would do better to make the difference of the past visible and let it destabilize our present.

---

[12] Michael Walzer, *Spheres of Justice: A Defense of Pluralism and Equality* (New York: Basic Books, 1983), p. 38.

[13] *New York v. Miln*, 36 U.S. 102, 132 (1837), quoting Vattel, *Law of Nations*, bk. 2, ch. 7, sec. 94.

If we look back at the historical record and take seriously America's history of rendering insiders foreign, can we be sure that terms such as "citizen" and "alien" can map neatly onto terms such as "insider" and "outsider" or "neighbor" and "stranger"? Over the centuries, Americans have named as aliens immigrants, but also blacks, Native Americans, and American women married to aliens. They have rendered foreign not only Asians and Latinos, but also millions of Asian Americans and Latino Americans by lumping them with immigrants of the same national background and removing them from communities. They have sought to absolve themselves of responsibility – and hence to exclude and remove – not only poor immigrants, but poor Americans from nearby towns, counties, and states, indeed their very next-door neighbors.

This historical record suggests that we not fall into the facile trap of fetishizing space, of allowing our sense of what we owe to neighbors and do not owe to strangers to turn on something as crude as "pure" physical presence or absence, which (as this book suggests) is always politically and legally mediated. Americans have long imbued physical "presence" and "absence" with political and legal meanings, marking Native Americans as aliens and placing them beyond the borders of their communities, for example, while welcoming European Protestant settlers into their communities as proto-citizens and giving them property and political rights. The positivist tradition according to which states may exclude and remove aliens has dictated neither what states have done nor what they should do.

Writing the history of attempts to render foreign, exclude, and remove insiders *and* outsiders does not spring out of any Burkean nostalgia for a world in which insiders and outsiders were all subordinate. If it invokes that world, it is rather to impel the reader to refuse to normalize any understanding of physical "presence" and "absence" that asserts that political and legal consequences follow ineluctably from it and to continue to interrogate citizenship and immigration regimes, past and present. By reminding us of the fact that "we" on the inside (blacks, Native Americans, women, the poor, and others) were ourselves once rendered foreigners, it seeks to provoke a different relationship toward immigrants, those in our midst and those beyond our borders. Like us, they are heirs to the many struggles that have made America what it is.

## The Structure of This Book; Terminology

The structure of this book is chronological, ranging from the colonial period to the end of the twentieth century. Drawing on legal materials (constitutions, statutes, cases, reports, petitions) at the federal, state, and local levels, non-legal materials of all sorts, and multiple historiographies, each chapter explores changing conceptions of citizenship and alienage – as well as the changing nature of immigration restriction – as Americans sought to welcome, regulate, exclude, and expel insiders and outsiders. When the chapters are put together, they reveal the gradual differentiation of citizen from alien, insider from outsider, and the emergence of an increasingly powerful centralized immigration regime focused more or less exclusively upon the alien.

Although each chapter has a different structure, each explores the parallels and intersections between the experiences of those from the territorial outside and those on the territorial inside. Thus, each chapter includes discussions of immigrants, Native Americans, blacks, women, the poor, and – where appropriate – Latinos and Asians. Discussions of federal constitutional law relating to immigration and citizenship begin in Chapter 4, but really pick up in Chapters 5–7, which cover the period from the late nineteenth century through the end of the twentieth century.

It is appropriate to include a brief discussion of terminology. The historian Mae Ngai has recently called for sensitivity to the terms used to describe migrants to British North America and the independent United States. In the colonial period, the term "colonist" or "settler" predominated; for much of the nineteenth century, the term "emigrant"; and, beginning in the late nineteenth century, the term "immigrant."[14] These terms show up in my text and in those I cite. However, because my primary interest is in tracking the history of the insider–outsider distinction, and because I need a neutral term to designate the object of the study that can work throughout the text, I rely principally upon the term "immigrant" to designate those seeking to enter the country from outside its limits. I use the term "black" to designate African Americans and "Native American" (and, less frequently, "Indian") to designate the country's indigenous populations.

[14] Mae M. Ngai, "Immigration and Ethnic History," in Eric Foner and Lisa McGirr, eds., *American History Now* (Philadelphia: Temple University Press, 2011), pp. 359–60.

Chapter 2 begins with early-seventeenth-century English conceptions of birthright citizenship and perpetual allegiance. It then
describes the various legal disabilities relating to property, voting, residence, and movement suffered by the majority of early modern British
subjects, with specific attention to women and the poor. It moves on
to discuss how North American colonists – even as they retained hierarchies from the mother country – manipulated British subjecthood
to attract wealthy European Protestant settlers, on the one hand, and
render Native Americans and blacks foreigners, on the other hand. It
concludes by examining "immigration restriction" during the colonial
period by focusing on the poor laws that managed the mobility and
residence of insiders and outsiders, British subjects and aliens. As part
of this discussion, it shows how eighteenth-century New Englanders
manipulated the poor laws to render their own poorer neighbors
foreigners.

Chapter 3 probes the many contradictions that accompanied the new
conception of volitional citizenship that emerged with the American
Revolution. Even as greater numbers of white males could claim the
right to be governed by their consent, this right was grounded in the
rendering foreign of Loyalists, women, blacks, and Native Americans.
The chapter goes on to discuss the constitutional division of authority between the federal and state governments in matters of citizenship and immigration. Although the federal government acquired
the authority to legislate on naturalization, immigration restriction
remained the province of the states. In the early Republic, immigration
restriction remained locally administered and governed by the poor
laws; states, counties, and towns excluded and removed from their
territories aliens and fellow Americans. A new development, brought
about by the growth of the free black population in the early Republic,
was the territorial restrictions that began to emerge at the state level to
exclude and remove free blacks.

Chapter 4 focuses on the antebellum period. During this period,
universal white male suffrage was achieved across the United States;
there were also judicial intimations that citizens of the various states
had the right to travel and reside anywhere in the United States. But
the majority of the resident population was slotted into second-class
citizenship status (women, the poor, free blacks) or non-citizenship
status (Native Americans and, in some cases, free blacks); the status

of slave was deemed antithetical to the status of citizen. The chapter pays considerable attention to the explosion of territorial restrictions on the movement and residence of free blacks and to attempts to remove Native Americans and free blacks from the country. It then examines how, at the level of constitutional law, the tolerance of territorial restrictions on the movement of free blacks became an obstacle to the emergence of a federal immigration regime, even as mass migration from Northwestern Europe was giving rise to calls for a shift from state-level to federal immigration restriction. Finally, describing anti-Catholic nativism directed against immigrants from Ireland, the chapter focuses on how the colonial era poor laws were adapted to regulate mid-nineteenth-century immigration. It shows how the mutual imbrication of the rejection of foreign-born paupers and the rejection of native-born paupers led to a centralization of immigration regulation at the state level.

Chapter 5 focuses on the late nineteenth century. With the ratification of the Fourteenth Amendment, all persons born in the United States were deemed citizens thereof. This brought an end to the formal non-citizenship of blacks and paved the way for the emergence of a federal immigration order. Even as formal citizenship was conferred on the native-born, the new federal immigration order came to be grounded in the new constitutional theory of plenary power, an inherent power grounded in sovereignty that immunized from substantive constitutional review the federal government's actions vis-à-vis immigrants in the context of exclusion, deportation, and naturalization. This contributed to the widening of the gulf between citizen and alien. In an attempt to manage the "problem" of Chinese immigration, the federal government began to exclude and deport on the grounds of race and national origin. Naturalization law, which had long barred non-whites, prevented Chinese immigrants from naturalizing. Even though formal citizenship was available to blacks (under the U.S. Constitution) and Native Americans (by statute), however, this did not mean that insiders were not rendered foreign. New and old practices and theories combined to do so: the spread of segregation, the extension of plenary power to Native Americans, the mingling of Chinese Americans with Chinese immigrants, the continuation of lesser citizenship for women; and regimes of territorial restrictions vis-à-vis the domestic poor.

Chapter 6 covers the period from 1900 to World War II. It begins by discussing the rise of racialist nativism, the "whiteness" naturalization cases, and the institution of racist national origins quotas by the 1920s. With the closure of borders came the rise of undocumented immigration. The chapter then discusses how, as the immigration regime undergirded by plenary power grew more powerful, the state began to focus much more on the regulation of resident immigrants. The focus here is on the multiplication of alien legal disabilities, Americanization movements, the denaturalization of immigrants, and the increasingly frequent use of deportation as an instrument of social policy to punish resident immigrants. If the subjection of immigrants to greater state power marks a further widening of the gulf separating insider from outsider, the chapter moves on to focus on various methods of rendering insiders foreign: the intensification of segregation and the rise of territorial restrictions on the poor during the Great Depression; the emergence of involuntary expatriation as a tool for converting citizens into aliens, which resulted in the rendering foreign of American women who married aliens; the denial of citizenship to the country's new colonial subjects; and the practice of mingling citizens and outsiders as illustrated by the repatriation of Mexican Americans and Mexican citizens to Mexico during the 1930s and the internment of Japanese immigrants and Japanese Americans in the 1940s.

Chapter 7 covers the second half of the twentieth century. It explores the rights revolution of the post–World War II period, focusing on three aspects thereof: the spread of norms of race and gender equality; the constitutionalization of a "right to travel" for the country's poor; and restriction of the government's right to expatriate American citizens against their will. All of these developments significantly enriched citizenship for Americans and made it harder to render them foreigners. It then shows how the rights revolution for citizens did and did not affect immigration and citizenship law. During the post–World War II period, the federal immigration regime grew exponentially and greatly increased its powers over immigrants. If immigration and citizenship law lost its formal racial trappings, the federal government's plenary power remained intact. With the sanction of constitutional law, the federal government excluded, deported, and discriminated against immigrants on grounds that would be constitutionally impermissible if used against citizens. Deportation in particular became a favored tool of federal social policy, allowing the state to use resident immigrants' formal non-citizenship against them long after they had entered the country and become part of the community. If the gulf between citizen and alien was never wider, the chapter shows the striking parallels between the treatment of immigrants and that of citizens as the rights revolution ebbed in the closing decades of the twentieth century.

Chapter 8 concludes the book by showing how joining the histories of immigrants with those of Native Americans, blacks, women, the poor, Asian Americans, and Latino Americans sparks a rethinking of U.S. citizenship history, on the one hand, and U.S. immigration history, on the other. It ends with a coda discussing developments in the early twenty-first century.

# 2

# Foreigners and Borders in British North America

## Introduction

Between the establishment of the first English settlements and the American Revolution, the North American colonies grew from tiny, fragile communities that could barely sustain themselves into diverse societies that collectively numbered multiple millions. Over the same period, they developed into major exporters of cash crops, significant markets for British exports, and challengers to the imperial trading system. This growth and development rested upon the accomplishment of various goals: clearing indigenous groups; settling lands; instituting systems of forced labor; and regulating nascent communities. Migration played a critical role. Approximately 900,000 people crossed the Atlantic during this period, almost three-fourths of them arriving in unfree statuses.

The pervasiveness of unfreedom in colonial era migration entails challenges for the historian seeking to identify an "immigration and citizenship law" for the period. Colonists on both sides of the Atlantic imagined, organized, and regulated membership, territory, and movement in ways very different from ours.

Borders were everywhere: between Great Britain and its overseas colonies; between British possessions and those of other European powers; between British possessions and Indian country; between the mainland colonies; between counties and towns within individual colonies; and within counties and towns themselves. These borders were enforced against individuals in different ways depending on their legal status: British subject, naturalized subject, denizen, alien, servant, redemptioner, convict, married woman, pauper, slave, free white, free black, Indian. The relationship between borders and statuses was complex. In some cases, legal status directly governed an individual's right to cross or remain within borders. In other cases, legal status worked more obliquely. Insofar as it shaped the distribution and content of political and social membership, it ended up determining rights to presence and movement. Communities were more likely to restrict, restrain, exclude, or remove individuals slotted into inferior legal statuses. By contrast, they were more likely to welcome as equals individuals granted superior legal statuses. This profusion of legal statuses and territorial borders makes visible a few signal interrelated features of the seventeenth- and eighteenth-century "immigration and citizenship regime" that are worth setting forth.

First, in both Great Britain and its North American colonies, membership in the community of allegiance – that is, being a British subject – did not entail either "full" social and political membership or rights to presence and mobility throughout the community's territory. Women and propertyless men lacked rights to vote and hold office. Married women suffered a range of legal disabilities when it came to property rights. Early modern British subjects also lacked rights to leave, enter, and remain within every part of the realm. The formal right to exit the realm had been denied British subjects from feudal times, although its denial was increasingly criticized by eighteenth-century legal commentators. There was no unassailable right to remain within the realm. Paupers and convicts could be transported against their will to places so far away that their hopes of returning to their communities were effectively extinguished. Neither could British subjects move freely throughout the realm. Systems of poor relief administration regulated the presence and mobility of the poor, who could be barred from entering local territories and returned to the places from which they came. Theorized as perpetual allegiance to the monarch on the basis of birth within his realm, British subjecthood by the early eighteenth century had become a prerequisite to rights to vote, exercise various offices, hold and devise real property, and participate in British commerce. This meant that aliens were denied such legal rights and privileges. However, so were the majority of British subjects. British subjects thus shared many of the legal disabilities of aliens, including the experience of territorial borders, exclusion, and involuntary removal.

Second, while all these British legal statuses and disabilities took root in Britain's North American colonies, the imperatives of life in a settler colony drove colonial Americans to instrumentalize British subjecthood, to make it a proxy of "immigration law" so as to draw in desirables and repel or manage undesirables. Eager to attract Protestant European settlers who would contribute labor, skills, and wealth, and often in the face of opposition from London, colonial Americans facilitated naturalization and loosened traditional links between British subjecthood, voting, officeholding, and property ownership. At the same time, they deployed British subjecthood against Native Americans and blacks. Although the Crown claimed sovereignty over Native Americans, they were declared aliens and foreigners, placed beyond the frontier of white settlement, hemmed in by borders in early prototypes of the Indian reservation, or subjected to the community's rules but not allowed to participate in their making. British subjecthood was also denied blacks. Slaves were consigned to a subordinate status well below that of white aliens to facilitate the exploitation of their labor. Free blacks shared many of the substantive legal disabilities visited upon slaves. In addition, they experienced a special kind of non-belonging: in certain colonies, they were required to leave the colony when they became free. They became removable foreigners as they passed from slavery to freedom.

Third, if manipulations of British subjecthood served to shape community in the North American colonies, everyday systems of territorial restriction remained local and not organized around the subject–alien distinction. To be sure, aliens from overseas were subject to exclusion and removal. But colonial Americans were equally, if not more, vociferous about excluding undesirables who were fellow British subjects (whether convicts, paupers, or Catholics). From the perspective of local poor relief officials, the officials charged with regulating access to and presence within territory, exclusion and removal applied to those from neighboring towns and counties as well as to those from "beyond sea." Membership in the wider community of allegiance meant little in local attempts to exclude and remove. Not surprisingly, those who were less than full members of society and polity – propertyless men, unmarried women, Native Americans, blacks – were most likely to be excluded and removed. However, colonial Americans went even further. New England offers numerous examples of the production of foreignness through the splitting of towns, the redrawing of borders, and the designation of former neighbors as excludable and removable outsiders. The larger point, however, should be clear. Aliens were not the only group, and most likely not even the most significant group, kept out of various territorial divisions in British North America. A "foreigner" might come from across the ocean, from relatively nearby, or from nowhere at all.

The remainder of this chapter consists of the following: first, an exposition of early modern English theories of subjecthood grounded in birth and perpetual allegiance and the multiple legal statuses that shaped the rights of British subjects; next, a discussion of colonial Americans' multiple strategies to include and exclude through grants and denials of subjecthood to aliens, Native Americans, and blacks; and finally, an exploration of the legal systems that regulated movement and presence across and within borders on a quotidian basis, with a focus on the English poor laws as transplanted in British North America and the territorial strategies communities used in order to disown the claims of outsiders. The chapter concludes with a discussion of the colonial world of multiple borders and statuses as exemplified in the 1763 declaration with respect to Native Americans that became such a potent source of colonial discontent.

## Subjecthood, Status, and Territorial Rights in Early Modern Britain

By the early seventeenth century in England, the principal difference between subject and alien had to do with the right to own real property (land and fixtures). The ownership of real property was a privilege restricted to English subjects. Aliens might acquire and enjoy real property, but their title to it was "defeasible," that is, subject to termination by the state, and therefore precarious. Because aliens lacked rights to real property, it followed that they were barred from bringing legal actions involving real property and from holding positions or exercising rights to which real property qualifications were attached. During the second half of the seventeenth century, a series of navigation acts prohibiting aliens from participating in England's expanding colonial trade exacerbated alien legal disabilities.

If the basic differences between subject and alien had coalesced by the early seventeenth century, however, they lacked sustained theoretical articulation. This gap was filled by the chief justice of the Court of Common Pleas, Sir Edward Coke, in his enormously influential opinion in *Calvin's Case* (1608). *Calvin's Case* grew out of litigation commenced in the name of Robert Calvin, an infant born in Scotland in 1606 – that is, after James VI of Scotland acceded to the English throne as James I. Calvin's counsel argued that their client had been barred from taking possession of lands in England that he had legally inherited. Opposing counsel maintained that Calvin was barred from inheriting and suing for lands in England because he was not an English subject. The dispute demanded a clarification of the nature of the recent union of the English and Scottish crowns, specifically with reference to the rights of subjects of one kingdom in the other.

Coke interpreted the problem in terms of "ligeance." The "ligeance" due from the subject to his sovereign followed from the subject's birth within the sovereign's domain. As Coke put it: "This ligeance and obedience is an incident inseparable to every subject: for as soon as he is born, he oweth by birth-right ligeance and obedience to his Sovereign."[1] Subject and sovereign were bound by reciprocal obligations: "for as the subject oweth to the King his true and faithful ligeance and obedience, so the Sovereign is to govern and protect his subjects."[2] Such reciprocity of allegiance and protection did not mean, however, that this was a contractual quid pro quo that could be shrugged off at will. The allegiance and obedience owed by the natural-born subject were perpetual. They subsisted even though the protection of the sovereign might be lost (for instance, if the sovereign lost the territory in which the subject lived as a result of military defeat).

According to Coke's rendering of birthright subjecthood, the core of the relationship between subject and sovereign was natural, an outgrowth of the subject's birth. The external expression of this relationship, however, was necessarily political and legal. To be sure, the subject owed allegiance to the natural body of the king. However, because the king could fulfill his obligation of protection only in his full political and legal capacity, he defined the community of allegiance

[1] *Calvin's Case*, 7 Coke Rep. 1a, 4b (1608).
[2] Id.

only upon acceding to the Crown. Thus, if subjects born in Scotland after the accession of James VI to the throne of England owed allegiance to James's natural body, James's protection of them flowed in his capacities as ruler of England *and* Scotland. From this, Coke reasoned that all *post-nati* Scotsmen – that is, those such as Calvin who were born after James VI of Scotland became James I of England – had necessarily to be considered natural-born subjects in Scotland *and* England. The Scottish-born Calvin would, as a result, not suffer alien legal disabilities in England. As a result of the rule in *Calvin's Case,* native-born Scotsmen, Irishmen, and Englishmen were all natural-born subjects of the king and exempt from alien legal disabilities in his various dominions.

If *Calvin's Case* clarified the rights of natural-born subjects, it said little about how aliens were to be incorporated into the community of allegiance. In the seventeenth century, two basic procedures – parliamentary acts of naturalization and royal letters patent of denization – accomplished this. Parliamentary acts of naturalization effected the legal fiction that the alien was natural-born. They allowed the alien to acquire title to lands through purchase, descent, or devise and also, subject to certain restrictions, granted him full political rights. Issued by the Crown, royal letters patent of denization got rid of fewer alien legal disabilities. A denizen might purchase and own real property, but could neither inherit nor transmit it through devise or descent. The denizen also lacked political rights. Nevertheless, denization remained a popular option because parliamentary acts of naturalization were expensive and cumbersome.

The seventeenth century was a time of bitter struggle between the Crown and Parliament. After the Glorious Revolution of 1688, Parliament emerged as the winner and the embodiment of English sovereignty. Its triumph was accompanied by an intellectual revolution, an important component of which was the new political theory of John Locke.

Rejecting Filmerian notions of the divine or patriarchal right of kings and natural social hierarchies, Locke argued that society and government emerged instead out of an originary social compact in which free individuals joined together of their own will to form political communities. Allegiance had no place in the state of nature. It could exist only in political society, where it was not a function of obligations owing at birth, but was entirely a creature of law. Although allegiance went to the king, Locke insisted, "'tis not to him as Supream Legislator, but as *Supream Executor* of the Law, made by a joint Power of him with others; *Allegiance* being nothing but an *Obedience according to Law*, which when he violates, he has no right to Obedience, nor can claim it otherwise than as the publick Person vested with the Power of the Law."[3] Thus, allegiance, as a creature of law, was ultimately a function of the individual consent that had given rise to laws in the first place.

In the late seventeenth century, the orthodox theories of *Calvin's Case* continued to dominate the legal framing of British subjecthood. The Lockean revolution made little immediate headway. However, after 1688, notions of consent slowly infiltrated understandings of subjecthood. The confused amalgam of Cokean and Lockean ideas is evident in Sir William Blackstone's mid-eighteenth-century rendering of the law of allegiance. Cleaving to Cokean ideas of perpetual, involuntary allegiance grounded in birth, Blackstone maintained that "[n]atural allegiance is such as is due from all men born within the king's dominions immediately upon their birth." Yet he also observed that the bond of allegiance might be sundered by "the united concurrence of the legislature."[4] For Blackstone and his contemporaries, in other words, even as they clung to older common law notions of natural, involuntary, and perpetual allegiance, it had become impossible to ignore increasingly influential Lockean theories that grounded society and government in consent and contract.

The drama of the contest between notions of political membership grounded in birth and those grounded in consent bypassed the majority of British subjects, who were denied full membership based on legal status regardless of the theory that informed subjecthood. In experiencing such denial, British subjects shared many of the legal disabilities of aliens.

This was especially true of the largest demographic group denied full membership: women. Whether married or unmarried, women

---

[3] John Locke, *Two Treatises of Government*, 2d ed., Peter Laslett, ed. (Cambridge: Cambridge University Press, 1988), p. 368 (emphasis in original).

[4] Sir William Blackstone, *Commentaries on the Laws of England: A Facsimile of the First Edition of 1765–1769*, vol. I (Chicago: University of Chicago Press, 1979), p. 357.

lacked rights to vote, hold public offices, and enter professions. The legal disabilities endured by married women were far greater than those imposed upon unmarried ones. Under the law of *baron* and *feme*, as the law of domestic relations was known, husbands controlled the physical persons of their wives. Such control extended to the right to inflict physical punishment. Built upon this initial premise was a highly articulated system of "coverture" according to which married women's legal and civic personalities were deemed occluded or "covered" by those of their husbands. Married women were thus represented to the outside world by their husbands, even when it came to controlling their own property. This legal invisibility is exemplified by the English law of "petit treason." From 1351 to 1790, women guilty of murdering their husbands were convicted of "petit treason." They were supposed to suffer the punishment meted out to female traitors: to be burned at the stake. Although women did not frequently suffer this punishment in the eighteenth century, the statute remained on the books. For our purposes, it is the legal structure of the crime that is revealing. A married woman's husband was, as far as she was concerned, akin to the state. Her primary legal duties and obligations were owing not to the state, but to him.

To be sure, women were hardly the only group who shared legal disabilities with aliens. Propertyless males were also denied the rights to vote and hold offices on the grounds that the ownership of real property gave men a unique stake in society and ensured that men would exercise such rights independently. Following this logic, all those dependent on public authorities for support – namely paupers – were excluded from any voice in government.

Equally important, and highly revealing of how British subjects and aliens shared legal disabilities, is the fact that rights to territorial presence and movement were not considered basic incidents of British subjecthood. British subjects could be barred from leaving the kingdom, denied rights to remain in the kingdom, and prevented from moving at will throughout the kingdom. In general, while women suffered all these restrictions, their rights to presence and movement were restricted even further because they were subordinated to, and followed from, the rights of their fathers and husbands.

A centuries-old tradition in English politico-legal thought required that Englishmen "attend at all times, the Service and Defence of their

King and Native Country when they shall be thereunto required."[5]
This meant that Englishmen were barred from leaving the kingdom
at will. A 1381 act prohibited "the Passage utterly of all Manner of
People ... except only the Lords and other Great Men of the Realm,
and true and notable Merchants, and the King's Soldiers ... out of
the said Realm, without the King's special Licence [*sic*]."[6] In 1606,
after James VI of Scotland became James I of England, an act of
Parliament repealed the 1381 act with a view to easing movement
between the two kingdoms. However, the 1381 act cast a shadow
over seventeenth-century emigration. Its imprint is evident in the first
Charter of Virginia (1606), which specifically authorized the departure
to America of "Sir Thomas Gates, Sir George Somers ..." and others to
"travel thitherward, and to abide and inhabit there, in every the said
colonies and plantations," provided "that none of the said persons be
such, as shall hereafter be specially restrained by us, our heirs or successors."[7] The second and third Virginia charters (1609 and 1612) and
the New England charter (1620) made a point of authorizing English
subjects' departure to these colonies, which suggests that exit rights
continued to be seen as subject to limitation. The same language
exists in the Carolina, Maryland, and Pennsylvania charters. By the
eighteenth century, mercantilist concerns had begun to play a role in
official attempts to discourage out-migration. If colonial Americans
were eager to attract the skilled and the propertied, the British government was concerned precisely to prevent such groups from leaving.
The Act of 1718 "to prevent the inconveniences arising from seduc-
ing Artificers in the Manufactures of Great Britain into foreign parts"
sought to retain such valuable workers in the kingdom.[8]

[5] Quote from Proclamation of 1635 restraining the "King's Subjects Departing out of the
Realm without License" into "the Kingdom, or Country of any Foreign Prince, State, or
Potentate," in John Rushworth, ed., *Historical Collections, the Second Part, Containing
the Principal Matters Which Happened from the Dissolution of the Parliament on the
10th of March 4 Car. 1 1628/29 until the Summoning of Another Parliament, Which Met
at Westminster, April 13, 1640* (London: John Wright & Richard Chiswell, 1680), p. 298.

[6] Statute of 1381 (5 Ric. II, St. 1, c. 2), in Owen Ruffhead, ed., *Statutes at Large, from
Magna Charta to the Twenty-Fifth Year of the Reign of King George the Third, inclusive*, vol. I (London: Charles Eyre & Andrew Strahan, Printers, 1786), pp. 330–32.

[7] Samuel Lucas, *Charters of the Old English Colonies in America* (London: John
W. Parker, West Strand, 1850), p. 5.

[8] 5 Geo. I, c. 27 (1718), in John Raithby, ed., *Statutes at Large, of England and of
Great-Britain: From Magna Carta to the Union of the Kingdoms of Great Britain &
Ireland*, vol. 8 (London: George Eyre & Andrew Strahan, 1811), pp. 216–18.

By the mid-eighteenth century, in the midst of widespread population movements within Europe and across the Atlantic, European legal thinkers began to represent a man's right to exit the realm as a natural right that could not be limited by royal prerogative. The Swiss international law thinker Emmerich de Vattel argued that men should be able to expatriate themselves if they were unable to earn a living, if society disregarded its obligations to them, or if the government under which they lived was changed without their consent.[9] The importance of the right of mobility was even recognized by Blackstone, who characterized "the power of loco-motion, of changing situation, or removing one's person to whatsoever place one's own inclination may direct" as a hallmark of the Englishman's personal liberty.[10] However, writing at a time when anxiety about population loss was running high in Great Britain, Blackstone was also careful to add that the right was open to abridgment.

If, by the mid-eighteenth century, there were voices in support of the Briton's right to leave the kingdom of his own volition, there was no question that the Briton could be removed from the kingdom against his will. From very early on, the North American colonies had been seen as a way of accommodating England's superfluous people, whose right to remain in England could be legally abridged. In his *Pamphlet for the Virginia Enterprise* (1585), Richard Hakluyt the Elder had argued that those who were "burdensome or hurtefull to this Realme at home" could be rendered "profitable members" by being shipped out to America.[11]

In the early seventeenth century, the English began to ship convicts to the New World. After the Restoration, following a lull during the middle decades of the century, the practice picked up. Over the last four decades of the seventeenth century, approximately 4,500 English felons were transported to the North American colonies. However, the practice really took off after the passage of the Transportation Act of 1718. Under the aegis of the Transportation Act, the British

---

[9] Emmerich de Vattel, *The Law of Nations*, vol. I (Northampton, MA: Thomas Pomroy, for S. & E. Butler, 1805), pp. 166–67.

[10] Blackstone, *Commentaries on the Laws of England*, vol. I, p. 130.

[11] Richard Hakluyt the Elder, "Pamphlet for the Virginia Enterprise" (n.d.), in E. G. R. Taylor, ed., *Original Writings and Correspondence of the Two Richard Hakluyts*, vol. II (London: Hakluyt Society, 1935), p. 340.

government devoted significant resources to shipping convicts out of Great Britain. Some 50,000 were transported to America in the eighteenth century. Transportation of convicts was the most important form of involuntary transportation to North America after African slavery. Two-thirds of all felons convicted at the Old Bailey, London's principal criminal court, suffered this fate.

Unlike the transportation of convicts, shipments of British paupers overseas never rose to the level of a concerted national policy. In 1618 and 1619, the City of London shipped 200 poor children to Virginia at a cost of about £500. Thereafter, although statistics are hard to obtain, individual parishes continued the practice of sending their paupers to the North American colonies all the way up to the American Revolution and thereafter. Such individuals had few legal options to resist such transportation.

British subjects also lacked the right to travel and reside throughout the kingdom. A complex grid of laws restricted the mobility and residence of, or forced mobility and residence upon, impoverished, mobile, "masterless" subjects. The Elizabethan poor laws were critical in this respect. Beginning in 1572 and stretching into the early seventeenth century, a series of acts sought to regulate the poor and punish vagrancy. But the crucial feature of English poor law administration was the fixing of responsibility for relief of the poor on local governments. This was formalized in the 1662 Settlement Law, which stipulated how local poor relief officials should determine who came under their jurisdiction for purposes of administering poor relief and how they could remove poor people to their home parishes. The critical legal concept of "settlement" or "inhabitancy" emerged to refer to local residence rights. Settlement determined where one belonged and, hence, where one could be returned against one's will.

From the preceding discussion, it should be clear that British subjects in the early modern period shared many of the legal disabilities imposed upon aliens. Based upon their status, many British subjects did not enjoy rights to participate in government, exercise control over property, and bring lawsuits. Neither did they enjoy unimpeded rights to leave, remain in, or travel throughout the kingdom. British subjecthood mattered. But statuses other than subjecthood shaped lives in far more powerful ways.

## Instrumentalizing Subjecthood in British North America

Colonial Americans replicated many of the gender and class statuses of the mother country. Full membership was not available to all who were nominally inside the community of allegiance. On the eve of the American Revolution, white men were required to own land or personal property of a specified value, or pay taxes, in order to vote. Paupers and servants were unable to vote in some colonies, religious minorities in others. Married women were, of course, always virtually represented by their husbands. In several colonies, laws expressly barred women from voting, although there were cases of propertied widows voting in Massachusetts and New York.

Even as colonial Americans retained inherited British hierarchies within their communities, however, they began to deploy subjecthood self-consciously as a tool to encourage the influx of desirable settlers from overseas or to mark as outsiders, foreigners, and inferiors those present among them. Easing access to subjecthood, or denying it, thus became a kind of "immigration regulation," a way of managing presence and movement in the shaping of nascent communities. Such instrumentalizations of subjecthood might even have altered colonial Americans' own understandings of subjecthood, pushing them away from Cokean notions of membership rooted in birth to Lockean ones rooted in consent and contract.

Colonial Americans were vocal about the need to facilitate naturalization in order to attract propertied European Protestant migrants. Such migrants would naturally want the security of property that British subjecthood assured. Accordingly, as early as 1700, promoters such as William Penn were urging that Parliament provide "that such foreigners that come to inhabit in any of the King's colonies that are by Act of Assembly declared freemen in the said Provinces, shall enjoy the rights and liberties of English subjects, except being masters or commanders of vessells [*sic*] and ships of trade."[12]

In 1709, Parliament tried out a general naturalization act for European Protestants. However, the act was short-lived. It was repealed in 1712 after German Protestant refugees Parliament hoped would head to North America flooded instead into London. Aliens

[12] John R. Brodhead, *Documents Relative to the Colonial History of the State of New York*, vol. IV (Albany, NY: Weed, Parsons & Co., 1854), p. 757.

were compelled once again to pursue expensive private naturalization acts in Parliament. In the absence of a general naturalization act, however, various colonies took the initiative and adopted aliens as subjects on their own. The exigencies of attracting and keeping valuable settlers led to a loosening of orthodox British practices.

Although neither the colonies' foundational documents nor common law principles explicitly granted colonial governments a naturalization authority, rights conferred upon them to admit to membership "any Person or Persons, as well Strangers and Aliens" were often read as rights to confer status as British subjects.[13] The procedures that emerged to admit aliens to the status of subjects varied from colony to colony. In New England, admission to freemanship served as the equivalent of naturalization. The central government and the towns participated in inducting aliens into the political community. Other colonies established general naturalization requirements administered by local courts. New York and Pennsylvania performed group naturalizations.

In general, colonial naturalizations proved easier to procure than parliamentary naturalizations in England. Colonial legislatures and governors paid little heed to basic distinctions between denization and naturalization. They reduced various deterrents to naturalization such as religious oaths and exorbitant fees. Although Protestants were clearly the desired migrants, on occasion even Catholics were naturalized. The relaxation of naturalization laws in the colonies stemmed at least in part from competition among colonies to attract propertied European settlers and fears that restrictive naturalization policies in one colony might drive desirable migrants to others. In 1761, New York's lieutenant governor, Cadwallader Colden, noted: "Should we in this Province refuse such acts of naturalization, which can easily be obtained in the neighbouring colonies, it would draw all foreigners, who are willing to settle and improve lands, from this Colony to the others."[14] Relaxed naturalization practices were thus of a piece with other enticements such as relaxation of traditional British alien legal disabilities. In the Carolinas, for example, proprietors relinquished

[13] James H. Kettner, *The Development of American Citizenship, 1608–1870* (Chapel Hill: University of North Carolina Press, 1978), p. 79.
[14] Cited in id., p. 110.

their right to escheats, thereby assuring migrants that they could pass their lands on to their heirs, devisees, or assignees. Certain colonies allowed aliens to exercise political rights. A Georgia law of 1761 permitted aliens who had resided in the colony for six months to vote if they were free, white, male, twenty-one years old, and owned fifty acres of land. Aliens in the colonies might even have been able to hold offices they would have been barred from holding in England, although this was not entirely free from doubt under the Act of Settlement (1701). In 1773, Parliament finally clarified the issue when it ruled that the provisions of the Act barring aliens from holding offices pertained only to Great Britain and Ireland.

In 1740, Parliament finally provided a general naturalization act for the North American colonies. The preamble of the act reflected prevailing mercantilist sentiments in stating that "the Increase of People is a Means of advancing the Wealth and Strength of any Nation or Country: And ... many Foreigners and Strangers, from the Lenity of our Government, the Purity of our Religion, the Benefit of our Laws, the Advantages of our Trade, and the Security of our Property, might be induced to come and settle in some of his Majesty's Colonies in America, if they were made Partakers of the Advantages and Privileges which the natural born Subjects of this Realm do enjoy."[15] The Act required applicants to reside seven years or more in any of the colonies. There were also requirements that applicants take oaths of allegiance and profess Christian beliefs (with exemptions for Quakers and Jews). The Act was welcomed: thousands naturalized under its aegis.

Despite the passage of the 1740 Act, however, colonies continued to pass local naturalization acts. These acts were often disallowed, to the dismay of colonies such as New York, Pennsylvania, and Virginia. In 1773, as part of a broader effort to crack down on loose colonial practices, London began to require colonial governments to invalidate local naturalizations. The tensions between the colonies and Great Britain over the naturalization and settlement of migrants would become one of the grievances of colonial Americans in their struggle to break from Great Britain.

---

[15] Preamble to An Act for naturalizing such foreign Protestants, and others therein mentioned, as are settled, or shall settle, in any of his Majesty's Colonies in America, 13 Geo. II, c. 7 (1740), in Ruffhead, ed., *Statutes at Large*, vol. VI, p. 134.

If practical concerns pushed colonial Americans to liberalize membership for propertied European migrants, practical concerns drove them to withhold membership from the Native Americans and blacks in whose midst they lived. If membership could be used to welcome, it could also be used to exclude.

The first exclusionary use of membership must be in the context of English dealings with Native Americans. In New England and the Chesapeake, early English colonists relied upon purchases, gifts, and treaties to acquire lands from Native Americans. But if such transactions implicitly recognized the preexisting rights of Native Americans in their lands, the English effortlessly moved from transacting with Native Americans to asserting sovereignty over them. The royal charters were claims of territorial sovereignty vis-à-vis other European powers, but could also be used to claim sovereignty over Native Americans. If certain legal discourses represented Native Americans as conquered subjects of the Crown, however, discourses on the ground often represented them as aliens.

Concrete proof of Native Americans' legal status as aliens in the early colonial period lies in the fact that it became meaningful to extend or deny naturalization to them, which means that they were seen by the English as outside the community of allegiance to begin with. The only unambiguous naturalization in New England before 1700 was a 1695 Connecticut act that declared the Indian Abimelech, grandson of Uncas, a subject of the king and granted him "the priuiledg and protection of his Maties lawes this Colony alowes his subjects here, provided he take the oath of allegiance."[16] The impulse behind this unusual act seems to have been to resolve a land title dispute. Someone must have alleged, in other words, that Abimelech was an alien and, as such, could not convey good title to real property. The naturalization would have taken care of that problem. Abimelech's naturalization was, of course, the exception that proved the rule. For the most part, Native Americans in New England remained a group ineligible to freemanship. The historian Yasuhide Kawashima argues that naturalization was "almost impossible" for Native Americans in Massachusetts

---

[16] Charles J. Hoadly, ed., *The Public Records of the Colony of Connecticut*, vol. IV (Hartford, CT: Case, Lockwood & Brainard, 1868), p. 153.

and that no recorded cases of Native Americans becoming British subjects exist.[17]

As English settlements and assertions of sovereignty grew in strength, and as Native American resistance was progressively broken down through disease, war, and westward migration, there emerged three distinct categories of Indians that differed on the basis of their relationship and proximity to English power: so-called "foreign Indians," "plantation Indians," and individual Indians who lived within English communities without tribal ties.

"Foreign Indians" was the term used to designate Native Americans who lived beyond the frontier of white settlement. Representations of Native Americans as "foreign" were never part of any genuine or stable recognition of native sovereignty. On the one hand, the English regularly engaged in diplomatic negotiations with frontier Native Americans just as they might with any other foreign government. They attended Indian conferences and signed treaties that promoted commerce, established protocols in respect of captives, and called for the renunciation of revenge. Until the 1760s, frontier Native Americans concluded treaties and violated them, playing the English and the French against one another. On the other hand, frontier Native American societies were rarely treated as sovereign equals in the way that another European power might be because of the reach of British sovereignty over them. In 1693, for example, the so-called "Eastern Indians" on Massachusetts's northern frontier pledged obedience to English law (except when it came to internal disputes within the tribes) and even gave up hostages to back up their pledge. In 1717, Massachusetts' Governor Shute told the sachems of the "Eastern Indians" that they, just like other colonial Americans, were subjects of the Crown. Similar assurances were given to Native Americans on Massachusetts's western frontiers and, indeed, in other colonies. Native Americans were thus not like other foreigners. Ultimately, representations of frontier Native Americans as "foreign" were designed to place them beyond the advancing frontier of white settlement and to define them as outside the community.

---

[17] Yasuhide Kawashima, *Puritan Justice and the Indian: White Man's Law in Massachusetts, 1630–1763* (Middletown, CT: Wesleyan University Press, 1986), p. 97.

The "plantation Indians" of Massachusetts lay not beyond the frontier of white settlement, but instead had frontiers drawn around them. They mark the beginning of the Indian reservation. In May 1677, the Massachusetts General Court passed an act requiring that all Indians within the colony, "Praying Indians as well as others," be restricted to one of the four plantations of Natick, Punkapaug, Hassanimesit, and Wamesit. In 1681, another act reduced the number of such towns to three (Natick, Punkapaug, and Wamesit) and ordered that, since there was "land sufficient to improve for many families more than are of them," those Indians found outside those reservations be sent to "the House of Corrections or Prison, until he or they engage to comply with this Order."[18] In other words, Native Americans were not permitted to stray beyond the borders of plantations designated for their use. A superintendent of Indian affairs supervised Indian villages in Massachusetts and would do so throughout the colonial period.

The final category of Native Americans, individuals who lived among the English, was, of course, entirely subject to the laws of the communities in which they lived. Such Native Americans were simply consigned to a lesser membership. They were generally barred from participating in colonial politics. If they were sporadically allowed to vote in Massachusetts, no Native American ever represented his town to the Massachusetts General Court.

Thus, despite frequent assurances by colonial officials that Native Americans were British subjects, Native Americans could be described and treated as foreigners and aliens on the basis of their changing relationship to settlers' power or in the context of their ability to transfer land titles. But what is interesting about the designation of Native Americans as aliens is the kind of aliens they were. Native Americans were made aliens not by having come from anywhere, but by having bounded territorial English communities literally emerge in their midst and name them as such. It was when these communities placed Native Americans beyond a frontier of the communities' making, or drew borders around them, that Native Americans became aliens.

Blacks represent another instance of the strategic denial of membership, but as much to control as to cabin, exclude, and remove. Although estimates vary, Europeans forcibly transported somewhere

---

[18] Id., p. 29.

between 250,000 and 400,000 Africans to the mainland colonies over the course of the seventeenth and eighteenth centuries. Like European migrants, African forced migrants played a crucial role in improving the value of lands. However, their experience of membership differed dramatically.

In the earliest decades of African presence in the colonies, Africans' status did not differ significantly from that of European indentured servants. But this changed after Virginia pioneered the legal codification of slavery in 1661. Slavery soon became the dominant status of blacks in every colony. In rapid succession, enslaved blacks lost a number of public and private rights. They were excluded from the political process; barred from testifying in courts; prohibited from engaging in commercial activity; and unable to form legally recognized families.

By the eighteenth century, small communities of free blacks existed in every colony, with percentages of free blacks proportionately higher in New England and the Mid-Atlantic colonies. There were some instances in the eighteenth century of free blacks' voting in local elections, serving in militias, and owning property. However, there is no doubt that, in general, free blacks occupied a subordinate status. In 1668, the Virginia Assembly stated that free blacks "ought not in all respects to be admitted to a full fruition of the exemptions and immunities of the English."[19] By the early eighteenth century, free blacks were widely denied many political and legal rights. Some of the restrictions of slave codes were extended to them.

Were slaves and free blacks British subjects? Under the logic of *Calvin's Case*, native-born slaves and free blacks should have been considered British subjects. Being slotted into an inferior legal status – as was the case of the propertyless, women, and paupers – was not necessarily at odds with simultaneously being a British subject. As the eighteenth century progressed, there was an emerging recognition in certain reformist circles that slaves might be entitled at least to some of the rights of British subjects. By the 1760s, some administrators in London had begun to argue that slaves in the North American colonies deserved greater protections than they enjoyed at the hands of their masters. In 1768, William Knox asserted that slaves merited "an

---

[19] Smith, *Civic Ideals*, p. 65.

impartial dispensation of the laws," one that prevented cruelties such as being "lacerated by whips [and] racked by every species of torture the most wanton tyranny can invent."[20] For a figure like Knox, the protection of slaves entailed precisely the greater parliamentary control over conditions in North America that made colonial Americans nervous. In the momentous case of *Somerset v. Stewart* (1772), Lord Mansfield granted a writ of *habeas corpus* to prevent a Virginia slave owner from forcibly transporting his slave out of England. Formally, the decision did not affect slavery in the colonies or even England, but it was widely viewed as supporting the position that slaves might turn to British courts for protection.[21]

As in the case of Native Americans, however, such scattered instances of recognition that free and enslaved blacks were entitled to some of the rights of British subjects went along with practices that marked blacks as foreigners. Colonial Americans routinely distinguished between "country-born" slaves and "outlandish" Africans. But they did so not so much to recognize the former as fellow subjects as to emphasize the rebelliousness of the latter. The spirit of resistance among "outlandish" Africans was, according to contemporaries, much harder to quell. "If he must be broke," wrote an English observer, "either from Obstinacy, or, which I am more apt to suppose, from Greatness of Soul, [i]t will require ... hard Discipline ... You would really be surpriz'd at their Perseverance ... they often die before they can be conquer'd."[22] "Outlandish" blacks were viewed as more likely to abscond than native-born ones. In the eighteenth century, owners of fugitive slaves regularly placed newspaper announcements in which they identified escapees in terms of their African origins, describing them as "Gambia men," for example, or as men from the "Fullah Country."

Far more revealing, South Carolina and Virginia required free blacks to leave the colony or be re-enslaved. This rule applied not to white indentured laborers, who were considered valuable settlers at the end

---

[20] William Knox, *Three Tracts Respecting the Conversion and Instruction of the Free Indians and Negroe Slaves in the Colonies; Addressed to the Venerable Society for the Propagation of the Gospel in Foreign Parts*, rev. ed. (London: J. Debrett, 1789), p. 31.

[21] *Somerset v. Stewart*, 98 Eng. Rep. 499 (1772).

[22] "Observations in Several Voyages and Travels in America" (July 1746), in Lyon G. Tyler, ed., *William and Mary College Quarterly Historical Magazine*, vol. XVI, no. 1 (Richmond, VA: Whittet & Shepperson, 1907), p. 7.

of their indentures, but *only* to blacks and regardless of where they had been born – that is, whether or not they were native-born. This suggests something significant about the nature of blacks' member-ship in colonial polities notwithstanding intimations from reformers in London that blacks were deserving of protections. Blacks' presence was tolerated in the colonies as long as they were slaves. When they became free, they could be ordered to leave. It was the moment of free-dom – that is, the moment when blacks were least dependent and most qualified to be full members of the polity – that made them excludable and removable from the community.

Those cast outside the community of allegiance – Native Americans and free blacks – could thus also be cast out of the territory of the community, their foreignness reinscribed in the process. However, where such groups could not be expelled, or when the desirability of their labor made expelling them non-feasible, spatial restrictions abounded. These were the internal analogue of external borders. Colonies instituted night watches and curfews to safeguard towns against the suspicious activities of Native Americans and free blacks. In 1703, Massachusetts established a curfew providing that no "Indian, Negro or Mulatto Servant or Slave may presume to absent from the Families whereto they respectively belong" after nine o'clock at night. Violators were to be jailed, subjected to physical punishment, and then restored to their owners. In 1732, the Long Island town of Brookhaven prohibited slaves from going out at night at all. Similarly, in 1737, Maryland forbade blacks "from Rambling, rideing or Going a Broad in the night." The enforcement of such laws varied from place to place. However, their pervasiveness suggests a general concern with controlling the presence and mobility of blacks and Indians.[23]

## "Immigration Law" in British North America

If manipulations of British subjecthood served to welcome, exclude, repel, and control, they did not constitute a general system of terri-torial restriction governing presence and movement. An examination

[23] Laws quoted in Sally E. Hadden, "The Fragmented Laws of Slavery in the Colonial and Revolutionary Eras," in Michael Grossberg and Christopher Tomlins, eds., *The Cambridge History of Law in America*, vol. I (Cambridge: Cambridge University Press, 2008), pp. 253–87, 267.

of the colonial analogues of "immigration law" – the legal systems regulating territorial presence and movement – reveals that the insider versus outsider distinction did not map onto the subject–alien distinction. Those most likely to be excluded and removed from nascent communities were fellow British subjects.

American opposition to new entrants from across the Atlantic was directed primarily at British policies that sought to get rid of undesirable sections of Britain's own population. By the mid-eighteenth century, there was vocal opposition to shipments of convict labor. In 1751, Benjamin Franklin famously accused Great Britain as follows: "Thou art called our MOTHER COUNTRY; but what good *Mother* ever sent *Thieves* and *Villains* to accompany her *Children*; to corrupt some with their infectious Vices, and murder the rest?"[24] Such opposition proved unavailing. The transportation of convicts continued until 1776, when Parliament repealed its 1718 decision to transport convicts to the North American colonies.

Shipments of British paupers also provoked opposition. In the early years, colonists had actively sought out British paupers. In the early 1620s, for example, the Council of New England sought "poor children of 14 years and upwards" from the City of London, procured a letter "from the King to the Lieut. of every shire for sending their poorer sort of people to New England," and suggested that "[a] Statute of Queen Elizabeth for binding poor children apprentices … be made use of for the benefit of the plantation."[25] But New Englanders were soon disappointed with such imports. By 1632, they were asking for "skilful artificers" instead of "the very scum of the earth sent over" earlier.[26] Other colonies expressed similar views. As in the case of opposition to shipments of convicts, authorities in London disallowed outright attempts to prevent British shipments of paupers.

Americans were even less enthusiastic about receiving British Catholics. Various colonies placed legal obstacles in the way of Irish Catholics' landing. There was a steadfast refusal to resettle Acadians or French Neutrals after the British government forcibly removed

[24] Benjamin Franklin, *Writings*, J. A. Leo Lemay, ed. (New York: Library of America, 1987), p. 358.
[25] As quoted in Marilyn C. Baseler, *"Asylum for Mankind": America, 1607–1800* (Ithaca, NY: Cornell University Press, 1998), p. 32.
[26] Id.

thousands around the time of the Seven Years' War. European Protestants might occasionally receive a frosty welcome. But the distaste for Irish Catholics and French Neutrals targeted fellow British subjects.

In keeping with this logic, colonial "immigration laws" covered not only migrants from across the Atlantic, but also migrants between and within the colonies. The most general and developed system of territorial restriction in colonial America was that of the poor laws. Descended from the English poor laws, colonial poor laws were a highly decentralized system that managed the presence and movement of individuals, whether they were British subjects or aliens, whether they were from "beyond sea," neighboring colonies, or neighboring counties and towns.

The principal fear of colonial Americans in regard to newcomers from "beyond sea" was that they would require public assistance and become a charge to the localities in which they were landed. The solution was typically to require shipmasters to provide lists of passengers and post bonds to indemnify ports for costs incurred. Some of these laws were directed at aliens alone. For example, a Rhode Island law of 1700, reenacted in 1729, required shipmasters bringing in foreigners from outside "Great Britain, Ireland, Jersey and Guernsey" to post a £50 bond to ensure that their passengers would not become public charges.[27] But the laws of jurisdictions like Massachusetts did not single out passengers from outside the community of allegiance as Rhode Island did, but simply targeted all passengers from "beyond sea."

Laws directed at passengers from "beyond sea" were merely an external dimension of the internal grid of colonial poor relief administration. In colonial New England, for example, poor laws provided that every individual possessed a settlement or inhabitancy in, or belonged to, a particular town, which meant that he or she had legally recognized claims only upon that town's treasury for purposes of poor relief and legally recognized rights of residence only within the territory of that town. There were various ways in which individuals could acquire a settlement, including uncontested residence within the town for a specified period of time. The law also bore the distinct stamp of legal coverture: a woman's legal residence followed that of her father or, if she was married, that of her husband. Vis-à-vis other towns, every

---

[27] Id., pp. 71–72.

town was compelled to accept the return of, and pay for the relief of, an individual who possessed a settlement in it.

Within this system, outsiders or "foreigners" were understood in terms of settlement in a town rather than in terms of membership in the community of allegiance. Just as ship captains were required to identify passengers they brought over on their ships, town inhabitants were required to identify to town authorities those outsiders whom they "entertained." In 1700, 1723, and 1726, in a series of "entertainment" statutes, Massachusetts enacted laws declaring that no strangers could be entertained in any town for more than a certain number of days without notice being given to town selectmen; penalties were imposed on town inhabitants who violated these provisions.

In eighteenth-century New England, outsiders could also be "warned out" of towns. In most cases, "warning out" consisted of providing the individual with formal notice to leave. Once such notice had been given, the town had met the legal requirements to ensure that such an individual could not obtain a legal settlement in the town. Such an individual's presence might then be tolerated: he or she could live, work, and pay taxes in the town without acquiring a settlement therein. When he or she became needy, the town could administer relief and charge the town of the individual's settlement for reimbursement. But in certain cases, when the claims of the individual upon the town treasury became excessive or chronic, or when the individual was deemed troublesome, the individual could be forcibly shipped out of the town to the town to which he or she "belonged." In order to assist their inhabitants in negotiating this system, towns often provided inhabitants with travel documents – species of internal passports – attesting that the inhabitants were in fact settled there and would be taken back if necessary.

During the colonial period, when migration into New England from "beyond sea" was not great, the principal targets of the poor laws were not aliens, but New Englanders themselves. The historian Ruth Herndon's study of "warning out" in Rhode Island between 1750 and 1800 finds that only a small fraction (3.4 percent) of "warned out" transients were foreign-born: the vast majority were native-born New Englanders.[28] Herndon's study uncovers a world in which thousands

---

[28] Ruth W. Herndon, *Unwelcome Americans: Living on the Margin in Early New England* (Philadelphia: University of Pennsylvania Press, 2001), pp. 13–14.

of individuals were routinely interviewed by town officials to discover where they were settled in order to determine whether or not they should be "warned out" of town and hence possibly returned to the towns where they belonged. Often, this was the result of a kind of popular policing: suspicious townspeople might report an annoying neighbor to town officials. Not surprisingly, single women, unmarried mothers, widows, the disabled, the sick, the aged, and subordinated racial groups were disproportionately represented among the ranks of those "warned out." Historians have identified a number of instances in which Native Americans were denied settlements in Massachusetts towns and ordered to leave.

But the poor laws were not merely ways of regulating the influx and presence of outsiders from "beyond sea" or neighboring towns. Just as colonial Americans manipulated British subjecthood to make European aliens subjects and Native Americans and blacks aliens or non-subjects, the poor laws furnished New Englanders opportunities to make outsiders. These outsiders were their former neighbors.

According to numbers compiled by David Grayson Allen for Massachusetts, in the seventeenth century a total of 14 towns were created through the division of older towns and, in the eighteenth century, a total of 119 towns. A whopping 65 percent of all towns created during the eighteenth century came into being through the division of older towns.[29] How are we to understand this incessant splitting?

The conventional story was that, as a town expanded, those living in outlying areas of the town (or "outlivers") found it difficult to participate in the life of the town (local government, attendance at the meetinghouse, sending children to school). Sheer physical distance prevented them from doing so. Therefore, as communities of outlivers coalesced, it made sense to petition the Massachusetts General Court to be incorporated into another town. In 1727, for example, outlivers of Scituate and Abingdon asked to be set off from their respective towns and formed into a new town, claiming that "most of ye Petitioners are situated at ye Westernmost part of sd. Town of Scituate near seven miles distant from meeting, & are obliged to Travail [sic]

---

[29] David Grayson Allen, "The Zuckerman Thesis and the Process of Legal Rationalization in Provincial Massachusetts," *William and Mary Quarterly* 29, no. 3 (1972): 443–60, 453.

near Ten miles to all Town Meetings & managing of Town Affairs, to
the very great dissatisfaction and disturbance of ye petrs in ye Civil
and Religious [matters]."[30]

But there is another story to be told about town-splitting that is far
less innocuous than the one of splitting towns to spare outlivers the
rigors of trudging along snowy New England roads to attend schools,
prayer services, and town meetings. Town centers were older than outlying areas. The neediest members of towns – the aged, widows, and so
on – tended to live in the town center. When outlivers were petitioning
to be set off into another town, they were doing so with full knowledge of the logic of settlement and "warning out." As a new town,
they would no longer have to support poor fellow townspeople who
were disproportionately settled in the town center. Furthermore, they
could, if need be, physically remove their former poorer neighbors
from their midst. We know about this other story from the complaints
of those living in town centers, who occasionally opposed the petitions to split the towns. The early-eighteenth-century dispute between
Boston and Muddy River (a hamlet belonging to Boston) makes this
clear. In 1701, the inhabitants of Muddy River had unsuccessfully petitioned Boston for permission to be set off from that town by reason of
"the remoteness of their Scituation, which renders them uncapable of
enjoying equall benefit and advantage with other of the Inhabitants,
of Publick Schools for the Instruction of their Children, relife of their
Poor, & repaireing of their Highways." Despite the denial of this initial
petition, Muddy River inhabitants kept arguing to be set off. However,
Boston's 1705 representation to the General Court in opposition to
the Muddy River petition tells a different story:

[W]e think it proper to lay before the Court the unreasonableness of their
demand, they having been hitherto supported by the Town [of Boston] while
they were not able to defray their necessary publick charges many of which
might be enumerated & the town charges now increasing upon us, & the
body of ye town abounding with poor & such as are not capable to defray
but rather greatly increase the charges for the Inhabitants of Muddy River at
such a time & being themselves grown more opulent and capable to be helpful to ye town to be rent from us seems most unreasonable, & in them very
ingrateful, & may be a bad example to others to endeavour the like, & to cutt

---

[30] Massachusetts Archives Collection, vol. 113: Towns, 1693–1729, p. 682.

the town into such shreds as will suit themselves without any due regard for the Publick Interest.

In the end, the inhabitants of Muddy River were successful. In being set off into a separate town called Brookline, they obtained important town privileges, those of no longer being obliged to support the poor of Boston and, if possible, of being able to ship undesirables out of Brookline back to Boston and other communities.[31] Similar stories were repeated in colonial Massachusetts, especially in the case of older port towns with larger numbers of poor residents (widows, transient sailors, etc.).

It should be evident that such instances of redrawing town borders had the effect of making foreigners out of one's former neighbors. Even if one's former neighbors were not rendered aliens in the formal legal sense, vis-à-vis the new town that had emerged, they lost their rights of residence and could be denied poor relief. From a legal perspective, they could be excluded and removed. There is a structural resemblance to the English practice of rendering Native Americans aliens in their own communities. Foreigners were made in colonial New England not just when they arrived from "beyond sea" and when they traveled from colony to colony, county to county, and town to town, but also when they had borders drawn around their places of residence to keep them out of emergent, more prosperous communities that sought to absolve themselves of responsibility for them.

## Conclusion

British North America was a world of multiple legal statuses and territorial borders. Subjecthood was only one of a number of important legal statuses. Most British subjects were slotted into legal statuses that meant that they shared legal disabilities with aliens when it came to voting, holding office, and even exercising rights over property. Like aliens, British subjects also lacked rights to enter and remain within every part of British territory. The poor law grid that governed movement and presence in the colonies did not distinguish between subject and alien.

In this world, there were many signs of a self-conscious and instrumental manipulation of British subjecthood and territorial borders

[31] Id., pp. 378–87.

to achieve concrete ends. Intent on attracting propertied European Protestant settlers, colonial Americans eased naturalization procedures for them. At the same time, even though Native Americans and blacks were frequently declared to be subjects of the Crown, practices on the ground sought to render both groups foreign in different ways. But instrumental uses of membership and territory were not confined to aliens, Native Americans, and blacks. Eighteenth-century New Englanders drew and redrew town boundaries in breathtakingly instrumental ways so as to designate their former neighbors as foreigners with a view to excluding them and absolving themselves of the legal responsibility of paying for their support.

For all its many and severe inequalities, the colonial world of multiple legal statuses and territorial borders was also a world that created a measure of equality arising from a shared subordination. This sense of shared subordination is captured by the term "subject." When one was a subject of the Crown, when nobody enjoyed absolute rights, rights could be adjusted, abridged, and curtailed so that, at least on occasion, subjects could be treated like aliens and whites restricted at the expense of groups they were accustomed to subordinating. Nothing embodies this sense of widespread subjection better than the Royal Proclamation of 1763 issued at the end of the Seven Years' War.

In the Proclamation, in an attempt to incorporate the former New France into the British Empire, the Crown promised Native Americans respite from the depredations of whites by acknowledging their rights over their lands. Without recognizing sovereignty or conferring true possession, the Proclamation declared that Native Americans were to have "such Parts of our Dominions and Territories as, not having been ceded to or purchased by Us, are reserved to them, or any of them, as their Hunting Grounds." White settlement was prohibited west of the Appalachians. The ban on settlement was ignored. Settlements had sprung west of the Proclamation line even before 1763. Nevertheless, the Proclamation's attempt to restrict white settlement became a source of conflict between the Crown and colonial Americans.

The Proclamation of 1763 was the product of a world in which Native Americans and whites, slave owners and slaves, subjects and aliens were variously limited by royal power. As we have seen, however, colonial Americans, through their instrumentalization of British subjecthood, were increasingly thinking of political membership in terms of consent and contract rather than in terms of birth. Thus reconceived, political membership could be granted or withheld, manipulated at will to achieve concrete ends. When the American Revolution came, "subjects" would be replaced by "citizens." Where all had once been subjects, Americans would enter a world in which some groups would experience an enhanced sense of possibility and others would experience new and intensified forms of subordination. Consent would bring about its own contradictions.

# 3

# Logics of Revolution

## Introduction

Conceptions of political membership played a critical role in the dispute that unfolded and culminated in the American Revolution. During the colonial period, Americans' dealings with aliens, Native Americans, and blacks had driven them to conceive of British subjecthood in instrumental ways, in ways more Lockean than Cokean. This tendency became far more pronounced as Americans moved from repudiating the authority of Parliament to interrogating their allegiance to the king. *Contra* Coke, Americans began to maintain that protection and allegiance were not mutual, perpetual, and independent obligations growing out of the allegedly natural tie between subject and sovereign. Instead, they were part of the quid pro quo of a Lockean contract, each given in exchange for the other. Were the colonial charters to be annulled, John Adams insisted, the king "would not be bound to protect the people, nor, that I can see, would the people here, who were born here, be, by any principle of common law, bound even to allegiance to the king. The connection would be broken between the crown and the natives of the country."[1] After the military skirmishes at Lexington, Concord, and Bunker Hill, and after George III declared the North American colonies in rebellion on August 23,

---

[1] John Adams, "Novanglus No. VIII," in Charles F. Adams, ed., *The Works of John Adams, Second President of the United States: With a Life of the Author*, vol. IV (Boston: Little, Brown & Co., 1851), p. 127.

1775, many Americans concluded that their obligations to their monarch could be suspended.

As Americans withdrew their allegiance from George III and severed their connection with Great Britain in formal, public, and communal acts, "citizenship" came to replace "subjecthood." Building upon American societies' own voluntary acts of expatriation, the new category of citizenship was supposedly grounded in volitional allegiance, an allegiance that could be assumed and cast off. In 1795, in the course of a legal argument, the Republican lawyer Alexander Dallas distinguished the new American citizenship from the old British subjecthood (which he labeled "allegiance") in the following terms:

Citizenship, which has arisen from the dissolution of the feudal system ... is a substitute for allegiance, corresponding with the new order of things. Allegiance and citizenship, differ, indeed, in almost every characteristic. Citizenship is the effect of compact; allegiance is the offspring of power and necessity. Citizenship is a political tie; allegiance is a territorial tenure. Citizenship is the charter of equality; allegiance is a badge of inferiority. Citizenship is constitutional; allegiance is personal. Citizenship is freedom; allegiance is servitude. Citizenship is communicable; allegiance is repulsive. Citizenship may be relinquished; allegiance is perpetual.[2]

But all these vaunted attributes of citizenship – consent, volition, compact, freedom, and equality – immediately generated their own set of contradictions, slippages, and exclusions.

Although the American revolutionaries cast off their allegiance to the British Crown in the name of "the people" of the colonies, it became immediately clear that the "people" were no monolith. A substantial percentage of the native-born population of the colonies insisted that it had no desire whatsoever to cast off allegiance to its monarch. Could allegiance to the revolutionary cause – portrayed as grounded in volition – then be compelled? In the heat of conflict, the revolutionaries proved utterly intolerant of those who did not share their political sympathies. Volitional citizenship emerged out of the coercion, intimidation, and expulsion of Loyalists.

Following the formation of the Republic at the end of the 1780s, the new category of U.S. citizenship emerged, but coexisted with – and in important respects remained subordinate to – citizenship of

[2] Alexander Dallas in *Talbot v. Jansen*, 3 U.S. 133, 141 (1795).

the various states. Both U.S. and state citizenship acquired meaning, furthermore, in terms of the British legal background. The shadow of perpetual allegiance proved long. Notwithstanding the revolutionaries' invocation of the right of voluntary expatriation, citizens of the new Republic had a difficult time claiming it. When England and revolutionary France went to war in the 1790s and the United States sought to preserve its neutrality, Federalist-dominated courts proved inhospitable to sailors who violated American neutrality by preying on British shipping and who claimed, upon prosecution, to have switched allegiance from the United States to France.

Neither was the new category of citizenship, whether at the federal or state level, characterized by what Dallas enthusiastically called "the charter of equality." Every independent state, and then the new federal government, retained the basic *jus soli* or birthright citizenship rule of *Calvin's Case*. But not everyone born in national or state territory would be considered a citizen at birth. Prominent legal voices argued that Native Americans and blacks were not citizens on the basis of their birth within territory. Instead, they were "aliens" or mere "inhabitants."

Even when it came to those who *were* considered citizens at birth, the rights of citizenship were not distributed evenly. As states shaped their electorates, working-class and propertyless white males began to enjoy more expansive suffrage rights than they had in the colonial period. In the first flush of revolutionary fervor, some states granted free blacks suffrage rights. By the early nineteenth century, however, many states took such rights away from free blacks. White women everywhere remained subject to the regime of coverture.

The era of the early Republic was one of vast territorial, political, and economic expansion. The organization of the Northwest Territory, the Louisiana Purchase of 1803, and the acquisition of Florida in 1819 added millions of acres and several new states to the United States. White migration away from the Atlantic seaboard to the trans-Appalachian West, combined with the transportation of hundreds of thousands of slaves into the old Southwest as a result of the spread of cotton cultivation, brought about a significant westward movement of population. Immigration played a major role not only in the westward push, but also in the growth of eastern cities such as Baltimore, Boston, New York, and Philadelphia. Scholars estimate that, between 1781 and 1819, some 350,000 to 400,000 immigrants entered the United States. Immigration was robust during the last two decades of the eighteenth century, dipped between 1800 and 1815 as war engulfed Europe, and picked up thereafter. The number of individuals arriving in unfree statuses – slaves, servants, redemptioners, and convicts – began to drop. By 1820, immigrants were largely free agents and were represented as such.

The federal structure of the new Republic affected how this in-migration was managed. The new constitutional order that emerged in 1789 vested explicit authority over naturalization in the federal government. When the new Republic wrote its naturalization laws, naturalization came to be – not surprisingly – a privilege extended only to whites. As in the colonial period, managing access to citizenship was an instrument of immigration policy.

As the French Revolution entered its radical phase, and as Federalist xenophobia mounted in the late 1790s, access to national citizenship was tightened in order to exclude aliens' participation in the polity. But when the Adams administration attempted through the Alien and Sedition Acts to arrogate to itself the power to deport aliens, Republican opposition was vigorous. Under the new constitutional order, Republicans argued, questions of access to, and presence within, territory were matters of state – not federal – competence. This was likely the understanding of many Americans in the early Republic.

Immigration restriction, then, remained a matter of state control. But what was "immigration restriction" in the early Republic? As in the colonial period, citizenship, whether at the state or national level, did not entail rights to move throughout, or reside within, every part of national territory. States regulated not only the massive inflow from outside the country, but also the large number of internal migrants. Aliens and citizens continued to be excluded and removed from state and local territories under state poor law regimes.

Alongside this essential continuity with the colonial period, there were new developments relating to the Republic's internal foreigners: free blacks and Native Americans. As the free black population increased, Northern and Southern states increasingly closed their borders to free blacks. The early nineteenth century witnessed the beginnings of efforts to remove free blacks from the United States and to ship them to Africa, where they allegedly "belonged." In the case of Native Americans, their foreignness vis-à-vis the polity widely accepted, the promises of the 1763 Proclamation to protect their lands from white encroachment were abandoned. Even as the federal government monopolized dealings with Native Americans, it proved unwilling or unable to halt the relentless advance of the frontier of white settlement. Native Americans were increasingly deported out of their lands to make way for white settlers.

The remainder of this chapter consists of the following: first, a discussion of the relationship of the new citizenship to the domestic population, with explorations of the removal of Loyalists, the limits on voluntary expatriation, and the uneven extension of citizenship among the native-born; next, an examination of the relationship of the new citizenship to aliens, covering federal naturalization law, federal and state alienage laws, and the brief aberration of the Alien and Sedition Acts; and finally, a discussion of late-eighteenth- and early-nineteenth-century "immigration law" – namely, the regimes designed to control the presence and movement of citizens and aliens, free blacks, and Native Americans.

### The New Citizenship and the Domestic Population

For many Loyalists, the American Revolution posed dilemmas of conscience, political theory, and law. In February 1778, Andrew Leet informed the Connecticut General Assembly that, "[f]rom the beginning of the present controversy," he had "esteemed it his duty to take no active part in it by taking up arms" because "he was born under allegiance to the King ... and never in his best judgment and conscience considered it justifiable to renounce that allegiance." Even if others might question his decision, Leet insisted, it was the product of the "most mature deliberation and thorough examination into the merits of the dispute." He was also quick to point out the contradictions in the position of those persecuting him. Supporters of the Revolution, allegedly fighting for liberty, should respect "the most sacred idea of ... liberty (viz) liberty of conscience."[3] Targeting Loyalists went against the putative spirit of the Revolution.

---

[3] Quoted in Robert McCluer Calhoon, *The Loyalists in Revolutionary America, 1760–1781* (New York: Harcourt Brace Jovanovich, 1973), p. 318.

Other Loyalists elaborated arguments grounded in social contract theory. As the revolutionary struggle was beginning, Peter Van Schaack returned to the major social contract theorists of the age to reflect on the dilemmas it raised. He concluded that, as one social order was giving way to another, "*every individual* has still a right to choose the State of which he will become a member; for before he surrenders any part of his natural liberty, he has a right to know what security he will have for the enjoyment of the residue." Once a society had coalesced, of course, matters were different. At that point, a majority might legitimately compel the allegiance and obedience of a minority.[4]

In the thick of military conflict, such moral, theoretical, and legal niceties were cast aside. On June 24, 1776, the Continental Congress declared that "all persons abiding within any of the United Colonies, and deriving protection from the laws of the same, owe allegiance to the said laws, and are members of such colony"; all persons "who shall levy war against any of the said colonies within the same, or be adherents to the king of Great-Britain ... are guilty of treason against such colony." Resolves were passed recommending that individual colonies pass laws punishing treason.[5] Overnight, then, a new political membership was thrust upon the resident population and allegiance compelled. Any attempt to repudiate this allegiance became legally punishable as treason.

After the Declaration of Independence, it became far easier to characterize dissent as treason. The June 24 resolutions provided individual colonies with the legal authority they needed to suppress Loyalist voices. Every colony sought to enforce the allegiance of its inhabitants by instituting oaths and declarations. Those who refused such oaths and declarations risked fines, disfranchisement, expropriation of their lands, and banishment. Those who took up arms against the revolutionaries or actively aided the British faced execution.

This legal onslaught proved remarkably effective. Accused of treason, Loyalists felt compelled to abandon their country. Upon leaving,

---

[4] Quoted in Henry C. Van Schaack, *The Life of Peter Van Schaack, LLD: Embracing Selections from his Correspondence and Other Writings During the American Revolution, and his Exile in England* (New York: D. Appleton & Co, 1842), p. 73 (emphasis in original).

[5] United States, *Journals of the Continental Congress, 1774–1789*, vol. V (Washington, DC: U.S. Government Printing Office, 1906), p. 475.

they became aliens vis-à-vis societies their families had inhabited for generations. In many cases, however, Loyalists might have been driven to leave even in the absence of sufficient evidence to support a treason conviction. The experience of Pennsylvania is illustrative. On March 6, 1778, Pennsylvania's legislature passed an act that named individual Loyalists and gave them until April 21, 1778, to give themselves up and stand trial for treason. If such individuals failed to comply, they would suffer forfeiture of their properties and, if apprehended, hanging. Between 1778 and 1781, Pennsylvania targeted nearly 500 individuals. Of those targeted, 386 did not appear within the set time limits and sought the protection of the British. Of the 113 who surrendered, fewer than 20 came to trial because of the insufficiency of the evidence. Of the 16 who actually stood for trial, only 3 were convicted.[6] Given the small number of those successfully prosecuted, it seems at least likely that some of the 386 individuals who fled could not have been successfully prosecuted. They were, nevertheless, intimidated into leaving.

Thus, despite the small number of actual convictions for treason, and an even smaller number of executions, an effective rendering foreign of the dissident population took place. The scale of this rendering foreign was immense. As the historian Maya Jasanoff has written: "Confronting real doubts about their lives, liberty, and potential happiness in the United States, sixty thousand Loyalists decided to follow the British and take their chances elsewhere in the British Empire. They took fifteen thousand black slaves with them, bringing the total exodus to seventy-five thousand people – or about one in forty members of the American population."[7] Relative to population size, the population outflow of Loyalists and their dependents was four to five times greater than that of the émigrés driven out by the French Revolution.

If volitional citizenship arose out of rendering Loyalists foreign, it was also mired in contradiction to the extent that the right of voluntary expatriation – the very right the revolutionaries claimed for themselves – proved difficult to vindicate in the new polity. English notions of perpetual allegiance died hard. In the 1779 Virginia law

---

[6] Calhoon, *Loyalists in Revolutionary America*, pp. 400-01.
[7] Maya Jasanoff, *Liberty's Exiles: American Loyalists in the Revolutionary World* (New York: Alfred A. Knopf, 2011), p. 6.

drafted by Thomas Jefferson, expatriation was declared a "natural right which all men have of relinquishing the country in which birth or other accident may have thrown them"; the law set forth various ways in which Virginia's citizens might abandon their citizenship.[8] After the formation of the Republic, in his capacity as secretary of state, Jefferson continued to subscribe to this position: "Our citizens are entirely free to divest themselves of that character by emigration, and other acts manifesting their intention, and may then become the subjects of another power, and free to do whatever the subjects of that power may do."[9] But there was also opposition to the idea of voluntary expatriation. In 1784, in a gesture of solidarity with the travails of Loyalists, Alexander Hamilton asserted: "The idea, indeed, of citizens transforming themselves into aliens, by taking part against the State to which they belong, is altogether of new invention, unknown and inadmissible in law, and contrary to the nature of the social compact."[10]

After the formation of the United States, American officials had an investment in pushing for recognition and acknowledgment of the individual's right of voluntary expatriation. The impressment controversies between the United States and Great Britain, which arose when Great Britain requisitioned the labor of British-born sailors who were naturalized American citizens, became a dispute lasting into the early nineteenth century. The United States insisted on the right of voluntary expatriation: British subjects who became American citizens should no longer be seen as Britons. Great Britain, cleaving to the doctrine of perpetual allegiance, denied its subjects' right of voluntary expatriation and treated them like Britons regardless of their American naturalizations.

However, when it came to adjudications of American citizens' right to expatriate, the American position – especially as articulated by a conservative, Federalist-dominated judiciary – was much more

---

[8] An Act declaring who shall be deemed citizens of this commonwealth, ch. 55 (May 3, 1779), in William W. Hening, *The Statutes at Large; Being a Collection of All the Laws of Virginia, from the First Session of the Legislature, in the Year 1619*, vol. X (Richmond, VA: George Cochran, 1822), p. 129.

[9] Thomas Jefferson to Gouverneur Morris, August 16, 1793, in Francis Wharton, ed., *State Trials of the United States During the Administrations of Washington and Adams* (Philadelphia: Carey & Hart, 1849), p. 89.

[10] Alexander Hamilton, "Letters from Phocion II," in Henry C. Lodge, ed., *The Works of Alexander Hamilton*, vol. IV (New York: G. P. Putnam's Sons, 1904), p. 256.

equivocal. The doctrine was set forth in the opinion delivered by Chief Justice Ellsworth in the case of *United States v. Williams* (1799). Isaac Williams, a citizen of Connecticut, had accepted a privateering commission from French authorities in violation of the treaty of amity between Great Britain and the United States. Williams's defense was that he had gone to France in 1792, had explicitly renounced his American citizenship, and had been naturalized in France. He had served in the French military before the treaty in question and had lived in French territories for three years. According to his counsel, these facts proved that Williams had expatriated himself from the United States.

Chief Justice Ellsworth refused to accept the argument. Stating that "the common law of this country remains the same as it was before the Revolution," Ellsworth argued that there were two "great principles" that the case implicated: first, "that all the members of civil community are bound to each other by compact" and, second, "that one of the parties to this compact cannot dissolve it by his own act." There was no default here on the part of the United States, nor was there any explicit governmental consent to Williams's expatriation. Indeed, Ellsworth continued, the United States was a nation "sparsely settled" with "no inhabitants to spare." Since neither explicit nor implicit governmental consent could be shown, Williams remained a U.S. citizen subject to legal penalties.[11]

Ellsworth's decision was read by the Jeffersonian-Republican press as a Federalist attempt to impose the old tyrannical principle of perpetual allegiance on the new Republic. Under the impact of such critiques, courts began to soften their denials of the right of voluntary expatriation. In Virginia and Kentucky, courts recognized the right of voluntary expatriation as a matter of natural law. However, the problem, even for those courts that recognized such a right, was that not every act of a citizen could be considered a valid act of expatriation. Were that to be the case, it would be an invitation to citizens to disregard their obligations to the polity's laws with impunity. Expatriation was a "reasonable and moral right which every man ought to be allowed to exercise," observed Judge Iredell, but it had to be subject to such limitations "as the public safety or interest requires, to which all

[11] *United States v. Williams*, 29 F. Cases 1330, 1331 (C.C.D. Conn. 1799).

private rights ought and must forever give way."[12] The ultimate act of volitional allegiance, namely the casting off of allegiance, thus had to be a creature of law determined in accordance with "public safety or interest." The conflict over the right of voluntary expatriation continued into the early nineteenth century, with Congress refusing to pass an act recognizing voluntary expatriation.

If the volitional nature of American citizenship was thus subject to qualification, so was the pretension that American citizenship was, as the lawyer Alexander Dallas put it, "the charter of equality." At both the state and federal levels, citizenship and the rights associated with it were not distributed evenly among the domestic population. Various statuses – Indian, slave, free black, married woman, pauper – determined access to the status of citizen and the rights of citizenship. The line that separated a denial of the status of citizen and a denial of many of the rights of citizenship (voting, officeholding, etc.) proved shadowy.

Although Americans insisted upon the volitional nature of allegiance, all the independent states and (after 1789) the federal and state governments ended up retaining the common law *jus soli* rule of *Calvin's Case*, according to which birth within territory served as the basic ground of citizenship. The feudal origins of the *jus soli* rule seem not to have bothered commentators excessively. Contemporaries such as South Carolina's David Ramsay explained away the contradiction between volitional allegiance and the retention of the *jus soli* rule by arguing that, at the age of twenty-one, "every freeman is at liberty to chuse his country, his religion, and his allegiance. Those who continue after that age in the allegiance under which they have been educated, become, by tacit consent, either subjects or citizens, as the case may be."[13]

There was a split between federal and state applications of the *jus soli* rule. Although the U.S. Constitution did not explicitly mention a *jus soli* rule for the United States, there was an assumption that *jus soli* would apply for purposes of determining who counted as a U.S. citizen. The U.S. Constitution required, for example, that the president be

---

[12] *Talbot v. Jansen*, 3 U.S. 133, 163 (1795).
[13] David Ramsay, *A Dissertation on the Manner of Acquiring the Character and Privileges of a Citizen of the United States* (Charleston, SC, 1789), p. 5.

a "natural born Citizen."[14] In the early Republic, however, there was no definitive legal pronouncement as to who did or did not count as a U.S. citizen under *jus soli* rules. In the meantime, states defined their citizenries through their own applications of *jus soli* rules. Across the states, there was considerable variation with respect to who counted as a citizen at birth. Nevertheless, it seems correct to state that *jus soli*, at the federal and state levels, applied most clearly only to native-born whites. When it came to Native Americans and blacks, birth within the Republic's territory might not confer citizenship. Indeed, they might be native-born foreigners.

Such denials of *jus soli* citizenship were especially true for Native Americans. The United States claimed sovereignty over the territories in which thousands of Native Americans lived. Even so, Native Americans were considered simultaneously within and without the polity. The U.S. Constitution conferred upon Congress the right to regulate commerce with "foreign Nations, and among the several States, and with the Indian Tribes," the very structure of the clause reflecting Native Americans' awkward suspension between the domestic and the foreign.[15] Congress soon executed a series of laws, known as the Trade and Intercourse Acts, as part of an Indian policy centered, tellingly, in the War Department.

This organization of the polity's relationship to its indigenous population was consistent with a widespread understanding that basic *jus soli* principles did not extend to Native Americans, especially if they lived beyond the frontier of white settlement. In *Jackson v. Wood* (1810), New York's celebrated jurist James Kent described the inapplicability of *jus soli* citizenship to Native Americans as follows: "Their political relation to this state is peculiar, and *sui generis*. If they are not *aliens* in every sense, because of their dependence as a tribe, and their right to protection, *they cannot be considered as subjects born under allegiance, and bound, in the common law sense of the term, to all its duties*."[16] Treaties between the United States and tribes often provided that individuals who left their tribes and accepted plots of land could thereby become citizens. The Cherokee treaties of 1817 and

---

[14] U.S. Const., art. II, § 1, cl. 5.
[15] U.S. Const., art. I, § 8, cl. 3.
[16] *Jackson v. Wood*, 7 Johns. Rep. 290, 295 (N.Y. 1810) (emphasis added).

1819, for example, stipulated that lands would be provided to heads of families "who may wish to become citizens of the United States."[17] Such attempts to incorporate Native Americans – which were in the first instance attempts to dissolve them as groups – underscore the fact that they were not viewed as citizens to begin with even as sovereignty was claimed over them.

The case of blacks was more ambiguous. The black community was slotted into two different legal statuses: slave and free black. During the colonial period, some might have considered slaves British subjects deserving of minimal protections. In the early Republic, however, the status of slave was generally considered antithetical to the status of citizen. But what of free blacks? In the first decades following the Revolution, slavery began to be phased out in the Northern states and anti-slavery sentiment in the South resulted in the legalization of manumission. Such developments resulted in an increase in the free black population. Black populations in the North were, of course, increasingly free. But free black populations in the South, especially in the Upper South, also grew. In states such as Delaware, Maryland, and Virginia the free black population grew as much as tenfold between the American Revolution and 1810.

Although there was no definitive legal pronouncement as to whether free blacks counted as U.S. citizens *jure soli*, at the state level, depending on the state, free black males enjoyed certain quintessential rights of citizenship. For example, free black males were permitted to vote in several states, including Maryland, Massachusetts, New York, North Carolina, Pennsylvania, and Vermont. The possession of suffrage rights suggests that they also likely qualified as citizens *jure soli* of such states. However, they were barred from voting in Georgia, South Carolina, and Virginia. Where free blacks lacked important rights associated with citizenship, it became intelligible to declare that they were not citizens at all. South Carolina's David Ramsay asserted in 1789: "Negroes are inhabitants, but not citizens."[18]

If free blacks were citizens of some states but not others, their suffrage rights proved precarious even where they might be

---

[17] Treaty with Cherokees, 7 Stat. 156, art. 8 (1817); Treaty with Cherokees, 7 Stat. 195, art. 2 (1819). The quoted text is from the treaty of 1817.

[18] Ramsay, *Dissertation*, p. 3.

considered citizens. What was given in the first flush of revolutionary fervor could be taken away. By 1820, as the free black population expanded all over the United States, states such as New Jersey,
Maryland, and Connecticut reversed an earlier trend and restricted
the franchise to whites. At its constitutional convention in 1821,
New York lifted property qualifications for whites, but effectively dis-
franchised its black population through a raft of property and residence requirements that applied only to blacks. As free blacks lost
suffrage rights, they also became – as will be discussed later in this
chapter – excludable and removable outsiders, a kind of foreigner.

Even for those to whom the principles of *jus soli* citizenship applied
more or less unequivocally (i.e., native-born whites), the rights associated with citizenship were not evenly distributed. In the aftermath of
the Revolution, suffrage reform expanded the white male electorate
at the state level (state suffrage laws determined who could vote for
members of the House of Representatives). Although the extent of suffrage reform varied from state to state, the overall thrust entailed a
reduction of colonial era property qualifications. Pauper exclusions
from voting, however, remained widespread.

While white men enjoyed expanded access to suffrage in the aftermath of the Revolution, women did not. New Jersey was the only
state that allowed women to vote. The state's 1776 constitution and a
1790 law granted the vote to all "inhabitants," a term that was interpreted to encompass property-owning women. By the early nineteenth
century, however, New Jersey's legislature excised women from the
electorate. With the exception of this brief interlude, women in the
early Republic were denied access to suffrage and officeholding, and
married women, legally designated *femes coverts*, remained subject to
the common law institution of coverture.

The legal subordination of women intersected with the law of citizenship. This is clear from the law of *jus sanguinis*, or citizenship
transmitted through blood. Under laws passed in the 1790s, white
American men were able to transmit their citizenship to children born
abroad, but white American women were not. Indeed, married white
women's lack of rights as *femes coverts* could even translate into
occasional assertions that they were akin to aliens vis-à-vis the polity.
This is illustrated in the case of *Martin v. Commonwealth* (1805), a
case in which the Supreme Judicial Court of Massachusetts addressed

whether a woman married to a Loyalist had any obligations to the state independent of those of her husband. If she did, she would be treated as a Loyalist and her property confiscated. The Massachusetts Confiscation Act was directed at "every *inhabitant* and *member* of the state." If it was clear that married women could be "inhabitants," it was not clear that they could be "members." Attorneys who spoke for the married woman's descendants argued that the Act could not be construed to extend to married women because, "[u]pon the strict principles of law, a *feme covert* is not a member; has no *political relation* to the *state* any more than an *alien*."[19]

What is noteworthy, of course, is the equation of the *feme covert* with the alien. If it did not formally espouse the equation of the married woman with the alien, the Massachusetts Supreme Judicial Court essentially adopted this view when it ruled that a married woman was compelled to follow her husband and that, by virtue of such compulsion, should not suffer the penalties of his having chosen British subjecthood over American citizenship. The Court put it thus: "A *wife* who left the country in the company of her husband did not *withdraw* herself; but was, if I may so express it, withdrawn by him. She did not deprive the government of the benefit of her personal services; she had none to render; none were exacted of her."[20]

In this particular case, then, a married woman's lack of agency at law redounded to the benefit of those claiming her property. The decision laid bare the relationship between a lack of rights and the possibility of slipping into the status of alien. Because of married women's lack of rights, they were politically and legally invisible. As such, it was meaningful to analogize them to aliens.

### Citizenship as Immigration Policy: The Federal Government, the States, and the Alien

While states enjoyed full control over naturalization and alienage laws during the Confederation period, the creation of the Republic produced a change. The federal structure of the new government resulted in different deployments of citizenship at the federal level, on the one

---

[19] *Martin v. Commonwealth*, 1 Mass. 347, 362 (1805) (emphasis in original).
[20] Id. at 391–92 (emphasis in original).

hand, and at the state level, on the other. As in the colonial period, however, citizenship functioned as a tool of immigration policy.

Article I, Section 8 of the U.S. Constitution conferred upon the federal government the power to establish "an uniform Rule of Naturalization."[21] The goal was to solve the problem of inconsistent naturalization laws that the states had promulgated during the Confederation period. But was this naturalization power exclusive to the federal government or did states enjoy a concurrent authority over naturalization? In the early 1790s, some courts found the federal and state governments to enjoy concurrent powers over naturalization.[22] By 1820, however, few disputed that the naturalization power was exclusive to the federal government. In *Chirac v. Chirac* (1817), Chief Justice Marshall observed that Congress's claim to sole power over naturalization "does not seem to be, and certainly ought not to be, controverted."[23]

Even as various segments of the domestic population were labeled or treated as "aliens" or mere "inhabitants," easing access to citizenship was considered a critical part of attracting the right sort of overseas settler. In keeping with the prevailing racialized nature of how citizenship was distributed among the native-born population, the first federal naturalization law passed in 1790 limited naturalization to a "free white person" who had resided in the United States for two years, had proved his "good character," and taken an oath "to support the constitution of the United States."[24] Although the first naturalization law did not bar naturalization by women, there is little evidence of single white women naturalizing. In general, women's naturalization followed that of their husbands.

Shaping access to the formal status of citizen was not the only way, however, in which overseas settlers were to be enticed or deterred. Both the federal government and states played an important role in shaping alien legal disabilities.

At the federal level, apart from citizenship requirements for holding federal office, there were bars on alien participation in the coastal trade. However, alien legal disabilities with respect to landownership

[21] U.S. Const., art. I, § 8, cl. 4.
[22] See, e.g., *Collet v. Collet*, 2 Dall. 294 (C.C.D. Pa. 1792).
[23] *Chirac v. Chirac*, 2 Wheat. 259, 269 (1817).
[24] Act of March 26, 1790, 1 Stat. 103.

and voting in the territories were relaxed to speed up white settlement. The Land Ordinances of 1784 and 1785 allowed aliens who resided in the Northwest Territory to purchase federal lands. The Northwest Ordinance of 1787 permitted aliens resident in the Northwest Territory to vote provided they owned fifty acres of land. In 1811, Congress abrogated these property qualifications and enfranchised all free white males, whether or not they were citizens, provided they were taxpayers and residents. The organizational acts for other territories required payment of taxes in order to vote or granted white male suffrage.

Because of the limited powers of the federal government, however, states played a relatively greater role in shaping immigration policy through the shaping of alien legal disabilities. The record in this regard was mixed. If some states eased some alien legal disabilities, others did not. Liberal impulses could overwhelm or be overwhelmed by restrictive ones.

In the late eighteenth century, state constitutions often conferred the franchise on "inhabitants." In many places, therefore, foreign-born men who had not been naturalized, but who met property, taxpaying, or residence requirements, were able to vote. However, the early years of the Republic witnessed a backlash against alien voting. Between 1800 and 1830, New Jersey, New York, Massachusetts, Connecticut, Vermont, Maryland, and Virginia amended their constitutions or passed statutes that restricted voting to "citizens." At the dawn of the Jacksonian era, aliens were denied the vote in most states.

In the last decade of the eighteenth century and the first decade of the nineteenth, several state legislatures also eased traditional alien real property disabilities. However, this was by no means a universal development. In many states, aliens continued to lack secure rights to own, devise, and inherit real property. If state authorities usually refrained from divesting aliens of their lands during their lifetimes, states regularly sought escheats when aliens died. Alien land disabilities were often also at issue in private disputes. Alien widows might be barred from dower rights in their deceased husbands' lands. In response to such property disabilities, aliens resorted to a range of legal devices (for instance, the trust) in order to acquire and transmit good title to lands.

States also barred aliens from holding public offices and participating in certain trades. Under New York City's charter of 1730, which remained in force until it was revised in 1827, "no person whatsoever not being a free citizen … [could] … use any art, trade, mystery, or occupation within the said city, liberties and precincts thereof; or shall by himself, themselves or others, sell or expose to retail, in any house shop, place, or standing within the said city … (save in the times of public fairs)." Such provisions placed a potent weapon in the hands of those eager to stamp out economic competition from immigrants. In 1784, New York City's ship carpenters complained to the City Council that George Gar, "a shipwright lately (about sixteen or eighteen Months) from Scotland[,] carries on his business in a manner hurtful to the Petitioners and their Brother Shipwrights. And that as the said George is not a Freeman but an Alien they conceive he is not entitled to carry on the said Business therefore they pray that he may [be] fined and prevented for the future from carrying on the said Business as the charter directs." In subsequent years, aliens in New York City were denied licenses as cartmen, butchers, tavern keepers, and surveyors and were also barred from serving on juries or as city watchmen.[25]

Events of the 1790s showed the manipulability of the line that separated the spheres of federal and state authority over aliens. As the French Revolution entered its radical phase and spread to France's colonies, and as counter-revolution intensified in Great Britain, refugees fled to the neutral United States. The United States attracted "discontented Englishmen, aristocratic Frenchmen, German pietists fleeing military service, French planters escaping from West Indian uprisings led by Toussaint l'Ouverture, and Irishmen in flight from British repression."[26] These were all migrants with passionate political beliefs. Not surprisingly, they contributed to the intensification of party conflict in the Republic just as the lines of division – federal versus state, commerce versus agriculture, pro-British versus pro-French – were hardening between Federalists and Republicans.

In the hands of the Federalist-led federal government, naturalization law rapidly became a tool for deterring undesirable aliens, minimizing the role they could play in the polity, and thereby striking at the Republican opposition. Under the Naturalization Act of 1790, the

---

[25] This entire paragraph is derived from Baseler, "*Asylum*," p. 221.
[26] James Morton Smith, *Freedom's Fetters: The Alien and Sedition Laws and American Civil Liberties* (Ithaca, NY: Cornell University Press, 1956), p. 23.

naturalization period – that is, the period of residence before an alien was eligible to naturalize – was a brief two years. The Naturalization Act of 1795 increased the naturalization period to five years. Federalists hoped that this relatively extended period would let future citizens assimilate better into the community and blunt the edges of the more radical among them.

Federalist hopes that the Naturalization Act of 1795 would result in domestic tranquility and strike at the Republicans' electoral base proved short-lived. Immigrant involvement in the protests surrounding Jay's Treaty, which was criticized by Republicans as binding the United States too closely to Great Britain, convinced Federalists that immigrants' participation in national politics had to be curbed. By 1798, with the United States in the throes of an undeclared war with France and Federalist-inspired paranoia about the presence of Jacobins everywhere, the Federalists sought to tighten naturalization laws even further and to increase the executive's control over aliens.

The Federalist onslaught against aliens in the late 1790s, and the Jeffersonian Republican response to it, afford an insight into how late-eighteenth-century Americans conceived the division of powers between the federal and state governments in matters of naturalization and immigration and how that division was breached as Federalists pushed aggressively to curb what they saw as a potent alien menace. The Federalist-sponsored Naturalization Act of 1798 extended the residence period for aliens seeking naturalization from five to fourteen years. At the same time, Federalists passed the Alien Enemies Act, which set up machinery to control the subjects of nations at war with the United States, and the so-called Alien Friends Act, which gave the executive (for a period of two years) the authority "to *order* all such aliens *as he shall judge* dangerous to the peace and safety of the United States ... to depart out of the territory of the United States."[27]

Republicans opposed these acts on various grounds. According to them, the fourteen-year waiting period threatened to create a class of perpetual foreigners in the United States. Representative Joseph McDowell of North Carolina argued that a fourteen-year waiting period would hinder the assimilation of immigrants: "When persons come here from foreign countries, it [is] our interest to attach them

---

[27] An Act Concerning Aliens (June 25, 1798), 1 Stat. 570–71 (second emphasis added).

to us, and not always to look upon them as aliens and strangers."[28]
The Alien Friends Act was seen as violating the federal constitutional
guarantees that "no person ... be deprived of life, liberty, or property,
without due process of law" and that "the privilege of the writ of
habeas corpus ... not be suspended, unless when in cases of rebellion or invasion the public safety may require it."[29] Such constitutional
limitations on Congress and the executive were, Republicans argued,
framed in universal terms to protect all persons.

However, an important and highly revealing argument against the
Alien Friends Act was that the power to deport aliens was simply
not one conferred by the U.S. Constitution upon the federal government, but, as part of a general control over immigration, was
reserved to the states. Representative Albert Gallatin of Pennsylvania
deemed it a truism "that every nation ha[s] a right to permit or
exclude alien friends from entering within the bounds of their society." However, that power, he argued, *"does solely belong to each
individual State."* Not only did the U.S. Constitution omit the right
to deport alien friends from among the enumerated powers conferred upon Congress, but the Tenth Amendment expressly guaranteed that "[t]he powers, not delegated to the United States by the
Constitution, nor prohibited by it to the States, are are [*sic*] reserved
to the States respectively, or to the people." Therefore, according to
Gallatin, "all the provisions in this bill [the Alien Friends Act] are
perfectly unconstitutional."[30]

Federalist responses to these arguments were wide-ranging. One
argument was that aliens, as outsiders, had no binding claim upon
the political community to fair treatment in matters of naturalization. Aliens were subject to absolute power and received what rights
they did as a matter of pure grace. According to Representative
James Bayard of Delaware, "Aliens cannot be considered as members of the society of the United States ... whatever is granted
to aliens is a mere matter of favor; and, if it is taken away, they
have no right to complain."[31] Another argument, used to justify the

---

[28]  5 Annals of Cong. 1776 (1798).
[29]  U.S. Const., amend. V; art. I, § 9, cl. 2.
[30]  U.S. Const., amend. X; Gallatin quote in 5 Annals of Cong. 1955 (1798) (emphasis
      added).
[31]  5 Annals of Cong. 1780 (1798).

expansion of executive power in the Alien Friends Act, rested upon highly expansive readings of the Preamble to the Constitution. Thus, Representative Samuel Sewall of Massachusetts argued that the Constitution "establishes the sovereignty of the United States, and that sovereignty must reside in the [federal] Government." Because congressional power "to provide for the general welfare and internal tranquility ... take[s] cognizance of everything which relates to aliens; ... if the residence of any aliens in this country would be likely, in their opinion, to endanger the public peace and tranquility, Congress have a right to take such measures respecting them as they shall think fit."[32]

Republicans read Federalists' expansive readings of the Preamble as a warning bell, a harbinger of what threatened to become an overweening federal power. If the language of the Preamble could justify action against aliens, they argued, there was no reason that the same language, vague and general as it was, could not be used to justify action against citizens. Edward Livingston of New York warned his Republican colleagues of the dangers of the Alien Friends Act: "[L]et no man vainly imagine that the evil is to stop here, that a few unprotected aliens only are to be affected by this inquisitorial power."[33]

Taken together, the opposed arguments of the Republicans and the Federalists reflected antinomies that would reverberate over time: whether aliens could avail of constitutional protections or whether whatever rights they received were matters of sovereign grace; whether governmental power over aliens could be read expansively as an incident of sovereignty or whether government had to be restrained by the language of the Constitution; and whether and what authority over aliens lay with the federal government versus the states. In the late-eighteenth-century United States, however, the Federalist attempt to exceed what were seen by the Republicans as firm constitutional limits on federal power backfired. Jefferson's election to the presidency in 1800 was followed quickly by a repeal of the Naturalization Act of 1798. A new law approved April 14, 1802, reinstated the five-year residence requirement of the 1795 Naturalization Act. The Alien Friends Act expired after two years. What was then understood by

---

[32] 5 Annals of Cong. 1957–58 (1798).
[33] 5 Annals of Cong. 2013 (1798).

many as constitutional order was restored. The federal government would have power over naturalization and alien legal disabilities in areas of federal competence such as federal territories. Although such uses of citizenship were undoubtedly tools of immigration law, the federal government was to have no direct power over alien legal disabilities in the states or the regulation of aliens' access to and residence within territory.

In the process of its dispute with the Federalists, the party of Jefferson became the party of immigrants. However, Republicans' insistence on limiting federal powers and on preserving state powers over aliens also had to do with the mutual imbrication of immigration, slavery, and controlling black mobility. After the Revolution, as anti-slavery sentiment grew and as slavery expanded, the slave states jealously guarded their powers over immigration into their territories in order to preserve the institution of slavery and to minimize dangers to it. From the perspective of pro-slavery politicians, an overweening federal power over aliens signaled a creeping federalization of control over the movement of persons generally, which could ultimately interfere with, or even threaten, the proper management of slavery. Opponents of the Alien Friends Act were careful to point out that the Act bore grave potential consequences for slavery. Representatives Edward Livingston of New York and Abraham Baldwin of Georgia both observed that, if Congress and the executive secured the power to deport non-citizens, nothing might prevent them from deporting African slaves.[34] Slavery would haunt questions of immigration restriction until the Civil War.

### Borders, Movement, and Presence in the Early Republic

The American Revolution effected a change in the institution of indentured servitude, which had facilitated the passage of hundreds of thousands of European migrants in the colonial period. Some of the opposition to indentured servitude clothed itself in the language of liberty. In 1784, some white New Yorkers criticized the arrival of indentured servants on the ground that the "traffick of White People" contradicted the "idea of liberty this country has so happily

---

[34] 5 Annals of Cong. 2019 (1798).

established."[35] But this was hardly the only cause of the decline of indentured servitude. British ship captains were hesitant to participate in the servant trade because they feared that American courts might no longer enforce contracts. The immigrant trade remained vital for Germans until about 1820. For others, it had disappeared long before that. The stage was set for the emergence of the "free" immigrant as a figure who "chose" America.

Even as this process was under way, however, prominent Americans participated in a public debate over the kind of immigrant America needed. Thomas Paine's famous revolutionary era call had urged Americans to "prepare in time an asylum for mankind," a place where Europe's downtrodden would find refuge.[36] However, in the 1780s and 1790s, the text that did as much or more to promote this image was Hector St. John de Crèvecoeur's *Letters from an American Farmer*, first published in London in 1782.

What is interesting about the *Letters from an American Farmer* is the kind of image of America it portrays, the text's intended reader, and the text's erasures. America's invitation and promise are for Europeans only. The redemptive drama of immigration is not for Native Americans and blacks. In the third letter, entitled "What is an American?", Crèvecoeur describes an "American race" that has come into being: "[Americans] are a mixture of English, Scotch, Irish, French, Dutch, Germans, and Swedes. From this promiscuous breed, that race, now called Americans, have arisen."[37] Even though Crèvecoeur is surely underplaying the significance of American anti-Catholicism, it is clear that, for him, Native Americans and blacks are not part of the "American race."

Europe's poor, Crèvecoeur wrote, had no real homeland: "Can a wretch, who wanders about, who works and starves, whose life is a continual scene of sore affliction or pinching penury; can that man call England or any other kingdom his country?" Only in America, through

---

[35] Quoted in Aaron S. Fogleman, "From Slaves, Convicts, and Servants to Free Passengers: The Transformation of Immigration in the Era of the American Revolution," *Journal of American History* 85, no. 1 (June 1998): 43–76, 63.

[36] Paine, "Common Sense," p. 31.

[37] H. St. John de Crèvecoeur, *Letters from an American Farmer* (New York: Oxford University Press, 1997) (1782), p. 42.

the acquisition of property, could Europe's poor finally come into their own. "Here," Crèvecoeur proclaimed, "they are become men." Blacks play a supporting role in this redemption narrative. Insofar as they are property, they make European immigrants true Americans. As Crèvecoeur puts it in one of his many portrayals of peaceable, generous, and content American farmers that stand as enticements for the European migrant: "Here liveth the warm substantial family, that never begrudgeth a meal of victuals, or a mess of oats, to any one that steps in. *Look how fat and well clad their negroes are.*"[38]

Not all thinkers about immigration painted quite as rosy a picture of immigration as Crèvecoeur did. Benjamin Franklin's *Information to Those Who Would Remove to America* (1784) argued that America needed immigrants of "mediocrity," and not aristocrats, military men, and "strangers possessing talents in the belles-lettres, fine arts, &c."[39] *Contra* Crèvecoeur, American thinkers also adamantly refused to accept the responsibility for regenerating Europe's outcasts. Pennsylvania's Tench Coxe argued that, with independence, the American states had finally won the "right to restrain that influx [of emigrants from abroad], whenever it is found likely to prove hurtful to us"; Americans could now exclude the "ship loads of wretches, too worthless for the old world."[40] Neither were American thinkers as cosmopolitan as Crèvecoeur suggested. One writer complained: "Emigrants arrive from Ireland, from Holland, from Germany, and from other parts of Europe. These all differ from us, and they differ from one another. They bring with them their peculiar habits, and their peculiar prejudices ... Thus a national character can never be established, and the sentiment of national honor can never be strongly felt."[41]

As the dispute over the Alien and Sedition Acts reveals, "immigration law" – the routine regulation of aliens' access to and presence

---

[38] Id., pp. 22, 42–43 (emphasis added).

[39] Benjamin Franklin, "Information to Those Who Would Remove to America" (1784), in *Writings*, p. 975.

[40] Tench Coxe, "An Enquiry into the Best Means of Encouraging Emigration from Abroad, Consistently with the Happiness and Safety of the Original Citizens. Read Before the Society for Political Enquiries, at the House of Dr. Franklin, April 20th, 1787," in *The American Museum, Or, Universal Magazine, for July 1791*, vol. 10 (Philadelphia: Carey, Stewart & Co., 1791), pp. 115, 165.

[41] Quoted in Douglas Bradburn, *The Citizenship Revolution: Politics and the Creation of the American Union, 1774–1804* (Charlottesville: University of Virginia Press, 2009), p. 161.

within territory – remained in the hands of the states and not the fed-eral government.[42] Americans were especially resolute when it came to refusing entry to British felons, a traffic they had complained about for decades. When news arrived about surreptitious shipments of British convicts, the Confederation Congress resolved, on September 16, 1788, "that it be, and it is hereby recommended to the several states, to pass proper laws for preventing the transportation of convicted male-factors from foreign countries into the United States."[43] In response, laws prohibiting the entry of criminals were passed in Connecticut, Georgia, Massachusetts, New York, New Jersey, Pennsylvania, South Carolina, and Virginia.

As in the colonial period, however, the governing logic of "immi-gration restriction" exercised by states derived from the poor laws. As such, it was directed at citizens *and* aliens, insiders *and* outsiders, the native-born *and* the foreign-born.

During the Confederation period, states sought to keep out indi-gent migrants from foreign countries and other states. This exclusion was explicitly contemplated by the comity clause of the Articles of Confederation, which excepted "paupers, vagabonds, and fugitives from justice" from the general obligation of states not to discriminate against "free inhabitants" of other states.[44] Thus, in 1782, Georgia passed an act to prevent "idle and disorderly Persons emigrating from any of the United States, or elsewhere becoming Citizens of this State"; the act targeted persons who did not "cultivate a sufficient quantity of land, or follow some trade or Occupation, whereby themselves and families can be supported," and "all idle Persons, who may be found Wandering from place to place of suspicious Character."[45] In 1788, New York's Act for the Better Settlement and Relief of the Poor man-dated that shipmasters report "the names and occupations of every

---

[42] The only piece of congressional legislation in this period was a regulation of the passenger trade specifying sanitary requirements and requiring captains to provide manifests of entering passengers. Act of March 2, 1819, 3 Stat. 488.

[43] *Journal of the American Congress: From 1774 to 1788*, vol. IV (Washington, DC: Way & Gideon, 1823), p. 867.

[44] Articles of Confederation of 1777, art. IV.

[45] Quotes from Georgia's Act for Preventing Improper or Disafected [*sic*] Persons Emigrating from Other Places, and Becoming Citizens of this State and for other purposes therein mentioned (August 5, 1782), in Allen D. Chandler, ed., *The Colonial Records of the State of Georgia: Statutes, Colonial and Revolutionary, 1774–1805*, vol. XIX, no. 2 (Atlanta: Chas. P. Byrd, 1911), pp. 162–66.

person who shall be brought" into the port of New York. Shipmasters risked being fined £20 for each unreported person and, "if any person so neglected to be reported ... shall be a foreigner," £30 per unreported person. The law refused admission "to any person who cannot give a good account of himself or herself, to the mayor or recorder of New York city or "is like to be a charge to the said city." Such persons were to be transported by the master of their vessel "to the place from whence he or she came."[46]

After the creation of the Republic, states were bound under the U.S. Constitution by a duty of comity to extend to "citizens" of other states the privileges and immunities they extended to their own "citizens."[47] However, this duty of comity did not impose upon states the obligation to extend to citizens of other states rights of travel and residence they did not extend to their own citizens. In general, because state citizenship did not entail rights to enter and reside in every part of state territory, this meant that states were also not obliged to open their borders to all citizens of other states.

Heavy migration from overseas undoubtedly led to a heightened focus on entering indigent aliens. For example, New York's 1797 amendment of its 1788 poor relief statute required shipmasters to provide bonds to "indemnify and save harmless the ... city of New York," the country's principal port of entry, from all expenses associated with "emigrants from any foreign country."[48] However, even as it imposed a bonding requirement vis-à-vis entering aliens, New York's 1797 act imposed a reporting requirement on shipmasters to provide the name and occupation of "every person" entering New York, imposing fines of fifty dollars for failure to comply and seventy-five dollars for failure to comply if the person involved was a "foreigner."[49] In 1817, New York imposed

---

[46] Act for the Better Settlement and Relief of the Poor (March 7, 1788), in *Laws of the State of New York Passed at the Sessions of the Legislature Held in the Years 1785, 1786, 1787, and 1788, inclusive, Being the Eighth, Ninth, Tenth, and Eleventh Sessions*, vol. II (Albany, NY: Weed, Parsons & Co, 1886), pp. 731–44.

[47] U.S. Const., art. IV, § 2, cl. 1.

[48] An Act to Amend an Act Entitled "An Act for the Better Settlement and Relief of the Poor," ch. 101 (April 3, 1797), in *Laws of the State of New York Passed at the Sessions of the Legislature Held in the Years 1797, 1798, 1799, and 1800, inclusive, Being the Twentieth, Twenty-First, Twenty-Second and Twenty-Third Sessions*, vol. IV (Albany, NY: Weed, Parsons & Co., 1887), p. 135.

[49] Id., p. 134.

a fine of twenty-five dollars on any person who brought into the state "any poor or indigent person ... not having a legal settlement therein," a status that covered aliens and citizens of other states.[50] Similarly, in 1820, Massachusetts imposed a bonding requirement on shipmasters who brought into the state "any passengers ... who have no settlement within this Commonwealth," once again a category encompassing aliens and citizens from other states.[51]

The occasional statutory discrimination between citizens and aliens in the poor laws of the late eighteenth and early nineteenth centuries should not obscure the fact that, when it came to rights to residence, indigent citizens might be worse off than indigent aliens. When cities and towns physically removed outsiders from their territories, they were far more likely to remove those who were citizens than those who were not, for the simple reason that it was cheaper to send someone to a neighboring state than to ship him or her back to Europe. Connecticut's law of 1784 expressed an accepted principle of sound poor relief administration when it authorized the removal of all foreigners who became public charges, so long as the cost of transportation did not exceed "the Advantages of such Transportation."[52] According to Allan Kulikoff, 1,039 individuals were "warned out" of Boston in 1791. Of those, 237 were born in foreign countries, 62 in other states, and 740 in other Massachusetts towns.[53] Of course, the fact that these individuals were "warned out" means only that they were legally subject to being physically removed, not that they were actually physically removed. But evidence of actual physical removals out of state in late-eighteenth-century Massachusetts points toward removals to New York and Nova Scotia rather than to Europe or the

[50] An Act to amend the act for the relief and settlement of the poor, ch. 177, § 4 (April 5, 1817), in *Laws of the State of New York, Passed at the Thirty-Ninth, Fortieth, and Forty-First Sessions of the Legislature, from January 1816 to April 1818*, vol. IV (Albany, NY: Gould, Banks, & Gould, 1818), pp. 176–77.

[51] An act to Prevent the Introduction of Paupers, from Foreign Ports or Places, ch. 290 (February 25, 1820), in *Laws of the Commonwealth of Massachusetts Passed at the Several Sessions of the General Court, Beginning May 1818 and Ending February 1822*, vol. VIII (Boston: Russell & Gardner, 1822), p. 428.

[52] An Act to prevent Foreigners Carrying on insidious Designs or Practices in this State, in *Acts and Laws of the State of Connecticut in America* (New London, CT: Timothy Green, 1784), p. 82.

[53] Allan Kulikoff, "The Progress of Inequality in Revolutionary Boston," *William and Mary Quarterly* 28, no. 3 (1971): 375–412, 401.

West Indies. Furthermore, attempts to prevent the influx of Europe's poor might have been ineffective. New York City regularly prosecuted shipmasters for non-compliance with the terms of the 1788 Act and its 1797 revision. But such prosecutions did not always yield concrete results. Fines remained unpaid. Shipmasters easily circumvented the city's inspection by landing undesirable immigrants around the city.

While the regulation of the movement and presence of poor citizens and aliens formed the core of general "immigration restriction" in the early Republic, a distinct system of immigration restriction emerged to exclude and remove the Republic's expanding free black population, which was increasingly native-born. In the process, we observe not only how easily free blacks' lesser citizenship at the state level could be swept aside, but also how they could be rendered excludable and deportable foreigners.

Tolerance of the slave trade was deemed inconsistent with the spirit of the American Revolution. Although most states banned the slave trade, some Southern states continued to import African slaves right up until Congress, pursuant to its authority under the Migration and Importation Clause of the U.S. Constitution, banned the slave trade in 1807. Scholars have estimated that more than 100,000 African slaves were imported into the country between 1776 and 1808.

If official sanction for the international slave trade was withdrawn by 1808, official support for the domestic institution of slavery was another matter altogether. The expansion of cotton cultivation brought about a vast expansion of slavery, which in turn brought about a reversal of Southern anti-slavery tendencies that had flourished in the immediate aftermath of the Revolution. Southern states sought greater control over blacks, passed extensive black codes, bolstered their enforcement powers, and placed obstacles in the way of private manumissions.

At the same time, Southern states concerned about the presence of free blacks placed restrictions on their entry, residence, and movement. Such restrictions went back to colonial times but were renewed in the early Republic. In 1793, Virginia explicitly forbade the in-migration of "any free negro and mulatto."[54] Between 1790 and 1820, Delaware,

---

[54] An Act to prevent the Migration of Free Negroes and Mulattoes into this Commonwealth, ch. 164, §1 (December 12, 1793), in *A Collection of all such Acts of*

Maryland, Georgia, and South Carolina all – and in some cases, repeatedly – prohibited the in-migration of free blacks. Georgia's 1818 Act was typical. Any free person of color found in Georgia in violation of the prohibition was subject to a penalty not exceeding one hundred dollars and, if unable to pay the penalty, became "liable to be sold by public outcry, as a slave." If such a person was found in Georgia twenty days after the payment of a penalty, the entire prosecution process could begin again.[55] Southern states also sought to block reentry of their own free black residents if they left for extended periods of time or traveled to prohibited destinations. In 1803, Southern states pushed Congress into passing a statute forbidding the importation of foreign blacks into states that prohibited their entry.

Restrictions on the entry and residence of free blacks were not confined to the South. In 1788, Massachusetts provided that no "African or Negroe" who was not "a citizen of some one of the United States" could "tarry within" the Commonwealth of Massachusetts for more than two months. Any free black claiming to be a citizen of another state had to produce "a certificate from the Secretary of the State of which he shall be a citizen," a requirement that was probably difficult for most to meet.[56] In 1804 and 1807, the Ohio legislature passed laws requiring all migrating blacks to give a bond that they would not become a charge to the state. The poor law grid of New England was used particularly harshly against blacks in the 1780s and 1790s. As newly freed black men and women swelled the ranks of the transient, New England town officials relaxed their usual procedures and warned them out of towns en masse.

---

the *General Assembly of Virginia, of a Public and Permanent Nature, as are now in force* (Richmond, VA: Samuel Pleasants et al., 1803), p. 316.

[55] An Act Supplementary to, and more effectually to enforce an act, entitled "An Act prescribing the mode of manumitting Slaves in this state, to prevent the future migration of Free Persons of Colour thereto, to regulate such Free Persons of Colour as now reside therein, and for other purposes," § 3 (December 19, 1818), in Lucius Q. C. Lamar, *A Compilation of the Laws of the State of Georgia, Passed by the Legislature Since the Year 1810 to the Year 1819, Inclusive* (Augusta, GA: T. S. Hannon, 1821), p. 812.

[56] An Act for suppressing and punishing of Rogues, Vagabonds, common Beggars, and other idle, disorderly and lewd Persons, ch. 21 (March 26, 1788), in *The Laws of the Commonwealth of Massachusetts, Passed from the Year 1780, to the End of the Year 1800, with the Constitutions of the United States of America, and of the Commonwealth, Prefixed*, vol. I (Boston: Manning & Loring, 1801), p. 413.

As early as 1777, Thomas Jefferson had raised the possibility of sending blacks back to Africa as American colonists. Such speculations began to be put into practice toward the end of the 1780s. Americans learned that British abolitionists intended to create a colony in Sierra Leone to resettle unwanted free blacks in England and Nova Scotia, many of whom had accompanied fleeing Loyalists. Free blacks in New England appear to have grasped onto the idea as well. A group of blacks in Rhode Island sent an exploratory mission to Sierra Leone to investigate the possibility of relocation. The American Colonization Society, the stated goal of which was to repatriate blacks to Africa, had its first meeting in Washington, DC, at the end of 1816. The meeting was attended by the city's political and legal elite, including Henry Clay, Daniel Webster, Bushrod Washington, and Andrew Jackson. Henry Clay called the meeting to order and lauded the advantages of shipping America's free blacks to Africa: "Can there be a nobler cause than that which, whilst it proposed to rid our country of a useless and pernicious, if not dangerous portion of its population, contemplates the spreading of the arts of civilized life, and the possible redemption from ignorance and barbarism of a benighted quarter of the globe?"[57] In May 1818, Congress asked the U.S. government to negotiate treaties to obtain African territories to which free blacks might be shipped.

African colonization constituted, the historian Daniel Walker Howe has written, "one of the most grandiose schemes for social engineering ever entertained in the United States."[58] Although there were analogues to eighteenth-century laws requiring free blacks to leave colonies, the idea of requiring free blacks to return to Africa, notwithstanding generations of black presence in North America, was new. If Crèvecoeur had represented enslaved blacks as props to regenerate Europe's poor when they moved to America, the idea of African colonization makes clear that, if blacks were no longer to serve as props, they became excludable and removable foreigners with no place in America.

Territorial restrictions applicable to the United States' other major group of internal foreigners – namely, Native Americans – took a different course, that of progressive, yet inexorable, removal from their

---

[57] Quoted in P. J. Staudenraus, *The African Colonization Movement, 1816–1865* (New York: Columbia University Press, 1961), p. 28.

[58] Daniel Walker Howe, *What Hath God Wrought: The Transformation of America, 1815–1848* (New York: Oxford University Press, 2007), p. 265.

homes and communities as the frontier of white settlement advanced relentlessly westward. This was a complex process, with the federal government, states, and white settlers often working at cross-purposes.

Pursuant to its exclusive constitutional power to deal with Native American tribes, the U.S. government claimed a monopoly on dealings with Native Americans in matters of land. As realized in a series of Trade and Intercourse Acts, the goals of this policy were the achievement of peace with Native Americans, seeking negotiation rather than waging warfare, curbing white encroachment into Indian lands beyond established boundaries, and promoting trade. Settlers on the western frontier, however, disagreed. In 1798, Tennessee's governor, John Sevier, put it thus: "By the law of nations, it is agreed that no people shall be entitled to more land than they can cultivate. Of course no people will sit and starve for want of land to work, when a neighboring nation has much more than they can make use of."[59]

The pious principles of legislators in Washington thus ran headlong into the unprincipled practices of settlers. Various measures were taken to hold the frontier, some of which reinscribed the "foreignness" of Indians from the perspective of white communities. For example, an act of 1796 forbade whites from moving onto Indian lands and even grazing their cattle there. Whites were required to be in possession of special travel documents in order to enter Indian country south of the Ohio. In general, however, such initiatives did little to curb the incursions of settlers. In an oft-repeated pattern, in order to avoid confronting irate settlers who had set up homes and farms in contravention of the law, the federal government demanded land cessions from Indians and effectively legalized the depredations of whites. As this pattern suggests, the federal government itself was hardly committed to respecting Native Americans' land claims. Frustrated tribes that resorted to armed resistance faced a military response and met with defeat. Thus, Native Americans were continually pushed farther west. Long labeled "aliens" if they lived beyond white settlements, they were repeatedly required to cede their own lands and become "aliens" vis-à-vis such ceded lands. The idea of deporting Native Americans to a permanent reservation west of the Mississippi was adumbrated in 1803, when the

[59] Sevier to James Ore, May 12, 1798, in Robert H. White, ed., *Messages of the Governors of Tennessee*, vol. I (Nashville: Tennessee Historical Commission, 1952), p. 58.

Jefferson Administration acquired the Louisiana Territory, although it would not really take hold until after 1820.

## Conclusion

The new category of "citizenship" that emerged in the aftermath of the American Revolution was supposedly grounded in contract, consent, and volition. But the polity grounded in consent emerged out of the intimidation, persecution, expulsion, and rendering foreign of Loyalists. Furthermore, although the right of voluntary expatriation was claimed as a justification for breaking with Great Britain, that same right was denied American citizens in the 1790s. More important, as hierarchies of race, class, and gender survived the American Revolution, not everyone in the native-born population was deemed a citizen or granted the rights of one. Native Americans and free blacks could be classified as "aliens" or mere "inhabitants." In discussions of their relationship to the polity, white married women could also occasionally be likened to aliens. The poor were subjected to an extensive regime of internal borders.

Declaring portions of the native-born population outsiders, foreigners, aliens, or mere inhabitants, and restricting their rights of mobility and residence, shaped the nature of "immigration restriction" in the early Republic. At the turn of the eighteenth century, the United States was a country with foreigners at and within its borders. The federal structure of the Republic shaped the regulation of these foreigners.

While the federal government exercised constitutional authority over naturalization, the states continued to regulate access to and presence within their territories. Following the logic of the poor laws, they did so on the basis of settlement rather than citizenship. The result was that citizens and aliens, insiders and outsiders, the native-born and the foreign-born faced barriers to entry and residence. At the same time, there were new developments. The rise in the population of free blacks led to an intensification of territorial barriers directed against their movement and residence. Particularly in the South, managing the influx of free blacks was deemed critical to the survival of the institution of slavery. As before, Native Americans continued to experience a progressive, yet inexorable diminution of their lands as the frontier pushed westward.

# 4

# Blacks, Indians, and Other Aliens in Antebellum America

## Introduction

Beginning in the 1820s, although citizenship remained in most important respects shaped at the state level, a new substantive sense of membership in a national community slowly came into being and began to receive judicial recognition. In the late eighteenth and early nineteenth centuries, the Privileges and Immunities Clause of the U.S. Constitution, which provided that "the Citizens of each State shall be entitled to all Privileges and Immunities of Citizens in the several States," had meant simply that states could not discriminate against citizens of other states by imposing special disabilities on them.[1] But in *Corfield v. Coryell* (1823), Justice Bushrod Washington read the Clause as giving rise to a notion of national citizenship possessed of a substantive core of uniform "fundamental" privileges. He listed some of the most important as follows:

Protection by the government; the enjoyment of life and liberty, with the right to acquire and possess property of every kind, and to pursue and obtain happiness and safety; subject nevertheless to such restraints as the government may justly prescribe for the general good of the whole. The right of a citizen of one state to pass through, or to reside in any other state, for purposes of trade, agriculture, professional pursuits, or otherwise; to claim the benefit of the writ of habeas corpus; to institute and maintain actions of any kind in the courts of the state; to take, hold and dispose of property, either real or personal; and

---

[1] U.S. Const., art. IV, § 2, cl. 1.

an exemption from higher taxes or impositions than are paid by the other citizens of the state; may be mentioned as some of the particular privileges and immunities of citizens, which are clearly embraced by the general description of privileges deemed to be fundamental: to which may be added, the elective franchise, as regulated and established by the laws or constitution of the state in which it is to be exercised.[2]

The most cursory examination of this list of the "fundamental" privileges of citizenship suggests that one or more of them were unavailable to the vast majority of the United States' native-born population. Even as talk of a substantive national citizenship was growing, the country's native-born population continued to be slotted, at the federal and state levels, into a variety of legal statuses. These ranged from full political and social membership to lesser versions of membership to the status of alien, with a corresponding range of legal rights and disabilities. Justice Washington might wax eloquent about "[t]he right of a citizen of one state to pass through, or to reside in any other state, for purposes of trade, agriculture, professional pursuits, or otherwise." However, depending on an individual's legal status, internal territorial borders and restrictions on entry and residence were ubiquitous in antebellum America.

During the second quarter of the nineteenth century, the United States experienced the political empowerment of white males that historians have labeled "Jacksonian democracy." At the same time, the country underwent significant westward territorial expansion and economic transformation. By 1850, as a result of a colonial war of conquest under the banner of "Manifest Destiny," the United States' borders extended to the Pacific. Although the majority of Americans remained engaged in agricultural pursuits, there was a steady movement, especially in the North, toward industry and commerce. The judicial recognition of a right to travel and reside throughout national territory, referred to earlier, reflected growing economic and territorial integration. Legislatures, courts, capitalists, farmers, and laborers rendered the United States a single national market. A communications revolution – encompassing a vast expansion of road, canal, railroad, and telegraph networks – shrank distances and travel times.

---

[2] *Corfield v. Coryell*, 6 F. Cas. 546, 551–52 (E.D. Pa. 1823).

During this period, the United States became a country of mass in-migration. According to official statistics, approximately 650,000 individuals immigrated to the United States between the early 1830s and the early 1840s. Severe crop failures and devastating famines in Europe drove that number to more than 2.5 million between 1845 and 1855. Furthermore, official statistics for the period understate the actual number of entrants because they do not include overland crossings. The new immigration was not just unprecedented in scale. As distinguished from immigration in earlier periods, the new immigrants also differed from the native-born population when it came to religion and ethnicity. By the time the Civil War began, approximately 70 percent of the foreign-born nationwide were of Irish or German descent; the foreign-born were also heavily Catholic. The new immigrants fed America's emerging working class, contributed to the development of national markets, and played a major role in westward expansion.

Internal political fragmentation, however, meant that the incorporation of immigrants into polity and territory proceeded haphazardly. The federal government retained control of naturalization law, which remained largely unaltered. Meanwhile, states exercised control over immigrants' access to their territories.

Where immigrants were highly desired, as in the newly settled West, alien legal disabilities such as bars on voting and property ownership were relaxed to encourage white settlement. However, along the Atlantic seaboard, immigrants became targets of public vilification that had much to do with anti-Catholic and anti-Irish sentiment. Religious and ethnic prejudice aside, there was no doubt that the swell of immigrants placed a significant strain on the eleemosynary institutions of the eastern states. As these states sought to cope with the flood of immigrants, however, they found that their attempts to manage the problems of immigrant pauperism ran up against the country's internal fragmentation of status, rights, and territory along lines of race and class.

In the late eighteenth and early nineteenth centuries, there had been little question that the states were entitled to regulate access to their territories. In the decades leading up to the Civil War, however, what had once been a certainty was up for challenge. As states such as New York and Massachusetts adapted their eighteenth-century poor laws to cope with the new mass immigration, transatlantic shipping lines charged that such laws were an infringement on Congress's authority under Article I, Section 8 of the U.S. Constitution to regulate "Commerce with foreign Nations, and among the several States, and with the Indian tribes."[3]

It seemed clear to many that, at least in some cases, state laws regulating immigration could plausibly be seen as infringements upon federal authority to regulate foreign commerce. This might point the way to the emergence of a federal immigration order. However, any recognition of federal authority to regulate the influx of persons was viewed by pro-slavery apologists as a potential threat to the slave states' authority to regulate the influx and residence of free blacks.

At the level of constitutional law, the result was confusion. Throughout the antebellum period, torn between the view that state immigration laws were an infringement on Congress's foreign commerce powers and the need to reassure the slave states of their continued authority to regulate the influx and residence of free blacks, the U.S. Supreme Court sent inconsistent signals to the immigrant-receiving states, alternately upholding and striking down state immigration laws. In such an environment, state immigration regimes remained weak and inefficient. As long as slave states insisted on regulating the residence and movement of the country's internal foreigners, namely free blacks, the U.S. Supreme Court's constitutional jurisprudence blocked the emergence of a national regime to regulate the country's external foreigners. A federal immigration order would not emerge until *after* the Civil War, when, at least formally, blacks ceased to be foreigners vis-à-vis the polity.

Antebellum immigration restriction thus remained at the state level, where a reliance on the poor laws, which had traditionally failed to distinguish between the citizen poor and the alien poor, gave rise to considerable corruption and mismanagement. Notwithstanding Jacksonian era rhetoric about the rights of citizens, the diminished legal status of the native-born poor – another instance of antebellum America's internal political and territorial fragmentation – led local communities to attempt to get rid of this despised group in whatever way possible, often by passing off the native-born poor as the foreign-born poor or, in short, rendering native-born paupers foreigners of a sort.

---

[3] U.S. Const., art. I, § 8, cl. 3.

This eventually led states to abandon the eighteenth-century system of local immigration control and to centralize immigration controls. Mid-nineteenth-century centralized state immigration bureaucracies were prototypes of the federal immigration bureaucracies that would emerge in the late nineteenth century.

The remainder of this chapter begins with a canvassing of the plethora of legal statuses, rights, and disabilities assigned to the native-born, with specific attention to territorial rights and internal borders. It then discusses two instances of how the country's internal fragmentation along lines of race and class affected antebellum immigration regimes: first, how, at the constitutional level, slavery's long shadow fell over immigration so as to stymie and arrest federal assumption of control over immigration and, second, how antebellum impulses to get rid of paupers regardless of their citizenship status confounded and complicated state-level immigration regimes in ways that compelled their centralization by the middle of the nineteenth century.

### Citizenship, Alienage, and Borders for the Native-Born

In antebellum America, the native-born population was slotted into a variety of legal statuses that implied different rights. Millions could be classified as aliens, share legal disabilities with aliens, and be far less welcome than many aliens. Depending on one's legal status, the experience of internal territorial borders – accompanied by a fragility of rights of residence and mobility – was also a given.

For white males, democracy's march in the second quarter of the nineteenth century was unstoppable. Between 1816 and 1821, six new states entered the Union and provided in their constitutions for universal white male suffrage. Between 1820 and 1830, Massachusetts, New York, and Virginia held constitutional conventions in which they also substantially liberalized their rules regarding white male suffrage. By 1850, universal white male suffrage was standard everywhere and political parties were self-consciously cultivating working-class white male electorates. Widespread political power for white males, accompanied by territorial expansion, economic integration, and the communications revolution, contributed to increased white male mobility. Law played a significant role in this regard. Federal land grant policies favoring white males encouraged westward migration. In several states, especially in the Midwest, residency requirements for voting were relaxed explicitly to allow white male migrants to participate sooner in the affairs of the community.

However, not all native-born white males enjoyed the benefits of the political power and territorial mobility that were such a hallmark of Jacksonian democracy. In a context in which participatory citizenship was actively claimed by white workingmen, native-born paupers embodied the opposite of citizenship. As states liberalized suffrage rules, paupers were explicitly denied rights of suffrage in many states. Historian Alexander Keyssar has observed: "These pauper exclusions were not archaic carryovers of colonial precedents; they were generally new constitutional provisions, often adopted at the same conventions that abolished property or taxpaying requirements."[4] Similarly, as white male citizens' right to travel and reside throughout national territory was being affirmed, the exclusion and removal of paupers from state and local territories were considered an integral and legitimate part of state police power. In 1856, a dissenting opinion in a judgment of the Maine Supreme Court described the effects of pauperism on the rights of the citizen and explicitly analogized paupers to slaves:

Pauperism works most important changes in the condition of the citizen. Through its influence, he is deprived of the elective franchise, and of the control of his own person. The pauper may be transported from town to town, and place to place, against his will; he loses the control of his family, his children may be taken from him without his consent; he may himself be sent to the work-house, or made the subject of a five years contract, without being personally consulted. In short, the adjudged pauper is subordinated to the will of others, and reduced to a condition but little removed from that of chattel slavery, and until recently, by statute of 1847, c. 12, like the slave, was liable to be sold upon the block of the auctioneer, for service or support.[5]

White women had a different experience of lesser citizenship to the extent that their rights were thought to derive from those of men. In *Amy v. Smith* (1822), a Kentucky court ruled that woman and infants "are generally dependent upon adult males *through whom* they enjoy the benefits of ... rights and privileges."[6] Pursuant to the common law

---

[4] Alexander Keyssar, *The Right to Vote: The Contested History of Democracy in the United States*, 2d ed. (New York: Basic Books, 2000), p. 49.
[5] *Portland v. Bangor*, 42 Me. 403, 411 (1856) (Rice, J., dissenting).
[6] *Amy v. Smith*, 11 Ky. 326, 333 (1822) (emphasis added).

institution of coverture, married women lacked political rights and full control over their persons and property. In the late 1840s, activist women began the arduous struggle to obtain political rights. While the satisfaction of women's demands for political participation would come about only in the next century, incremental changes emerged in the antebellum period with the passage of Married Women's Property Acts that conferred upon married women greater rights over their own property. But these acts represented no thoroughgoing transformation. Not every state passed one; there was widespread variation among the acts passed by different states; and the acts reaffirmed patriarchal power in different ways. Furthermore, the force of Married Women's Property Acts could be blunted by laws that rendered married women's domicile derivative of that of their husbands. Through the simple expedient of moving to a jurisdiction that accorded wives fewer rights, husbands could change their wives' domicile and thus their wives' rights. To be sure, coverture was an insufficient – if rhetorically powerful – argument for denying women rights. *All* women, not just married ones, were deprived of political rights and access to many professions and occupations.

During this period, there were occasional legal recognitions of women's capacity to exercise volition in matters of citizenship. For example, in *Shanks v. Dupont* (1830), writing for the majority of the U.S. Supreme Court, Justice Joseph Story argued that, under the common law, "marriage with an alien, whether a friend or an enemy, produces no dissolution of the native allegiance of the wife"; married women could retain or abandon their citizenship as they wished.[7] However, for the most part, the sense that women's political, property, and domiciliary rights derived from those of their husbands reigned supreme. Women's lesser social and political membership fed into the view that women's formal membership in the polity was also derivative of the formal membership of their husbands.

This was underscored when Congress wrote the principle of marital unity into naturalization law. In 1855, Congress provided that "any woman who might lawfully be naturalized under the existing laws, married, or who shall be married to a citizen of the United States, shall be deemed and taken to be a citizen."[8] Marriage to an American

[7] *Ann Shanks et al. v. Abraham Dupont et al.*, 28 U.S. 242, 246 (1830).
[8] Act of February 10, 1855, ch. 71, 10 Stat. 604.

man automatically conferred citizenship upon his alien wife. The rule brought American practice into conformity with those of European countries and guaranteed that foreign-born widows would not be barred from inheriting their American husbands' property on the ground that they were aliens. For our purposes, however, the rule shows how the lesser legal status of women intersected with rules regarding the nationality of women. American men were able to confer citizenship upon their alien wives, who were deemed to have lost nothing as a result. "[W]omen possess no political rights," observed Representative Francis Cutting of New York in the congressional debate preceding the passage of the law, so "where you confer on her the political character of her husband, it is a relief to the husband, it aids him in the instilling of proper principles in his children, *and cannot interfere with any possible right of a political character.*"[9] It followed that American women were unable to confer citizenship upon their alien husbands. Lacking political rights, they had no citizenship to confer. These and other rules implied the tenuousness of women's relationship to the polity, a point that was not lost upon women's rights activists. In an 1838 address to the Massachusetts legislature, the abolitionist Angelina Grimké would ask: "Are we aliens, because we are women? Are we bereft of citizenship, because we are mothers, wives, and daughters of a mighty people? Have women *no* country – *no* interests staked in public weal – no liabilities in common peril – no partnership in a nation's guilt and shame?"[10]

If white women and paupers were slotted into lesser citizenship statuses, such that the deprivation of political, property, personal, and territorial rights they experienced made meaningful the occasional analogy to aliens, the denial of citizenship to Native Americans and free blacks – and their casting out of the polity – worked to far more devastating effect. Between 1820 and the Civil War, issues surrounding the citizenship, presence, and movement of Native Americans and free blacks – none of which were new – intruded upon the national public sphere with unprecedented intensity. Both groups were denied

---

[9] Cong. Globe, 33d Cong., 1st Sess. 170 (1854) (emphasis added).

[10] Angelina Grimké, "Address to the Massachusetts Legislature" (February 1838), quoted in Gerda Lerner, *The Grimké Sisters from South Carolina: Pioneers for Women's Rights and Abolition*, 2d ed. (New York: Oxford University Press, 1998), p. 7 (emphasis in original).

citizenship and characterized variously as "occupants," "denizens," non-citizens, and aliens. Such legal characterizations enabled communities everywhere to deny Native Americans and free blacks meaningful control over their own lives, to regulate their movement and presence, and, eventually, to call for their expulsion from the boundaries of the nation. The mass expulsion of Native Americans to the trans-Mississippi West was largely accomplished by the 1850s. The attempted expulsion of free blacks, while the larger system of which it was a part wreaked havoc on the lives of many, remained a dream.

As in earlier periods, questions surrounding the citizenship of Native Americans were often linked to questions surrounding their right to possess and transfer sound legal title to property. Those who attacked titles derived from Native Americans argued that, as groups outside the community of allegiance, Native Americans had no power to hold or confer valid titles. In *Goodell v. Jackson* (1823), in a dispute involving lands transferred by a member of the Oneida Tribe, New York's Chancellor Kent characterized Native Americans as outsiders to the political community incapable of conferring property rights. After listing various attributes of national and state citizenship that Native Americans lacked, ranging from voting to jury service to subjection to general laws, Kent concluded: "I apprehend, that ... [Indians] are regarded as dependent allies and *alien communities* ... In my view of the subject, they have never been regarded as citizens or members of our body politic, within the contemplation of the [New York] constitution." *Jus soli* principles thus did not apply to Native Americans: "Though born within our territorial limits, the *Indians* are considered as born under the dominion of their tribes. They are not our subjects ... because they are not born in obedience to us."[11] If Native Americans were characterized as alien communities unable to convey sound title to property, American courts in the 1820s also held that Native Americans' own property rights, such as they were, could be extinguished at will by the sovereign. In *Johnson v. M'Intosh* (1823), the U.S. Supreme Court, upon characterizing Native Americans as "occupants ... incapable of transferring the absolute title to others," observed: "All our institutions recognize the absolute title of the crown [from which the United States' title was

[11] *Goodell v. Jackson*, 20 Johns. Rep. 693, 710 (N.Y. 1823) (emphasis added).

derived], subject only to the Indian right of occupancy, and *recognise the absolute title of the crown to extinguish that right*."[12] All Native Americans had, then, was a "right of occupancy," which illustrates more clearly than anything else that depictions of Native Americans as "aliens" were never intended to recognize them as sovereign equals possessed of full control over their own lands.

By the 1820s, government-supported initiatives to "civilize" Native Americans had begun to bear fruit, with several tribes – especially the Five Civilized Tribes of the southeastern United States – adopting external markers of white society. Marriage between white men and Christianized Native American women was often advocated as a means of making Native Americans disappear into American society. In 1827, however, the Cherokees adopted a constitution modeled on the U.S. Constitution and proclaimed themselves an independent nation with full sovereignty over tribal lands in Georgia, North Carolina, Tennessee, and Alabama. In doing so, they made clear that they repudiated completely all legal attempts to characterize them as mere "occupants" of the soil whose property rights could be destroyed at will. In asserting a genuine sovereignty, they were also using to their advantage centuries of white settlers' characterizations of Native Americans as "aliens."

The Cherokee Nation's declaration of sovereignty brought to a head disputes between the federal government, states responsive to white settlers, and the tribes themselves. Andrew Jackson was an energetic proponent of the position that the removal of Native Americans to the trans-Mississippi West was essential to safeguarding the United States. His public espousal of this view played a significant part in his victory in the 1828 presidential election. Thereafter, Georgia, Alabama, and Mississippi passed acts asserting sovereignty over all Native Americans living in their territories. The acts were intended to conflict directly with the Cherokees' claim to sovereignty. The hope was that this action would force a resolution of the issue.

The ploy worked. Despite energetic opposition in the late 1820s, particularly from missionary groups who had long worked with Native American tribes, Congress passed the Indian Removal Act in the spring of 1830. Under the Act, the president was authorized to offer Native

[12] *Johnson v. M'Intosh*, 21 U.S. 543, 591, 588 (1823) (emphasis added).

Americans lands in the trans-Mississippi West in exchange for their lands in the East. Native Americans were to receive good legal title to western lands, compensation for all improvements on lands they surrendered, as well as assistance in emigrating.

Such initiatives did not go unopposed. In 1830, the Cherokee Nation filed suit in the U.S. Supreme Court to enjoin Georgia from interfering with its rights to soil and self-government on the ground that it was a "foreign state, not owing allegiance to the United States, nor to any state of this union, nor to any prince, potentate or state, other than their own."[13] The Court was urged to accept jurisdiction under Article III, Section 2 of the U.S. Constitution, which gave the Court jurisdiction in cases "between a State, or the Citizens thereof, and foreign States, Citizens or Subjects" and original jurisdiction over cases "in which a State shall be a Party."[14] The Cherokee Nation was thus insisting on its foreignness and alien character vis-à-vis the United States to bolster its claim to a genuine sovereignty. However, in *Cherokee Nation v. Georgia* (1831), the Marshall Court rejected the Cherokee Nation's claim to be a foreign nation. Far from being bona fide foreign nations vis-à-vis the United States, Native Americans were "domestic dependent nations," their relationship to the United States analogized to that of a ward to his guardian.[15] Thus, while they were excluded from the rights of citizenship and designated aliens and mere "occupants" when it came to denials of their property and territorial rights, Native Americans would also not count as aliens when it came to acceptance of their sovereignty. The contradiction implicit in the view that Native Americans were aliens, yet not like other aliens, played out in subsequent years. In the 1857 *Dred Scott* case, Chief Justice Taney suggested that Native Americans could, if they left their tribes and took up residence among whites, "be entitled to all the rights and privileges which would belong to an emigrant from any other foreign people."[16] At roughly the same time, however, the U.S. attorney general observed that Native Americans were barred from naturalizing because naturalization was available only to white aliens and

---

[13] *Cherokee Nation v. State of Georgia*, 30 U.S. 1, 3 (1831).
[14] U.S. Const., art. III, § 2, cl. 1–2.
[15] *Cherokee Nation v. State of Georgia*, 30 U.S. at 17.
[16] *Scott v. Sandford*, 60 U.S. 393, 404 (1857).

because Native Americans were not actually aliens insofar as "they are in our allegiance."[17]

*Cherokee Nation v. Georgia* was widely viewed as a triumph for the administration. The government moved swiftly to negotiate removal treaties with individual tribes. The process was marred by subterfuge, intimidation, violence, and corruption. For example, on December 29, 1835, representatives of the War Department concluded a removal treaty with the Cherokees notwithstanding the refusal of delegates of the Cherokee National Party, who represented nearly 16,000 of the 17,000 Cherokees in the South, to consent. The Senate nevertheless ratified the treaty. Brigadier General John E. Wool warned the Cherokees that delaying would be useless: "You will be hunted up and dragged from your lurking places and hurried to the West."[18] When the government's goal of removing the Cherokees had not been accomplished by the deadline of 1838, Martin Van Buren authorized the use of force. Driven out of their ancestral homes at the point of rifles and bayonets, approximately 4,000 men, women, and children perished from malnutrition, exposure, and cholera on the "Trail of Tears" to present-day Oklahoma.

Thus, the United States engaged in the first large-scale deportation of "foreigners" from out of its midst. By the time Andrew Jackson left office, the United States had compelled approximately 50,000 Native Americans to migrate westward and had wrested approximately 100 million acres of land from them. Roughly 50,000 were driven westward in the ensuing decade. However, the forced westward migration of Native Americans ended up creating an Indian enclave at what became, following the 1848 war with Mexico, the very geographic heart of the expanded United States. Thereafter, advocates of Indian removal demanded cessions of lands from the relocated tribes. In the 1850s, the Office of Indian Affairs began to focus on reacquiring lands promised to Native Americans.

---

[17] C. C. Andrews, ed., *Official Opinions of the Attorneys General of the United States: Advising the President and Heads of Departments, in Relation to Their Official Duties, and Expounding the Constitution, Treaties with Foreign Governments and with Indian Tribes, and the Public Laws of the Country*, vol. 7 (Washington, DC: Robert Farnham, 1856), p. 749.

[18] Quoted in Ronald N. Satz, *American Indian Policy in the Jacksonian Era* (Lincoln: University of Nebraska Press, 1975), p. 100.

Even as the United States was accomplishing the removal of tens of thousands of Native Americans from their ancestral lands, there were renewed efforts across the nation to deny free blacks' citizenship and to exclude and remove them from the nation, states, counties, and cities. In contrast to earlier decades, however, such efforts sparked national controversy and rapidly acquired a constitutional dimension.

In December 1820, a dispute arose in Congress over a clause in the proposed Missouri constitution barring free blacks from entering the state. Opponents of the clause argued that since free blacks were "not aliens or slaves, ... [they] were of consequence free citizens."[19] As citizens of states and the Union, they could not be barred from entering another state. Southern spokesmen were outraged by such arguments. A Virginia congressman responded as follows: "It is not every person who is born in a State, and born free, that becomes a member of the political community. The Indians born in the States continue to be aliens, and so, I contend, do the free negroes ... [N]ature seems to have made the negro a perpetual alien to the white man." Where free blacks were not aliens, they might perhaps be considered "denizens," but under no circumstances could they be citizens.[20] In the end, Congress agreed to the admission of Missouri on the condition that the clause in dispute never be construed to authorize the exclusion of "any citizen of [any] of the States of this Union ... from the enjoyment of any of the privileges and immunities to which such citizen is entitled under the Constitution of the United States."[21] However, the underlying question about the citizenship status of free blacks remained.

Whether in the North or the South, free blacks were denied important political and civil rights. Every state admitted after 1819 denied blacks the vote. By 1855, only five states treated blacks with formal impartiality when it came to the suffrage. These were all in New England, which accounted for a tiny fraction of the country's free black population. The federal government barred free blacks from the vote in the territories.

---

[19]  16 Annals of Cong. 93 (1820) (statement of Sen. Harrison Gray Otis).
[20]  16 Annals of Cong. 556–57 (1820) (statement of Rep. A. Smyth).
[21]  James Monroe, "Proclamation Respecting the Admission of the State of Missouri into the Union" (August 10, 1821), quoted in *Laws of the State of Missouri; Revised and Digested by Authority of the General Assembly*, vol. 1 (St. Louis: E. Charless, 1825), p. 70.

However, Northern and Southern courts interpreted this denial of rights in very different ways. Northern courts subscribed to the position that native-born free blacks remained state citizens notwithstanding a diminution of rights. Free blacks were akin to white women and children, who were denied many political rights but did not therefore forfeit their basic status as citizens. Most Southern courts took a different approach, insisting that free blacks' general lack of political and civil rights rendered them something other than citizens. The diminished status of free blacks traveled under different names: "denizens";[22] "subjects";[23] "wards";[24] something "associated still with the slave in this State."[25]

The uncertainties surrounding free blacks' citizenship at the state level played into determinations of their national citizenship. In the antebellum decades, in confirmation of the view that federal citizenship was derivative of state citizenship, U.S. attorneys general and secretaries of state tended to hold that free blacks could not be citizens of the United States because they were not full citizens at the state level. Free blacks were thus barred from positions restricted to U.S. citizens, unable to obtain U.S. passports, and denied the protection of U.S. consuls when outside the country. A definitive (albeit controversial) interpretation came only with the U.S. Supreme Court's infamous decision in *Scott v. Sandford* (1857). According to Chief Justice Taney's opinion, on grounds of their race, blacks could not be U.S. citizens by reason of birth on U.S. soil (*jus soli*), birth to a citizen father (*jus sanguinis*), or naturalization. Taney argued that blacks had not been citizens of the states that had joined to form a national community in 1789. Therefore, they were not within the contemplation of the national community that had arisen then. States conferring citizenship upon free blacks subsequently could not therefore force such individuals upon the national community.[26] Thus, even if free blacks were citizens of Northern states, the Privileges and Immunities Clause of the U.S. Constitution would not impose upon Southern states a duty to treat them like their own citizens. Ohio might "confer citizenship on

[22]  *Rankin v. Lydia*, 9 Ky. 467, 476 (1820).
[23]  *Hardcastle's Estate v. Porcher*, 16 S.C.L. 495, 501 (S.C. 1826).
[24]  *Cooper and Worsham v. Savannah*, 4 Ga. 68, 72 (1848).
[25]  *Bryan v. Walton*, 14 Ga. 185, 202 (1853).
[26]  *Scott v. Sandford*, 60 U.S. 393 (1857).

the chimpanzee or ourang-outang," wrote Judge Harriss of Mississippi in 1859, but nothing under the U.S. Constitution would force "States not thus demented, to forget their own policy ... and lower their own citizens."[27]

The chorus of denials of free blacks' citizenship through the decades leading up to the *Dred Scott* decision translated into harsh restrictions on free blacks' rights to movement and residence within the United States. The U.S. Supreme Court repeatedly acquiesced in states' attempts to exclude and remove free blacks on the ground that regulating undesirables' access to territory was fully part of a state's traditional police power to act for the health, welfare, and benefit of the community. In *Moore v. Illinois* (1852), Justice Grier stated:

In the exercise of this power, which has been denominated the police power, a State has a right to make it a penal offence to introduce paupers, criminals or fugitive slaves, within their borders ... Some of the States, coterminous with those who tolerate slavery, have found it necessary to protect themselves against the influx either of liberated or fugitive slaves, and to repel from their soil a population likely to become burdensome and injurious, either as paupers or criminals.[28]

Thus, even as federal courts were proclaiming whites males' rights to move freely throughout national territory as an incident of *their* citizenship, state territorial borders were activated under sanction of constitutional law against native-born free blacks, who became as a result a species of internal foreigner comparable to the "illegal alien" of the next century: restricted at borders, vulnerable to exploitation and intimidation because they might be present in violation of law, punishable with expulsion and other sanctions.

In the North, restrictions on free blacks' entry and residence were common even in states that saw themselves as bastions of anti-slavery sentiment. In 1822, in a report entitled *Free Negroes and Mulattoes*, a Massachusetts legislative committee emphasized "the necessity of checking the increase of a species of population, which threatens to be both injurious and burthensome."[29] Denials of suffrage rights were explicitly intended as deterrents to the influx and residence of free

[27] *Mitchell v. Wells*, 37 Miss. 235, 264 (1859).
[28] *Moore v. Illinois*, 55 U.S. 13, 18 (1852) (Grier, J.).
[29] Massachusetts, General Court, House of Representatives, *Free Negroes and Mulattoes* (Boston: True & Green, 1822), p. 1.

blacks. So were other forms of legal discrimination against free blacks in respect of holding real estate, making contracts, and bringing lawsuits. But states also resorted to more direct measures. Midwestern states and territories obliged free blacks seeking residence to provide bonds that they would not become public charges. In some cases, there were even flat prohibitions on blacks' moving into states. Fears were especially acute in border states. Senator Stephen A. Douglas defended the Illinois statute restricting the entry of free blacks on the ground that his state was reluctant to serve as "an asylum for all the old and decrepit and broken-down negroes that may emigrate or be sent to it."[30] Indiana declared its refusal to become "the Liberia of the South."[31]

Northern states' legislation prohibiting the entry of free blacks appears to have been enforced only sporadically. But such sporadic enforcement allowed communities to intimidate and exploit blacks, subject them to violence, and render their presence insecure. This is clear from the events in Cincinnati in the late 1820s. Even though Ohio had passed laws in 1804 and 1807 imposing bond requirements on free blacks seeking to enter the state, such laws had not been enforced consistently. However, in 1829, Cincinnati officials concerned about the spurt in the city's free black population announced that the laws would henceforth be enforced: blacks were to comply or leave within a month. The city's black community procured a time extension, petitioned the Ohio legislature for a repeal of the laws, and considered relocating to Canada. Meanwhile, white mobs attacked Cincinnati's black section, intimidating residents and destroying their property. According to estimates, between 1,000 and 2,000 blacks left Cincinnati in 1829, many of them for Canada.

The paranoia about the influx and presence of free blacks was, of course, far greater in the slave states, where free blacks' presence was thought to give the lie to the increasingly strident racial justifications for slavery and to increase the possibility of slave revolts. As the struggle over slavery intensified, the situation of free blacks deteriorated. Free blacks were required to carry evidence of their freedom and

---

[30] Cong. Globe, 33d Cong., 1st Sess., App. (Part 2), 1664 (September 12, 1850).
[31] *Report of the Debates and Proceedings of the Convention for the Revision of the Constitution of the State of Indiana*, vol. 1 (Indianapolis: A. H. Brown, 1850), p. 446.

proof of support at all times. Slave state legislation barred the entry and residence of out-of-state free blacks. States even prohibited the return of their own free black residents who traveled outside the state. Individual cities placed barriers on the entry of free blacks from other parts of the same state. For example, in 1839, the City of Savannah passed an ordinance requiring any free person of color entering the city from any part of Georgia to pay a sum of one hundred dollars on pain of arrest and confinement until such sum was paid: the law was upheld.[32] In the late antebellum period, several slave state legislatures debated forcing their free black populations to elect between re-enslavement and leaving the state. Arkansas passed such legislation.

The panoply of restrictions on free blacks' residence and movement in both North and South makes clear that, from the perspective of many, there was to be no place for blacks in the United States once they were not slaves. At the point of freedom, blacks became aliens of a sort, excludable and removable. The Tennessee Supreme Court put it thus in 1834: "All the slaveholding states, it is believed, as well as many of the non-slaveholding, like ourselves, have adopted the policy of exclusion. The consequence is the freed negro cannot find a home that promises even safety in the United States, and assuredly none that promises comfort."[33]

Representing itself, as the occasion called, as both pro-slavery and anti-slavery, the American Colonization Society stepped up its efforts in the antebellum decades to encourage free blacks to return to its privately established colony of Liberia. Colonization won extensive public support, particularly in the Upper South. Legislatures in Delaware, Maryland, Kentucky, Tennessee, and Virginia appropriated moneys to facilitate colonization. Certain slave owners made leaving the United States a condition of manumission. Despite the pressure on free blacks, colonization proved a failure. Only about 15,000 blacks were actually repatriated (or "chose" to return) to Africa. For the most part, blacks and white abolitionists mobilized against colonization. In 1852, Martin Delaney put it as follows: "We look upon the American Colonization Society as one of the most arrant enemies of the colored man, ever seeking to discomfit him, and envying him of every privilege

---

[32] *Cooper and Worsham v. Savannah*, 4 Ga. R. 68 (1848).
[33] *Fisher's Negroes v. Dabbs*, 16 Yer. 119, 130 (Tenn. 1834).

that he may enjoy."[34] In keeping with this sentiment, free blacks in the Upper South congregated in cities in defiance of laws intended to remove them, converting them into centers of black life. Between 1820 and 1860, the free black population of the South, concentrated in the Upper South, doubled, reaching about 260,000.

Given the considerable political, legal, and rhetorical investment in denying blacks' legal citizenship, in insisting upon their foreignness, and in excluding and removing them, it is not surprising that at least some Southern state courts *formally* assimilated out-of-state free blacks to the status of aliens. In 1838, the Tennessee Supreme Court upheld a statute prohibiting the entry of free blacks on the ground that "every free State has a right to prevent foreigners going to it, and to punish those who violate such laws."[35] Formal determinations of the alien status of free blacks could, furthermore, turn on legal determinations of their race. In the late antebellum period, widespread racial justifications of slavery led to considerable litigation about the racial status of individuals that drew upon both racial "science" and common knowledge. In the typical case, legal determinations of race determined whether an individual would be free or enslaved. But they could also determine whether an individual might legally be classified as an alien, denied entrance to and residence within a state, and be subjected to alien legal disabilities. This is clear from the Mississippi Supreme Court's decision in *Heirn v. Bridault* (1859). The case involved the claim of Marcelette Marceau, originally from New Orleans but resident in Mississippi, to inherit under the will of a deceased Mississippi white male with whom she had been cohabiting. The contestants of the will paraded a series of witnesses who testified about Marceau's racial status. One witness described Marceau as "a bright mulatto, and ... a free woman of color; her son is still darker; her hair is kinky." Another added that she "never saw a white person of [Marceau's] color." Yet another insisted that "[Marceau's] negro blood is very apparent," but confessed that she had never seen Marceau's hair "as she always wore a handkerchief on her head." All of this testimony about hair and skin color convinced the court that Marceau was black. This meant

---

[34] Martin R. Delaney, *The Condition, Elevation, Emigration, and Destiny of the Colored People of the United States* (1852; reprint, New York: Arno Press, 1968), p. 31.
[35] *State v. Claiborne*, Meigs Reports 331, 341 (Tenn. 1838).

that she became an alien not legally present in the state and therefore someone unable to inherit property under the contested will. The court offered the following rationale: "[F]ree negroes [in Mississippi in violation of law] are to be regarded as alien enemies or strangers *prohibiti*, and without the pale of comity, and incapable of acquiring or maintaining rights of property in this State which will be recognized by our courts."[36]

## The Long Shadow of Slavery: Keeping Immigration Restriction at the State Level

During the antebellum period, the federal government's role in regulating immigrants was largely restricted to establishing the requirements for naturalization and the requirements for alien ownership of federal lands. Both policies remained unchanged relative to the early nineteenth century, with two exceptions: (a) the provision allowing alien wives of U.S. citizens to become citizens upon marriage, discussed earlier, and (b) a provision that aliens seeking to buy federal lands have declared their intent to naturalize. To the extent that being white was a prerequisite for naturalization *and* ownership of federal lands, the federal government obviously played a significant part in facilitating white immigration and settlement.

One major exception to this federal policy of promoting white citizenship and settlement was a by-product of the country's mid-nineteenth-century war of colonial conquest and acquisition. With the Treaty of Guadalupe Hidalgo in 1848, Mexico ceded to the United States more than half of its territory, comprising all or part of present-day Arizona, California, Colorado, Kansas, Nevada, New Mexico, Oklahoma, Texas, Utah, and Wyoming. The Treaty had a profound impact on the lives of the estimated 75,000 to 100,000 Mexicans who lived in the ceded territories. Article VIII of the Treaty provided that this population had a year from the effective date of the Treaty to elect Mexican or American citizenship. If no election had been made, individuals would be deemed American citizens. This grant of citizenship to Mexicans became the subject of racial anxieties. In the *Dred Scott* case, Justice McLean observed: "On the question of

---

[36] *Heirn v. Bridault*, 37 Miss. 209, 213, 214, 215, 233 (1859).

citizenship, it must be admitted that we have not been very fastidious. Under the late treaty with Mexico, we have made citizens of all grades, combinations, and colors."[37]

Many white Americans took comfort, however, in the thought that the territories were sparsely settled and would be transformed by white migration. The populations that remained in the ceded territories suffered discrimination, violence, and expropriation. Native Americans suffered the most. In 1851, California state governor Peter Burnett presaged "a war of extermination" that would endure "until the Indian race becomes extinct."[38] California's Native American population fell by two-thirds between 1845 and 1855. Although the Treaty of Guadalupe Hidalgo had guaranteed existing property rights, the states that emerged out of the Mexican cession also placed heavy burdens on holders of Mexican land grants who attempted to validate their titles under the new regime, which resulted in massive dispossessions. White settlement thus transformed power structures and demographics.

If the federal government exercised authority over naturalization and territorial questions, throughout the antebellum period, states shaped most alien legal disabilities and regulated immigration. Appreciation for the role played by immigrants varied across the states. This variation is reflected in the alienage laws of the period. Although aliens were increasingly barred from the polls in the eastern states, western states seeking settlers welcomed immigrants by giving aliens the vote (even as they denied it to blacks and Native Americans). Wisconsin's 1848 constitution inaugurated the policy of granting the franchise to aliens who had declared their intent to naturalize. By the beginning of the Civil War, Indiana, Kansas, Louisiana, Michigan, Minnesota, and Oregon all granted declarant aliens the vote. At the conclusion of the Civil War, historian Alexander Keyssar writes, outside of the Northeast, "noncitizen suffrage ... became commonplace, permitting hundreds of thousands of previously excluded voters to go to the polls."[39]

The same imperatives that drove western states to open the polls to aliens also led them to liberalize common law rules regarding alien

---

[37] *Scott v. Sandford*, 60 U.S. at 533 (McLean, J., dissenting).
[38] Howe, *What Hath God Wrought*, p. 810.
[39] Keyssar, *Right to Vote*, p. 33.

ownership of real property. In the eastern states, alien legal disabilities with respect to real property ownership remained (although they were liberalized in certain states). James Kent's *Commentaries on American Law* observed that an alien remained "exposed to the danger of being devested [sic] of [a] fee, and of having his lands forfeited to the state."[40] In 1834, Massachusetts' Chief Justice Lemuel Shaw stated that the rule against alien inheritance of real property was "as among the first principles of the law of real property."[41] But in the West, matters were different. Between 1840 and 1850, Iowa, Wisconsin, California, and Michigan did away with alien legal disabilities regarding property ownership.

Despite the many positive contributions that immigrants made, and notwithstanding the welcome given them by the western states, the antebellum United States experienced a growing swell of nativist paranoia – particularly in the Atlantic seaboard states – as it tried to come to terms with a largely non-British and non-Protestant mass immigration. The nativism of the period drew upon many different and interrelated sources. One of the most significant was anti-Catholicism, the roots of which went back centuries. The influx of large numbers of Catholic immigrants had resulted by the 1830s in a visible expansion of the presence of the Roman Catholic Church. Given Rome's open hostility to political liberalism, many Americans worried that a large Catholic population would subvert the young Republic on orders from Rome. Concerned citizens attended public lectures with titles like "Is Popery Compatible with Civil Liberty?"[42] Protestants' insistence on the teaching of the King James Bible in public schools was designed to re-educate, but also to intimidate, the country's Catholic minority. Lurid fabricated accounts of the goings-on in convents resulted in violence, such as the 1834 burning of the Ursuline convent in Charlestown, Massachusetts.

In some cases, the activities of American nativists drove Catholics out of the country. The story of the Charlestown Ursuline convent is a case in point. After their convent was burned down, the Ursulines

[40] James Kent, *Commentaries on American Law*, 2d ed., vol. II (New York: O. Halstead, 1832), p. 61.
[41] *Slater v. Nelson*, 32 Mass. 345, 350 (1834).
[42] Ray Allen Billington, *The Protestant Crusade, 1800–1860: A Study of the Origins of American Nativism* (New York: Macmillan, 1938), p. 60.

struggled to find another location, lived with the threat of subsequent attacks, and were unable to attract students. The mother superior and her followers departed for Canada in 1838. For the most part, however, Catholics fought back. They started newspapers to combat anti-Catholic writings. They demanded equal treatment in public institutions such as schools and then created separate institutions when such demands went unmet. They also began to participate in the political process. The Democratic Party came increasingly to reflect the interests of Irish and German Catholic immigrants, even as the Party's identification with white workingmen occasionally led it to oppose the influx of those who might depress white workingmen's wages.

American anti-Catholicism was intimately intertwined with entrenched racial attitudes toward the "simian race" of the Irish, a race long associated in English thought with unruliness, drunkenness, laziness, and animal behavior. In antebellum America, Catholic immigrants (especially the Irish) were frequently blamed for the coarsening of public discourse and behavior. In the 1830s, the nativist Samuel F. B. Morse lamented the fact that "the American character has within a short time been sadly degraded by numerous instances of riot and lawless violence in action, and a dangerous spirit of licentiousness in discussion." The cause, for Morse, was "FOREIGN IMMIGRATION."[43] Of course, Irish immigrants were hardly solely responsible for mob behavior, which was a common feature of antebellum political life. In many cases, furthermore, Irish groups were responding in kind to the attacks of nativists. In the 1830s, 1840s, and 1850s, nativist groups regularly sought to provoke Irish Catholics by parading in their neighborhoods. When trouble ensued, it was often the homes and churches of Irish Catholics that suffered destruction.

Nativists also complained, with more reason, that mass immigration placed a significant strain on the resources of eastern seaboard cities and states, where the impoverished segments of the immigrant stream – consisting primarily of Irish immigrants – tended to concentrate (Germans tended to move westward). The strain on public resources built up gradually as Irish famine migration peaked in

[43] Samuel F. B. Morse, *Imminent Dangers to the Free Institutions of the United States Through Foreign Immigration, and the present state of the naturalization laws* (1835; reprint, New York: Arno Press, 1969), pp. iii, iv.

the late 1840s and early 1850s. New York, the state containing the country's principal port, suffered the most under the burden of immigrant pauperism. According to an 1855 report to the state's legislature, the State of New York supported 80,324 native-born paupers and 119,607 foreign-born paupers.[44] Immigrants (especially the Irish) not only tended to rely on the public fisc at disproportionately higher rates, but were disproportionately represented when it came to the social ills of disease, crime, and juvenile vagrancy.

Finally, particularly after the Panic of 1837, nativists complained regularly of competition from immigrant labor, which tended to reduce American workingmen's wages and bargaining power. In 1844, a newspaper protested that "laboring men" were "met at every turn and at every avenue of employment, with recently imported workmen from the low wages countries of the old world" and that public projects "thronged with foreigners."[45] Occasionally, native-born workers resorted to violence to express their frustration over the hiring of aliens by city and state governments. Their resentments fueled the growth of nativist parties.

Throughout the antebellum period, nativists tried assiduously to reduce immigrants' participation in American political life. In order to curb immigrants' political activity, they pushed for lengthening the naturalization period and for giving the federal courts a monopoly over the naturalization of aliens. Not always without reason, nativists saw state court naturalization practices as lax and corrupt; they accused state court judges of naturalizing immigrants in contravention of legal standards on the eve of elections in order to guarantee Democratic victories at the polls. The Democratic Party's dominance of Congress ensured, however, that nativist petitions registered few successes. Democrats were reluctant to diminish one of the major sources of their electoral strength.

Meanwhile, the states of the eastern seaboard were left to cope as best they could with growing numbers of poor immigrants disembarked on their shores. They did so by turning to the legal structures that had traditionally served the purpose of regulating paupers' influx into, and residence within, territory, namely the poor laws. In the

[44] Foreign Criminals and Paupers, H.R. Rep. No. 34-359, 7–8 (1856).
[45] Quoted in Billington, *Protestant Crusade*, p. 200.

1830s, 1840s, and 1850s, although disease and criminal background were also bases of exclusion, state-level immigration regimes remained oriented as before around the exclusion of the poor. Although many state statutes formally focused as they had in the past on alien *and* citizen passengers, the economic panic of the late 1830s, the mounting problem of immigrant pauperism, and the ire of nativists gave rise to an increased focus on immigrants.

For the very first time, however, such initiatives came under constitutional attack from shippers worried about the profitability of the immigrant-carrying trade and encouraged by the centralizing tendencies of the Marshall Court's Commerce Clause jurisprudence. The U.S. Supreme Court was called upon to opine on the appropriate locus of constitutional authority to regulate immigration. The formal question was whether state-level immigration regimes were legitimate exercises of traditional state police powers to legislate for the health, welfare, and safety of the population, which authorized the exclusion of paupers, convicts, and blacks, or whether they constituted unconstitutional interferences with Congress's power under Article I, Section 8 of the U.S. Constitution to regulate "commerce with Foreign Nations."[46]

In *Mayor of the City of New York v. Miln* (1837), the U.S. Supreme Court's first examination of the constitutionality of state immigration statutes, the Court upheld a New York law that required shipmasters to report passenger information and post bonds for passengers who might become chargeable as paupers to New York City.[47] The Court grounded its decision on a rather basic territorial logic. New York was not interfering with the transportation of passengers, which was subject to Congress's exclusive foreign commerce power, but was merely attempting to mitigate fiscal problems associated with passengers who had landed in New York, which fell within the purview of New York's police power. Distinguishing this case from two of the Marshall Court's great Commerce Clause cases, *Gibbons v. Ogden* (1824) and *Brown v. Maryland* (1827), Justice Thompson endorsed the New York law as a legitimate exercise of the state's police power and as no interference whatsoever with Congress's Commerce Clause powers: "For although

[46] U.S. Const., art. I, § 8.
[47] *Mayor of New York v. Miln*, 36 U.S. 102 (1837).

commerce, within the sense of the Constitution may mean intercourse, and the power to regulate it be co-extensive with the subject on which it acts ... it cannot be claimed that the master [of the ship], or the passengers, are exempted from any duty imposed by the laws of a state, after their arrival within its jurisdiction; or have a right to wander, uncontrolled, after they become mixed with the general population of the state; or that any greater rights or privileges attach to them, because they come in through the medium of navigation, than if they come by land from an adjoining state." A little later, he asked rhetorically: "Can anything fall more directly within the police power and internal regulation of a state, than that which concerns the care and management of paupers or convicts ... ?"[48]

Emboldened by the decision in *Miln*, states such as Massachusetts and New York switched from demanding bonds to charging per capita fees for alien passengers landed in their ports. Fees collected upfront were viewed as a more secure way of recouping the costs of supporting immigrants than suing on bonds. The collected funds were to be used to defray the costs of supporting the immigrant poor. Once again, shippers challenged New York and Massachusetts laws charging alien passenger fees on the ground that they constituted an interference with Congress's foreign commerce power. The cases were consolidated as the *Passenger Cases* (1849).

The dispute in the *Passenger Cases*, while it resulted in the invalidation of the alien passenger taxes, divided the Court sharply. The published arguments and opinions run almost 300 pages in the *United States Reports* and consist of seven lengthy opinions (including three rambling dissents). Although the Court had acquiesced in New York's requirement of bonds in *Miln*, the alien passenger taxes at issue in the *Passenger Cases* seemed to go much further, representing a clearer interference with Congress's foreign commerce powers. New York and Massachusetts appeared to be taxing navigation itself, which was unconstitutional. But this is where the Court's solicitude for states' rights to control the residence and movement of America's internal foreigners, namely free blacks, cast a shadow upon the realm of immigration.

---

[48] Id. at 147, 148; *Gibbons v. Ogden*, 22 U.S. 1 (1824); *Brown v. Maryland*, 25 U.S. 419 (1827).

The justices were acutely aware of how any decision scaling back states' rights to control access to their own territories would be read by an ever vigilant and increasingly paranoid South. Southern spokesmen such as John C. Calhoun had earlier insisted upon "the very important right, that the states have the authority to exclude the introduction of such persons as may be dangerous to their institutions: a principle of great extent and importance, and applicable to other states as well as slaveholding, and to other persons as well as blacks, and which may hereafter occupy a prominent place in the history of our legislation."[49] Accordingly, Justice Wayne sought directly to assure the South that the Court's decision striking down the New York and Massachusetts laws was not a cause for concern:

The fear expressed, that if the States have not the discretion to determine who may come and live in them, the United States may introduce into the Southern States emancipated negroes from the West Indies and elsewhere, has no foundation ...

... [S]hould this matter of introducing free negroes into the Southern States ever become the subject of judicial inquiry, ... they have a guard against it in the Constitution, making it altogether unnecessary for them to resort to the *casus gentis extraordinarius*, the *casus extremae necessitatis* of nations, for their protection and preservation. They may rely upon the Constitution, and the correct interpretation of it, without seeking to be relieved from any of their obligations under it, or having recourse to the *jus necessitatis* for self-preservation.[50]

Thus, highly solicitous of states' rights views, the justices in the *Passenger Cases* were careful to signal that, while they were striking down the alien passenger taxes, they were *not* interfering with the basic police powers of the states to regulate undesirables' access to their territories. Because slave states could exclude free blacks, the eastern seaboard states could continue to demand securities from immigrants to indemnify the public from costs associated with immigrant pauperism as had been the case in *Miln*. The federal government

---

[49] John C. Calhoun, "Speech on the Bill to Prohibit Deputy Postmasters from Receiving and Transmitting through the Mail Certain Papers Therein Mentioned" (April 12, 1836), in *Speeches of John C. Calhoun, Delivered in the Congress of the United States from 1811 to the Present Time* (New York: Harper & Brothers, 1843), p. 216.

[50] *Smith v. Turner (Passenger Cases)*, 48 U.S. 283 (1849), 428–29 (Wayne J., concurring).

did *not* possess the authority to regulate the immigration of undesirables. Justice Wayne put it thus:

> But I have said the States have the right to turn off paupers, vagabonds, and fugitives from justice, and the States where slaves are have a constitutional right to exclude all such as are, from a common ancestry and country, of the same class of men. *And when Congress shall legislate ... to make paupers, vagabonds, suspected persons, and fugitives from justice subjects of admission into the United States, I do not doubt it will be found and declared ... that such persons are not within the regulating power which the United States have over commerce.*[51]

In the aftermath of the *Passenger Cases*, therefore, the Northern immigrant-receiving states continued to have the right to request bonds from incoming passengers, even if they could not impose taxes or fees. New York and Massachusetts instantly tailored their practices to fit the Court's ruling. They demanded bonds of all passengers, but offered shipmasters the option of commuting the bonds by paying a fee instead. The fee levels were exactly the same as that of the taxes that the Supreme Court had struck down in the *Passenger Cases*.

The most important consequence of the *Passenger Cases* is that they arrested growing efforts to bring a federal immigration order into being. By the mid-1850s, the influx of vast numbers of immigrants and the explosion of immigrant dependency, combined with the collapse of the second party system brought about by conflict over the expansion of slavery, had given birth to the American, or Know-Nothing, Party, America's first nativist political party. In 1854–55, the Know-Nothings triumphed in New England, New York, Pennsylvania, and California, secured a strong presence in the House of Representatives, and even seemed poised to win the presidency in 1856. While they were able to push through anti-immigrant legislation in the states where they had won, however, the Know-Nothings were unable to push through federal regulation prohibiting the landing of convicts, paupers, and the infirm. States such as Massachusetts and New York, fully aware that they lacked the resources to regulate immigration adequately, also ran into obstacles when they urged federal involvement in the regulation of immigration. Strong opposition to a federal immigration order

---

[51] Id. at 426 (Wayne, J., concurring) (emphasis added).

repeatedly insisted on the point – echoing the *Passenger Cases* – that Congress could not intervene in the sphere of police powers reserved to the states.

The constitutional uncertainties that stood in the way of a federal immigration order are revealed clearly in an 1856 congressional report on immigration commissioned by a Know-Nothing-dominated House of Representatives. As a matter of international law, the authors of the report observed, it was clear that every community had a right to protect itself against the evils associated with the influx of outsiders. But in the context of the United States, where exactly did the power to regulate immigration lie? The report's equivocal response reveals a great deal: "The power exists *somewhere*, either in the States, or in the general government, or in both of them." The locus of the power to regulate immigration was "not well settled even to the present time." The entire issue was plagued by "difference of opinion."[52] Before the Civil War, that "difference of opinion" had everything to do with slavery and the accompanying need to control the mobility and residence of free blacks. As long as free blacks were internal foreigners subjected to a regime of borders, a national regime focused on external foreigners could not come into being.

### Immigration Restriction "on the Ground": Separating Native from Alien Paupers in Antebellum Massachusetts

If slavery and paranoia about the mobility of free blacks blocked the emergence of a federal immigration order before the Civil War, what took place "on the ground" in immigrant-receiving states reveals another story involving the imbrication of external and internal foreigners, in this case immigrant paupers and native-born paupers. This is clear from the experience of antebellum Massachusetts.

Of all the antebellum immigrant-receiving states, New York and Massachusetts developed the most sophisticated immigration bureaucracies. To be sure, New York handled vastly more immigrants than Massachusetts. It was also generally less severe vis-à-vis immigrants than Massachusetts. Nevertheless, New York and Massachusetts both show the same trend, that of moving from immigration laws

---

[52] Foreign Criminals and Paupers, H.R. Rep. No. 34-359, 23 (emphasis added), 25.

administered by local officials to establishing centralized state bureaucracies by the mid-nineteenth century, a phenomenon triggered by the
need to separate out native-born paupers from alien paupers. This section will focus on the experience of Massachusetts.

What we observe in antebellum Massachusetts is the emergence of
a legal-bureaucratic order dealing specifically with immigrants from
out of the older matrix of the poor laws. As discussed earlier, in the
eighteenth and early nineteenth centuries, in Massachusetts as elsewhere, the concept of legal settlement (and not citizenship) determined
rights to entry, residence, and poor relief. Going back to the seventeenth century, however, there had always been in Massachusetts a
small category of those who needed poor relief and who could not
point to a settlement in any Massachusetts town. When such outsiders fell in need, they became the charge of the Province – or, after the
Revolution, the Commonwealth – and were labeled "state paupers,"
to distinguish them from "town paupers," who possessed a settlement in a Massachusetts town. Because of the decentralized system of
poor relief, when an individual lacking a settlement fell in need, town
authorities administered relief to the "state pauper" in question and
then charged the central authorities for the costs of care.

Perverse economic incentives coursed through the logic of settlement. Massachusetts's last major eighteenth-century revision of its
settlement law in 1794 made it extremely difficult for outsiders to
acquire a settlement in a Massachusetts town. Citizenship of one of
the American states was made a prerequisite for acquiring a settlement. Because Massachusetts retained alien property disabilities,
aliens were risky prospects from the perspective of towns wary of
granting settlement to indigent outsiders. This meant that immigrants
could not obtain a settlement in Massachusetts. From the perspective
of the manufacturing towns that expanded as Massachusetts experienced an economic revolution, the structure of the settlement law was
ideal. Immigrants might live, work, and pay taxes in the town, but
when they turned to town authorities for assistance, the costs of supporting them would be passed on to the Commonwealth. To be sure,
aliens were not the only ones who found obtaining a Massachusetts
settlement difficult; citizens of other states did too.

But the logic of disowning the poor was carried even further. In a
species of cheating or corruption, towns administering care to "state

paupers" often inflated their requests for reimbursement from the Commonwealth and thereby sought to reduce the burden of caring for their own poor. Towns thus got rid of their own poor by passing them off as immigrant poor. If this problem was already apparent in the late eighteenth century, it became much more acute when mass immigration picked up after 1820. In the 1820s, 1830s, and 1840s, investigations of town reimbursement claims revealed over and over again that towns were cheating the Commonwealth (in one year, an investigation found approximately half of the total claim amount in accounts submitted by 196 towns to consist of illegal overcharges). In an environment characterized by high immigration, because it was often unclear whether individuals were in fact citizens, the slightest question as to a pauper's antecedents led town poor relief officials to represent him or her as an alien. An 1847 investigative commission revealed the following regarding the state pauper accounts of the Town of Tyngsborough regarding a state pauper named John Thompson:

Tyngsborough claims [Thompson] is a foreigner, and returns him as an Irishman; but Mr. Blodgett, one of the overseers, testified that no person had ever been able to ascertain where he was born, or anything of his history before he came to that town, and this we found confirmed by other persons. Elizabeth Thompson, the wife of John Thompson, states that her husband always assured her that he was born in Virginia, or, to use her own words "in the State where Washington lived."

In this case, although Thompson would have acquired a settlement in Tyngsborough had he been an American citizen, the investigating commissioners did not think that Thompson's nativity was clearly made out and the charge was allowed.[53] But the point should be evident. As a general matter, towns in Massachusetts often represented the native-born poor as foreign-born.

In disowning their own poor and passing them off as foreigners, towns were driven by cold financial logic: in successfully arguing that a native-born individual was foreign-born, towns avoided responsibility for them. But the drive to get rid of the native-born poor by disowning

---

[53] Commonwealth of Massachusetts, *Report of the Commissioners Appointed Under the Resolve of 16 April 1846, to Examine the Claims Presented to the Legislature of that Year for the Support of State Paupers*, House Document No. 21 (Boston: Dutton & Wentworth, 1847), pp. 52–53.

their claims also had a great deal to do with the fact that native-born paupers – like native-born free blacks – *were* a type of internal foreigner, degraded vis-à-vis other citizens and generally excludable and removable from the community. One result of this systematic disowning of the native-born poor was that it becomes impossible to measure the precise extent of antebellum immigrant pauperism. The state pauper expense, an expense routinely blamed by nativists on dissolute immigrants dumped on Massachusetts's shores, was constantly inflated, to a degree that can never be adequately measured, by the expenses of supporting citizens that towns did not want to accept as their own.

A deep-seated suspicion of towns' incentives and practices, justified by inquiry after inquiry, finally led the Commonwealth, at the height of the Irish famine migration, to end the localized and decentralized system of territorial controls and poor relief administration that had been in place since the seventeenth century. What emerged was a centralized legal-bureaucratic structure in which the state assumed a direct and special relationship with immigrant paupers, separating them out from the rest of the pauper population. By the late 1840s, the Commonwealth assumed control over the regulation of immigrants' entry; by the early 1850s, it had taken over direct control of poor relief administration for state paupers.

With centralized control over immigrants established by the mid-1850s, and with Massachusetts in the grip of Know-Nothing hysteria, the Commonwealth was able to step up activities against immigrants in ways that town officials had been unable or unwilling to do. Know-Nothing governor Henry Gardner called for increasing the number of removals. As he put it in early 1855: "The average expense of supporting an alien pauper is not far from sixty dollars per annum; the cost of sending them to Liverpool ... would not exceed twenty dollars each, including a comfortable outfit."[54] To be sure, the *Passenger Cases* had created an atmosphere of uncertainty. New York's commissioners of immigration believed that "this direct power [of deportation] is not granted by the existing laws of the State, and is perhaps a regulation

---

[54] Commonwealth of Massachusetts, *Address of his Excellency Henry J. Gardner, to the Two Branches of the Legislature of Massachusetts, January 9, 1855*, Senate Document No. 3 (Boston: William White, 1855), pp. 18–19.

of the intercourse with foreign nations, not within the competence of the State legislature."[55] But Massachusetts officials did not suffer from such qualms.

The state afforded immigrants few formal protections when it came to deportation beyond a hearing before a justice of the peace. Even these minimal protections were, however, not accorded on occasion. Most often, Massachusetts's newly created Board of Commissioners of Alien Passengers and Foreign Paupers (the name itself illustrating the intrinsic link between immigration restriction and poor relief) attempted to represent removals as voluntary. But this was clearly not always the case. In 1855, one of the commissioners, Peleg Chandler, launched a diatribe against the ad hoc practice of sending "lunatic" immigrant paupers out of the state and country.

[S]ince the commencement of the present year, paupers have been taken from one of the lunatic hospitals and sent over the sea to their alleged homes, and this at the expense of the State, but without any complaint to a justice of the peace, and, in fact, in the face of the law. It is said that these people *consented* to go. *The consent of lunatics!* When it is one of the wisest and most humane maxims of the law that a lunatic can give no consent to any thing.[56]

Chandler was critical not just of practices in violation of the law, but of the law itself because it placed the power of removal in the hands of a justice of the peace without trial by jury, right of appeal, and other procedural protections. Indeed, he questioned the very justice of the Commonwealth's removal of immigrant paupers:

Some of them have been laborious men, honest, useful citizens, and have in their small way contributed to the wealth of the State. Some of them have paid "head money" when they came here; and for some bonds have been given for their support in case they become paupers. If the Commonwealth desires to adopt the policy of preventing foreign immigration entirely, if she chooses to hold her sister States or foreign countries responsible for sending paupers here, let her do so in a suitable manner, with all proper firmness, *let her select antagonists about her own size*, and not wreak her vengeance on poor wretches whose only fault is poverty and whose only heritage is misery.[57]

---

[55] Zolberg, *Nation by Design*, p. 159.
[56] Commonwealth of Massachusetts, *Report of the Commissioners of Alien Passengers and Foreign Paupers, House Document No. 123* (Boston: William White, 1855), p. 46 (emphasis in original).
[57] Id., p. 47 (emphasis in original).

The Know-Nothing General Court appointed a legislative committee that dismissed Chandler's charges as groundless. Deportations continued apace. The bulk of the removals were to New York, where the immigrant paupers had landed, although there were also removals to Liverpool. At least 50,000 destitute persons were removed from Massachusetts between the 1830s and the early 1880s, some American citizens of Irish descent.

But even as the Commonwealth sought to separate alien paupers from native-born paupers, thereby creating a separate legal regime specific to aliens, it could not escape the problem of towns attempting to disown their own paupers by passing them off as immigrants. After state almshouses exclusively for state paupers – that is, for the immigrant poor – opened in 1854, the state employed an agent, John Locke, whose task was to visit the new state almshouses and ascertain whether inmates sent there by towns might not actually possess a Massachusetts settlement. Locke's task was to sift through the mass of purported immigrant paupers, find native-born paupers, and compel their communities to take them back. In the mid-1850s, Locke discovered hundreds of paupers alleged to be state paupers who were actually settled in Massachusetts and neighboring states.

By midcentury, the inability of the old poor law system to cope with mass immigration had brought the system itself under attack. In the words of one commentator, by the early 1860s "the effect of [the creation of an industrial labor force in Massachusetts], together with the influx of foreigners, has been to *unsettle* (in the poor law sense) nearly half the inhabitants of New England."[58] Things were already changing in the 1850s: alien property disabilities were lifted for aliens in Massachusetts in 1852 and citizenship was removed as a prerequisite for the acquisition of a settlement in 1868. Some of the perverse incentives that had driven towns to pass off citizens as aliens were thereby extinguished. But the experience of antebellum Massachusetts shows that the emergence of a central legal-bureaucratic structure to deal with immigrants had to do not only with a desire to minimize the scale of immigrant pauperism, but also with the need to prevent local communities from disowning their own by passing them off as immigrants.

[58] F. B. Sanborn, "The Poor Laws of New England," *North American Review* 106 (1868), 483–514, 496 (emphasis in original).

## Conclusion

During the second half of the 1850s, possibly as a reaction to bad economic conditions and news of anti-immigrant legislation, immigration dropped dramatically. The Civil War depressed immigration even further. This sparked concern among American industrialists, who, with a wary eye on trade unionism, called for increased immigration and began to argue that immigration's benefits outweighed its costs. Such voices in support of immigration, but, more important, the acceleration of the sectional conflict and the rise of the Republican Party, brought a swift end to the Know-Nothing Party. After the Civil War, capital and labor would clash over the continued unrestricted admission of labor.

In the meantime, German and Irish Catholic immigrants, despite the violence and resentment they suffered, won a place for themselves on the American landscape. By 1860, Aristide Zolberg has written, America was transformed from "the bounded community of 'Anglo-Americans' into a more diverse and segmented 'nation of immigrants.'"[59] Irish and German immigrants' incorporation into the polity is evidenced by their ability to push successfully for an expatriation law. In 1868, under pressure from immigrants who faced conscription or imprisonment in their native countries, the United States recognized the right of expatriation as a "natural and inherent right of all people"; reversing a policy of long standing, it pledged to extend protection to naturalized Americans in their native countries.[60]

It is important to underscore, however, that German and Irish Catholic immigrants became Americans at least in part by acceding to "whiteness" and at the expense of Native Americans and blacks. The Democratic Party, which cultivated German and Irish immigrants as an electoral base, self-consciously positioned itself as a party of white males; it was largely pro-slavery and pro–Indian removal. The Party's immigrant base demonstrated its whiteness and party loyalty by distancing itself from America's internal foreigners. In New York City's draft riots of 1863, for example, Irish immigrants manifested their

---

[59] Zolberg, *Nation by Design*, p. 165.
[60] An Act Concerning the Rights of American Citizens in Foreign States (Act of July 27, 1868), 15 Stat. 223.

opposition to the anti-slavery cause by attacking blacks and symbols of black life in the city.

Furthermore, if German and Irish Catholic immigrants succeeded in becoming Americans, not all foreigners would be welcome in the newly reimagined "nation of immigrants." The late 1840s had seen the beginning of Chinese immigration to the United States. Chinese immigrants were drawn to California, as others were, by the Gold Rush. But unlike others, Chinese immigrants would face a spate of discriminatory measures at the state level, from prohibitive taxes to racial bars to testifying against whites to prohibitions on entry. California's mid-nineteenth-century measures against the Chinese would become precursors to federal action against the Chinese in the late nineteenth century.

# 5

# The Rise of the Federal Immigration Order

## Introduction

The Civil War resulted in a major recalibration of federal vis-à-vis state authority, making the United States a more centralized polity than it had been. In significant part, this had to do with the postwar federal government's new role in articulating and defending the rights of freedmen. In the decade that followed the conclusion of the War, a Radical Republican–dominated Congress pushed through three constitutional amendments and a raft of major civil rights statutes. These initiatives were directed at ending slavery, enabling newly emancipated slaves' formal incorporation into the polity, and guaranteeing them a measure of protection against violence, exploitation, and discrimination in the defeated South.

The results were, to say the least, mixed. As a formal politico-legal institution, slavery disappeared. But in many other respects, Radical Republicans' solicitude for freedmen encountered stiff resistance. John Wilkes Booth was driven to assassinate Lincoln, after all, because of the latter's commitment to "nigger citizenship."[1] Lincoln's successor, Andrew Johnson, claiming that "[negroes] have shown a constant tendency to relapse into barbarism," worked hard to stymie change.[2] By

---

[1] Quoted in James McPherson, *Battle Cry of Freedom: The Civil War Era* (New York: Oxford University Press, 1988), pp. 851–52.

[2] Andrew Johnson, Third Annual Message (December 3, 1867), in James D. Richardson, ed., *A Compilation of the Messages and Papers of the Presidents, 1789–1908*, vol. 6 (New York: Bureau of National Literature & Art, 1908) (1897), p. 565.

the beginning of the 1880s, in the midst of political brokering, the promise of Reconstruction had faded.

From the perspective of immigration and citizenship law, however, the postwar constitutional order brought about a change of critical import. Ratified in 1868, the Fourteenth Amendment to the U.S. Constitution provided: "All persons born or naturalized in the United States, and subject to the jurisdiction thereof, are citizens of the United States and of the State wherein they reside."[3] The Fourteenth Amendment thus formalized the common law *jus soli* principle that had hitherto operated unequivocally only for native-born whites and made it theoretically applicable to all. It also made state citizenship follow from national citizenship as a function of residence, and thus took away states' ability to declare native-born blacks non-citizens. Although there would be struggles over the precise contours of the Fourteenth Amendment's *jus soli* principle in the decades that followed, it unambiguously put an end to one of the most egregious forms of internal foreignness: that imposed upon native-born blacks.

In *Crandall v. Nevada* (1867), the U.S. Supreme Court struck down a Nevada tax on persons leaving the state by means of public transportation on the ground that national citizenship encompassed the right to travel from state to state.[4] With the recognition of native-born blacks as citizens of the nation and of the states where they resided, it would follow that blacks possessed at least a formal right to travel and reside throughout national territory. This robbed states' insistence on controlling access to their territories of much of its persuasive power. In 1874, striking down a California immigration law, Justice Stephen Field acknowledged that both *New York v. Miln* (1837) and the *Passenger Cases* (1849) had upheld "the right of the state to exclude from its limits any persons whom it may deem dangerous or injurious to the interests and welfare of its citizens." However, Field continued, such a right on the part of a state was inextricably linked to slavery and was thus a relic of the past: "[W]e cannot shut our eyes to the fact that much which was formerly said upon the power of the state ... grew out of the necessity which the southern states, in which the institution of slavery existed, felt of excluding free negroes from

---

[3] U.S. Const., amend. XIV, § 1.
[4] *Crandall v. Nevada*, 73 U.S. 35 (1867).

their limits ... But at this day no such power would be asserted, or if asserted, allowed, in any federal court."[5]

Field was saying, essentially, that the constitutional grant of national citizenship to native-born blacks made it possible to reopen the question of the constitutionality of state-level immigration regimes and pave the way for the emergence of a federal immigration regime. This was precisely what occurred. Between 1870 and 1890, as courts chipped away at state immigration regimes, a federal immigration regime came into being.

Between the end of the Civil War and the turn of the nineteenth century, the United States became a leading industrial power. As heavy industry emerged and the railroad network expanded, corporations of national scope came to dominate the economic landscape. Cities grew enormously. These developments drove the final push to settle the Far West, which would supply food for America's cities and raw materials for its industries.

None of these economic transformations would have been possible without massive immigration, which swelled the ranks of workers and consumers. Between 1871 and 1901, approximately 12 million immigrants entered the United States. Almost 750,000 entered in 1882, the nineteenth century's peak year. The new immigrant pool was more diverse than ever before. In addition to coming from traditional sending countries in Northwestern Europe, immigrants came from Southern and Eastern Europe as well as Asia. Immigration rose and fell in keeping with economic cycles, with immigrants moving back and forth regularly between the United States and their countries of origin, many eventually returning permanently to the latter.

The federal immigration regime that emerged to regulate this expanded, diverse, and mobile immigrant pool built upon the state immigration regimes it displaced, adopting traditional bases of exclusion, but rapidly adding new ones. Perhaps the clearest way of seeing what was distinctive about it, however, is through an examination of the experience of Chinese immigrants.

Under the new federal immigration and citizenship regime, what was perceived as the "problem" of Chinese immigration resulted in the passage of racist exclusion and deportation laws. Immigrants' ability

---

[5] *In re Ah Fong*, 1 F.Cas. 213, 216–17 (C.C.D. Cal. 1874).

to naturalize had long been restricted on the ground of race. Now their ability to enter and remain on U.S. soil came to be thus restricted as well. Chinese immigrants' protracted legal struggles against racist immigration laws resulted in the becoming visible of the constitutional architecture of the new federal immigration and citizenship order. As interpreted by the U.S. Supreme Court, the new federal immigration power was an inherent, sovereign, "plenary power," one not grounded in any portion of the constitutional text, not limited by any particular provision of the U.S. Constitution, and largely immune from substantive judicial review. Plenary power would also extend to naturalization law. This is not to suggest that governmental power over immigrants in the late nineteenth century was entirely unfettered. Thanks to Chinese immigrants' skillful use of the courts, both federal and state powers came to be limited in certain ways. Nevertheless, as citizenship was formally extended to the entire native-born population, the extension of plenary power to matters of immigration and naturalization marked a widening of the gulf between citizens and aliens.

The subjection of immigrants to largely unfettered federal power even as citizenship was formally extended to the native-born population did not mean that those who were nominally citizens did not continue to share many legal disabilities with aliens. A yawning gap between formal and substantive citizenship still made it possible to render millions foreigners. Native Americans found that they did not qualify as *jus soli* citizens under the Fourteenth Amendment. After citizenship was extended to them by statute, their continued foreignness was revealed in the fact that they were subjected to a plenary power bearing an eerie resemblance to the plenary power that governed immigrants. Blacks experienced such harsh conditions in the post-Reconstruction rural South that they chose not only to leave the South to go north and west, but also (albeit in far smaller numbers) to return voluntarily to Africa. Mexican Americans in territories like New Mexico were denied statehood until the territory's demographics tilted in favor of whites. Chinese Americans were frequently subjected to the same treatment as Chinese immigrants. The inferior legal status into which American women were slotted resulted, albeit sporadically, in the involuntary expatriation of American women who married alien men. State poor laws continued to prevent the indigent from traveling to or residing in places as they liked. As states lost the power to exclude blacks from their territories, blacks (but also Asians and Latinos) experienced hardening borders of segregation as residential neighborhoods, schools, hospitals, places of entertainment, and modes of transportation were shut off to them.

The remainder of this chapter begins by tracing the emergence of the late-nineteenth-century federal immigration and citizenship order. The focus here is heavily on the Chinese immigrant struggle, which gave rise to the articulation of plenary power as the constitutional underpinning of the federal immigration regime. The chapter then discusses the postwar regime of unequal citizenship and internal foreignness visited upon the domestic population and canvasses the regime of internal borders that truncated many Americans' rights to movement and presence, rendering them strangers in their own country.

## The Postwar Federal Immigration and Citizenship Order: Chinese Immigrants and Plenary Power

Chinese had been immigrating to the United States since the late 1840s. In 1868, the United States and China signed the Burlingame Treaty, which recognized reciprocal rights of travel "for purposes of curiosity, of trade, or as permanent residents."[6] From the perspective of the United States, the Treaty was driven by the desire to expand commerce with China, but also by appreciation for Chinese labor. The labor contributions of Chinese immigrants were indeed significant. The overwhelming majority of the workers who built the Central Pacific Railroad were Chinese. Curiosity about Chinese workers was also on the rise in the post–Civil War South, where planters were exploring alternatives to employing recalcitrant freedmen.

As the Chinese presence grew in the West, however, so did anti-Chinese sentiment. There was a widespread perception that Chinese labor was akin to slave labor, a highly charged analogy in a country that had just concluded a war to extirpate slavery. White laborers saw in the allegedly "slavelike" Chinese a dangerous threat to their hard-won standards of living. The manifesto of an "Anti-Chinese Convention" held in San Francisco in 1870 demanded an eight-hour workday and supported the exclusion of the Chinese, thereby

---

[6] Treaty of July 28, 1868, 16 Stat. 739, at 740.

underscoring the intimate link between worker demands and resentment of Chinese labor. Such fears were not entirely unjustified. In the early 1870s, Chinese workers were brought from California to break strikes as far away as the Northeast.

Slowly, anti-Chinese sentiment in the West seeped into national attitudes. By 1876, the Democratic Party's platform was demanding steps to "prevent further importation or immigration of the Mongolian race."[7] Justice Stephen Field, the author of some of the U.S. Supreme Court's important late-nineteenth-century immigration opinions, openly opposed Chinese immigration. "[T]he practical issue," Field maintained, "is, whether the civilization of this coast [i.e., the West Coast], its society, morals, and industry, shall be of American or Asiatic type."[8] Field's campaign literature when he was a presidential hopeful urged that the country protect itself from "the oriental gangrene."[9]

Mounting anti-Chinese sentiment in the West in the 1870s coincided with a distinct set of developments in the East. State immigration regimes had been conducting a brisk business since the Civil War. Over its fifteen-year life, for example, the Massachusetts Board of State Charities removed more than 30,000 paupers, roughly twice the number removed by its predecessor body, the Commissioners of Alien Passengers and Foreign Paupers, between 1851 and 1863. However, in the mid-1870s, the U.S. Supreme Court, no longer concerned with placating slave states paranoid about the influx of free blacks, dealt New York's immigration regime – by far the country's most important – a devastating blow. In *Henderson v. New York* (1875), the Court put an end to the state's long-standing practice of requiring bonds or commutation fees from incoming passengers as a safeguard against immigrant pauperism.[10] According to the Court, restriction of the influx of immigrants into territory was possessed of an "international" dimension: "[I]t belongs to that class of laws which concern the exterior relation of this whole nation with other nations and governments."[11] A uniform, national policy had, therefore, to be

---

[7] Smith, *Civic Ideals*, p. 358.

[8] Carl B. Swisher, *Stephen J. Field: Craftsman of the Law* (Hamden, CT: Archon Books, 1963), p. 221 (citation omitted).

[9] Paul Kens, *Justice Stephen Field: Shaping Liberty from the Gold Rush to the Gilded Age* (Lawrence: University Press of Kansas, 1997), p. 205.

[10] *Henderson et al. v. Mayor of the City of New York*, 92 U.S. 259 (1875).

[11] Id. at 273.

brought into being: "The laws which govern the right to land passengers in the United States from other countries ought to be the same in New York, Boston, New Orleans, and San Francisco."[12] A wide variety of state immigration regimes had not been troubling before the Civil War; now they were.

What ensued was a confused period of transition from a state immigration order to a federal one. In 1862, in legislation similar to legislation barring the international slave trade, Congress had barred American citizens from participating in the transportation of Chinese "coolies" "to any foreign country, port, or place whatever."[13] This was not, strictly speaking, an immigration law. In 1875, bowing to western demands, Congress finally passed the very first piece of federal immigration restriction, the Page Law, aimed at excluding "coolie labor" and Chinese prostitutes.[14] Stemming from cultural anxieties that female immigrants from China were prostitutes or engaged in polygamous marriages, the Page Law sharply reduced the number of female immigrants from China.

Meanwhile, following the *Henderson* decision, with an important source of revenue cut off, New York's commissioners of emigration instituted a campaign to secure national legislation that would authorize states to collect head money, but encountered resistance from shippers. The result was that state and federal immigration law coexisted for several years. In 1883, however, the U.S. Supreme Court definitively declared all state immigration laws unconstitutional.[15] With New York's commissioners of emigration now threatening to shut down the Castle Garden immigrant-receiving station unless the federal government passed a national immigration law, a federal immigration regime was finally ushered into being.

Early federal immigration legislation was modeled upon the state immigration laws it displaced. The Immigration Act of 1882 imposed a fifty-cent head tax on entering immigrants and denied entry to "any convict, lunatic, idiot, or any person unable to take care of himself or herself without becoming a public charge."[16] However, federal

---

[12] Id.

[13] Act of February 19, 1862, 12 Stat. 340.

[14] Act of March 3, 1875, 18 Stat. 477.

[15] *People v. Compagnie Generale Transatlantique*, 107 U.S. 59 (1883).

[16] Immigration Act of 1882, 22 Stat. 214.

immigration law rapidly moved into uncharted territory. Organized labor called for immigration restriction to protect American workers from the competition posed by immigrant labor. In 1885, Congress obliged with the first of many alien contract labor laws. The 1885 contract labor law prohibited employers from subsidizing the transportation of aliens, voided transportation contracts, and imposed fines upon violators. Initially, the federal government contracted with state boards of immigration to administer its laws. In 1891, however, Congress created its own immigration bureaucracy.

For the most part, generally applicable federal immigration laws – that is, laws applicable to the general immigration pool – turned away very few: slightly more than 1 percent of the total number of entrants. At the same time, the federal government held out incentives for European migrants. The Homestead Act of 1862 encouraged white immigration by allowing white immigrants to make homestead claims so long as they filed a declaration of intent to naturalize. In the 1860s, multiple states and territories also granted declarant aliens the vote.

Matters were very different for Chinese immigrants, who came to be subjected to an immigration and citizenship regime altogether distinct from the one that governed all other immigrants. The Chinese became the first immigrant group to be formally excluded from the United States on grounds of race. Federal officials enforced Chinese exclusion laws rigorously. The rejection rates of Chinese immigrants were far higher than those for the general immigration pool, in some years reaching more than 30 percent.

Immigration laws directed at the Chinese would have been far less effective had naturalization laws not also worked against them. Denying Chinese immigrants the right to naturalize rendered them permanent aliens, subject to the threat of exclusion and removal, unable to shield themselves from racist alienage laws, and barred from participating in the affairs of the community regardless of the length of their presence there.

In the 1860s and 1870s, there was a successful push to bar Chinese immigrants from naturalizing. Since 1790, naturalization had been restricted to white persons. When the Reconstruction Congress discussed eliminating barriers to black citizenship, Radical Republican senator Charles Sumner of Massachusetts proposed striking out the word "white" from the 1790 law and making naturalization available to any immigrant who met the residence requirements. However, the proposal immediately faced opposition, especially from westerners. Senator William Stewart of Nevada declared: "I do not propose to hand over our institutions to any foreigners [i.e., the Chinese] who have no sympathy with us, who do not profess to make this country their home, who do not propose to subscribe to republican institutions, who cling to paganism and to despotism, and who are bound to contracts which make them slaves."[17] As a result, the 1870 naturalization law was expanded only to include "aliens of African nativity and ... persons of African descent."[18] The Fourteenth Amendment, construed at the time as applicable only to the states, did not act as a barrier to blatantly racist *federal* naturalization laws.

Because the 1870 naturalization law had not explicitly prohibited Chinese immigrants from naturalizing, several Chinese immigrants attempted to naturalize under its provisions. Attorneys bringing naturalization petitions on behalf of Chinese immigrants argued that the term "white" in the 1870 naturalization law should be interpreted to include the Chinese. In 1878, however, a California court rejected a Chinese petitioner's claim to naturalize as a white person on the ground that a white person was of the Caucasian race and that the Chinese were of the "Mongolian race."[19] In 1882, the first of the Chinese exclusion acts got rid of all ambiguities by expressly prohibiting Chinese immigrants from naturalizing. Thereafter, resident Chinese immigrants became a class of permanent aliens.

By a quirk of history, Mexicans were permitted to naturalize despite the legal restriction of naturalization to blacks and whites. At a time of rising nativist racism in the United States, it was precisely the colonial context of the acquisition of the Southwest that left naturalization open to Mexicans. In 1897, a federal district court considering the question of Mexicans' eligibility for citizenship declared that "[i]f the strict scientific classification of the anthropologist should be adopted, [the petitioner] would probably not be classed as white." However, the Treaty of Guadalupe Hidalgo and other foundational documents either "affirmatively confer[red] the rights of citizenship upon Mexicans, or tacitly recognize[d] in them the right of individual naturalization."

---

[17] Cong. Globe, 41st Cong., 2d Sess. 5150 (1870).
[18] Act of July 14, 1870, 16 Stat. 254.
[19] *In re Ah Yup*, 5 Sawy. 155 (1878).

Furthermore, because these instruments had not distinguished among Mexicans on the basis of color, all Mexicans would be eligible to naturalize.[20] Thus, the United States' obligations to its colonized Mexican population ultimately ended up benefiting Mexican immigrants.

After successfully blocking naturalization as an option for Chinese immigrants, anti-Chinese nativists sought to deprive the Chinese of *jus soli* citizenship. During the 1880s, under the impact of the Chinese exclusion laws, many entrants of Chinese descent began to allege – some undoubtedly falsely – that they had been wrongfully excluded because they were citizens by virtue of birth on U.S. soil or derivative citizens (children born abroad to U.S. citizens of Chinese descent). The federal courts often proved receptive to their arguments. In response to such developments, a movement began to deny Chinese Americans' birthright citizenship claims. In the 1880s, commentators attacked the *jus soli* principle as undesirable, at odds with federalism, and generative of double allegiances. Such arguments were presented before the U.S. Supreme Court in the case of Wong Kim Ark, a laborer born in San Francisco who had lived his entire life in California. When Wong Kim Ark attempted to enter the United States in August 1895 following a trip to China, he was denied entry on the ground that he was not a citizen of the United States and was subject to the Chinese exclusion laws. The federal government's arguments against birthright citizenship for the Chinese reveal how, a full thirty years after the passage of the Fourteenth Amendment, antebellum ideas denying the citizenship of the native-born remained vital. The United States' solicitor general invoked as precedents antebellum cases in which courts had denied the citizenship of native-born free blacks on the ground that it was the rights and privileges to which individuals were entitled, and not their place of birth, that conferred upon them the status of citizen. The argument was that Chinese resident immigrants, deemed unfit to naturalize, transmitted their alien status to their native-born children.

Such arguments failed. In March 1898, the U.S. Supreme Court ruled that the Fourteenth Amendment was intended to reaffirm "the ancient and fundamental rule" of birthright citizenship at common law.[21] Native-born individuals of Chinese descent were U.S. citizens

---

[20] *In re Rodriguez*, 81 Fed. 337, 349, 354 (W.D. Tex. 1897).
[21] *United States v. Wong Kim Ark*, 169 U.S. 649, 693 (1898).

under the Fourteenth Amendment. The Court was acutely aware that a contrary ruling "would be to deny citizenship to thousands of persons of English, Scotch, Irish, German, or other European parentage, who have always been considered and treated as citizens of the United States."[22] In this way, a constitutional principle intended to benefit blacks ended up redounding to the benefit of Chinese Americans and all other immigrants.

This was a rare victory in the ratcheting upward of restrictions targeting Chinese immigrants. In 1880, the United States renegotiated the Burlingame Treaty to give itself the right to "regulate, limit or suspend" the immigration of Chinese laborers whenever their entry or residence in the United States "affects or threatens to affect the interests of that country, or to endanger the good order of [the United States] or of any locality within the territory thereof."[23] Shortly thereafter, in 1882, Congress enacted the first of a series of Chinese exclusion laws suspending the immigration of Chinese laborers.

When the 1888 Chinese exclusion law was challenged before the U.S. Supreme Court, the Court articulated the plenary power doctrine. In the case at issue, the returning Chinese alien, Chae Chan Ping, had met every possible legal requirement to secure his right to return to the United States, only to have the law change while he was out of the country. His assets in the United States were suddenly inaccessible to him. The law was, furthermore, in conflict with the treaty with China.

Nevertheless, in *Chae Chan Ping v. United States* (1889), the Court declared that its hands were tied because Congress's power to exclude aliens was absolute: "The power of exclusion of foreigners being an incident of sovereignty belonging to the government of the United States, as a part of those sovereign powers delegated by the Constitution, the right to its exercise at any time when, in the judgment of the government, the interests of the country require it, cannot be granted away or restrained on behalf of any one."[24] The source of the federal government's exclusion power – a power that had not even *existed* as a federal power at the country's founding – now came to be grounded in an inherent "sovereignty" essentially unrestrained by the Constitution.

---

[22] Id. at 694.
[23] Treaty of November 17, 1880, 22 Stat. 826.
[24] *Chinese Exclusion Case (Chae Chan Ping v. United States)*, 130 U.S. 581, 609 (1889).

Shortly thereafter, the Court moved to extend plenary power to the deportation of resident immigrants. The 1892 Geary Act required Chinese laborers living in the United States to obtain a "certificate of residence" from the collector of internal revenue within one year of the passage of the Act. Under regulations promulgated pursuant to the Act, the government would issue a certificate only on the "affidavit of at least one credible [white] witness." Any Chinese alien who failed to obtain the certificate could be "arrested ... and taken before a United States judge, whose duty it [was] to order that he be deported from the United States."[25] Contemporaries remarked upon the resemblance of the law to restrictions on blacks' movement during slavery. During the Senate debates on the Geary Act, Senator John Sherman of Ohio criticized the Act as follows: "[T]hey are here ticket-of-leave men. Precisely as under the Australian law a convict is allowed to go at large upon a ticket of leave, these people are allowed to go at large and earn their livelihood, but they must have this ticket of leave in their possession." He continued: "This inaugurates in our system of government a new departure, one, I believe, never before practiced, although it was suggested in conference that some such rules had been adopted in the old slavery times to secure the peaceful and quiet condition of society."[26]

Despite the fact that the Geary Act was racist on its face, the Court upheld it, arguing that "[t]he right of a nation to expel or deport foreigners who have not been naturalized, or taken any steps towards becoming citizens of the country, rests upon the same grounds, and is as absolute and unqualified as the right to prohibit and prevent their entrance into the country." Even worse, the Court ruled that deportation "is not a punishment for crime," but only "a method of enforcing the return to his own country of an alien." The implication of interpreting deportation as a civil, rather than a criminal, sanction was that the deported alien was not entitled to the constitutional protections ordinarily applicable in the criminal context.[27]

The very harshness of plenary power in the exclusion and deportation contexts led to the invigoration of two different sets of legal

---

[25] Geary Act of 1892, 27 Stat. 25–26.
[26] 23 Cong. Rec. 3870 (1892).
[27] *Fong Yue Ting v. United States*, 149 U.S. 698, 707, 730 (1893).

distinctions that would become a hallmark of modern immigration law – namely, the territorial inside–outside distinction and the
procedure–substance distinction. First, with respect to the territorial
inside–outside distinction, the U.S. Supreme Court made it clear that
the Fourteenth Amendment to the U.S. Constitution would protect
all "persons" who happened to be on the territorial inside from discriminatory legislation by state governments. In *Yick Wo v. Hopkins*
(1886), the first case in which the Fourteenth Amendment was applied
to protect aliens, the Court struck down a San Francisco laundry ordinance that was being applied in a blatantly discriminatory manner.[28]
Constitutional protections for aliens were not just available vis-à-vis
the states. In *Wong Wing v. United States* (1896), the U.S. Supreme
Court also invalidated a federal law subjecting Chinese found present
in violation of law to punishment at hard labor. Although immigrants
could be subjected to criminal punishment, the Court ruled, the government had to provide immigrants with the constitutionally mandated safeguards of a trial.[29] However, these limitations on state and
federal power were themselves subject to limitation. The application of
the Fourteenth Amendment to explicitly racist action at the state level
did not invalidate traditional state alienage distinctions, which could
still be crafted to racist ends. Between 1868 and 1890, seven states –
Alabama, Arkansas, Colorado, Florida, South Dakota, West Virginia,
and Wyoming – added constitutional provisions lifting alien property
disabilities. But this liberalizing trend was reversed on the West Coast
as part of the onslaught against Asian immigrants. Prefiguring an
early-twentieth-century trend, a California constitutional provision of
1894 allowed aliens to enjoy property rights if they were of "the white
race, or of African descent, eligible to become citizens of the United
States under the naturalization laws thereof."[30] Correspondingly,
limitations on federal power in the context of criminal sanctions visited upon immigrants did not reach the federal government's overall
plenary power to exclude and deport on the basis of race.

---

[28] *Yick Wo v. Hopkins*, 118 U.S. 356 (1886).
[29] *Wong Wing v. United States*, 163 U.S. 228 (1896).
[30] California Constitution 1879, art. I, § 17, amendment adopted November 6, 1894, in
*The Federal and State Constitutions, Colonial Charters and Other Organic Laws of
the States, Territories, and Colonies Now or Heretofore forming the United States of
America*, vol. I (Washington, DC: U.S. Government Printing Office, 1909), p. 451.

Second, with respect to the procedure–substance distinction, as the federal government's substantive power to exclude and deport aliens was progressively immunized from judicial review under the plenary power doctrine, immigrants' strategies focused increasingly upon procedural issues. Federal judges often tended to use their *habeas corpus* jurisdiction to overturn immigration officials' decisions to exclude Chinese immigrants, thereby leading to considerable tension between courts and bureaucrats, with the latter accusing the former of subverting the administration of the Chinese exclusion laws. In 1891, frustration with immigrants' strategic recourse to courts drove Congress to shield immigration officials' decisions from judicial review. Immigration inspection officers' decisions were to be final. Appeals could be taken to the superintendent of immigration and then to the secretary of the treasury. Judicial review of administrative decisions was eliminated for entering immigrants. In 1892, when a Japanese immigrant was denied admission on the ground that she would become a public charge challenged the procedural arrangements of the 1891 Act as a denial of due process, the U.S. Supreme Court dismissed her claims.[31] However, the Court displayed somewhat more solicitude for the procedural rights of aliens subject to deportation because they were already inside the country. In *Yamataya v. Fisher* (1903), the Court ruled that immigration officials could not "cause an alien who has entered the country, and has become subject in all respects to its jurisdiction, and a part of its population ... to be taken into custody and deported without giving him all opportunity to be heard upon the questions involving his right to be and remain in the United States." Constitutional due process required as much.[32]

Subject to the aforementioned limitations, as it developed in the last three decades of the nineteenth century, the constitutional architecture of the new federal immigration and citizenship regime made aliens subject to the virtually unfettered power of the federal government in the areas of exclusion, deportation, and naturalization, while also allowing states to discriminate against them through the crafting of alienage laws. Most aliens were only theoretically subject to such absolute governmental power, but the Chinese felt it directly. The federal

---

[31] *Nishimura Ekiu v. United States*, 142 U.S. 651 (1892).
[32] *The Japanese Immigrant Case (Yamataya v. Fisher)*, 189 U.S. 86, 101 (1903).

government's concerted attempts to shrink the Chinese presence in the
United States proved successful. While the 1875 Page Law resulted in
a sharp drop in the number of Chinese female immigrants, the Chinese
exclusion laws kept out a significant number of Chinese males. The
Chinese immigrant male–female ratio was especially adverse (about
27 to 1 in 1890) and prevented the Chinese from creating families in
the United States. Bars to naturalization prevented resident Chinese
immigrants from naturalizing and prevented their foreign-born children from claiming derivative citizenship. Although estimates vary, the
population of Chinese origin diminished from a peak of approximately
110,000 in 1890 to a low of approximately 60,000 in 1920. Although
numbers slowly increased, as of 1940 there were still fewer Chinese in
the United States than at the beginning of the twentieth century. The
political scientist Aristide Zolberg has argued that "this willful reduction of a national group stands to date as the only successful instance
of 'ethnic cleansing' in the history of American immigration."[33]

## Foreignness for the Native-Born in Post–Civil War America

In the post–Civil War period, as the *jus soli* principle was constitution-
alized, a much greater proportion of the native-born population was
formally classified as citizens than before. Certain kinds of state activity – formal, state-sponsored attempts to expel the native-born from
the country – no longer seemed possible. In one sense, then, especially
as the federal government was given unfettered authority over immigrants, the gulf between native-born and foreign-born, citizen and
alien, widened. In another sense, however, the gulf did not widen all
that much. Many older forms of rendering the native-born population
foreign on the ground of race, class, and gender, along with internal
territorial regimes of long standing, endured. More important, new
forms of rendering the native-born foreigners, fitted to the post–Civil
War constitutional order, came into being.

Strategies for rendering the native-born foreign in their own country were various. They included formal denials of birthright citizenship; subjection to plenary power free of constitutional constraints
just as immigrants were; the opening of a gulf between formal and

---

[33] Zolberg, *Nation by Design*, p. 192.

substantive citizenship; subjection to surveillance, suspicion, and border controls like immigrants of the same racial background; involuntary expatriation; and controlling movement and presence through territorial controls, discrimination, and violence. I examine the distinct (but also overlapping) experiences of Native Americans, blacks, Chinese Americans, Mexican Americans, women, and the poor.

Congressional debates over the Fourteenth Amendment and its precursor, the Civil Rights Act of 1866, suggested that Native Americans were not imagined as members of the post–Civil War national polity. In 1866, Senator Lyman Trumbull of Illinois successfully pushed for the exclusion of "Indians not taxed" from the Civil Rights Act on the ground that "the wild Indians who do not recognize the Government of the United States at all, who are not subject to our laws, with whom we make treaties, who have their own regulations, whom we do not pretend to interfere with or punish for the commission of crimes one upon the other [were not] subjects of the United States in the sense of being citizens."[34]

In the post–Civil War years, such assertions about the allegedly separate, self-governing character of Native Americans rang false. The state was dropping even the pretense that it took Native American sovereignty seriously. In 1870, the U.S. Supreme Court ruled not only that Congress could legislate directly for the tribes, but also that it could annul existing treaties unilaterally.[35] Thereafter, Congress ceased to negotiate treaties with Native Americans. Treaties had been based on the idea – respected more in theory than in practice – that the Native American tribes were sovereign equals. Their abandonment suggests that Congress had ceased to view the tribes in this way even theoretically.

Nevertheless, in *Elk v. Wilkins* (1884), the U.S. Supreme Court lent the idea of Native American tribes as sovereign equals its imprimatur to deny Native Americans *jus soli* citizenship under the Fourteenth Amendment.[36] John Elk was a Native American who had left the tribe in which he was born and become a Nebraska resident. When Elk attempted to vote, however, he was prevented from doing so. Nebraska

---

[34] Cong. Globe, 39th Cong., 1st Sess. 527 (1866).
[35] *The Cherokee Tobacco*, 78 U.S. 616 (1870).
[36] *Elk v. Wilkins*, 112 U.S. 94 (1884).

refused to recognize Elk as a voter on the ground that he was not a citizen as mandated by state law. As presented to the U.S. Supreme Court, the question was whether, under the Fourteenth Amendment, Elk was a citizen by virtue of birth "subject to the jurisdiction" of the United States.

The Court ruled that the words "subject to the jurisdiction thereof" in the text of the Fourteenth Amendment meant "not merely subject in some respect or degree to the jurisdiction of the United States, but completely subject to their political jurisdiction, and owing them direct and immediate allegiance." Native Americans such as Elk failed this test: "Indians born within the territorial limits of the United States, members of, and owing immediate allegiance to, one of the Indian tribes, (an alien though dependent power,) although in a geographic sense born in the United States, are no more 'born in the United States and subject to the jurisdiction thereof,' ... than the children of subjects of any foreign government born within the domain of that government."[37]

What were the implications of this ruling for Elk, an individual who had been born within a tribe but had left it? Considered a non-citizen at birth, Elk found himself in a legal no-man's-land upon leaving his tribe. Justice Harlan's dissent observed sharply that Elk could be taxed by Nebraska, was subject to the jurisdiction of its courts, and even served in its militia. Harlan also noted that the Court had upheld congressional power over the tribes, thus making the majority's equation of Native American tribes with foreign countries highly questionable. If the majority's interpretation of the Fourteenth Amendment stood, Harlan insisted,

then the fourteenth amendment has wholly failed to accomplish, in respect of the Indian race, what, we think, was intended by it; and there is *still* in this country a despised and rejected class of persons with no nationality whatever, who, born in our territory, owing no allegiance to any foreign power, and subject, as residents of the states, to all the burdens of government, are yet not members of any political community, nor entitled to any of the rights, privileges, or immunities of citizens of the United States.[38]

The Court in *Elk* indicated that, although citizenship was unavailable to Native Americans under the Fourteenth Amendment's *jus*

---

[37] Id. at 102.
[38] Id. at 122–23 (Harlan, J., dissenting) (emphasis added).

*soli* clause, it could be conferred upon them by the polity's consent (i.e., through a kind of naturalization that reinscribed their prior foreignness). In the 1887 Dawes Act, Congress expressed precisely such consent. Designed to destroy Native American communities, fracture reservations, and open up lands for white settlement, the Dawes Act and its progeny conferred citizenship upon those Native Americans who accepted individual allotments. Thus, ceding land – which added up to approximately 80 million of the 138 million acres held by the tribes – was made a precondition to receiving federal citizenship. Not surprisingly, although reformers critical of the corruptions of the reservation system were the most outspoken proponents of allotment, railroad companies and white settlers also became enthusiastic supporters. Not without irony in a polity in which citizenship was supposed to be grounded in individual consent, the decision to cede land and accept citizenship was vested not in the tribes, but in the president. The executive was empowered, in other words, to seize Native American lands and enfold Native Americans into the polity. If Jacksonian era Indian removal had insisted upon Native Americans' alien character in order to expel them and seize their land, the Dawes Act implicitly recognized Native Americans' initial alienage and imposed citizenship upon them in order to accomplish the very same end. The Dawes Act and its progeny, as President Theodore Roosevelt observed in 1901, were "a mighty pulverizing engine to break up the tribal mass."[39]

If Native Americans became citizens on condition of giving up their lands, they learned that they remained foreigners notwithstanding the grant of citizenship to the extent that they were subject to congressional plenary power just as immigrants were. The plenary power era for Native Americans began with the case of *United States v. Kagama* (1886).[40] The case was a constitutional challenge to the 1885 Major Crimes Act, which had extended federal criminal jurisdiction to certain crimes between Native Americans, both in Indian country and on reservations. The *Kagama* Court based its decision to uphold the Act on what it considered Congress's inherent powers over Native Americans. Justice Miller put it thus: "The power of the General

---

[39] Theodore Roosevelt's First Annual Message (December 3, 1901), in Fred L. Israel, *State of the Union Messages of the Presidents, 1790–1966*, vol. 2 (New York: Chelsea House, 1967), p. 2047.
[40] *United States v. Kagama*, 118 U.S. 375 (1886).

Government over these remnants of a race once powerful ... must exist in that Government, because it never has existed anywhere else; because the theater of its exercise is within the geographical limits of the United States; because it has never been denied; and because [the United States] alone can enforce its laws on all the tribes."[41] "The most remarkable aspect of Justice Miller's analysis," constitutional scholar Sarah Cleveland writes, "was the complete absence of any reliance on the Constitution as the basis for national authority."[42] This idea of powers inherent in sovereignty was precisely the basis of congressional plenary power over immigrants.

Congressional plenary power over Native Americans overrode their constitutional rights as U.S. citizens. *Cherokee Nation v. Hitchcock* (1902) and *Lone Wolf v. Hitchcock* (1903) were both Fifth Amendment challenges to congressional control over Native American lands.[43] *Cherokee Nation* was a challenge to the Curtis Act, which authorized the United States to lease Cherokee lands for mining purposes. Congress had granted the Cherokees citizenship by a 1901 statute and the U.S. Constitution extended to Indian country in Oklahoma. Accordingly, the Cherokees maintained that their property rights should be protected just like those of "citizens of Massachusetts and descendants of the Pilgrim fathers."[44] This argument failed to persuade the Court. Notwithstanding the grant of citizenship, the Court insisted, Indians remained "in a condition of pupilage or dependency, ... subject to the paramount authority of the United States."[45] Furthermore, Congress's relationship with the tribes concerned a "political question" – exactly like relations with foreign governments – that lay beyond the purview of the courts: "The power existing in the Congress to administer upon and guard the tribal property, and the power being political and administrative in its nature, the manner of its exercise is a question within the province of the legislative branch to determine, and is not one for the courts."[46]

---

[41] Id. at 384–85.

[42] Sarah H. Cleveland, "Powers Inherent in Sovereignty: Indians, Aliens, Territories, and the Nineteenth Century Origins of Plenary Power over Foreign Affairs," *Texas Law Review* 81, no. 1 (2002): 1–284, 62.

[43] *Cherokee Nation v. Hitchcock*, 187 U.S. 294 (1902); *Lone Wolf v. Hitchcock*, 187 U.S. 553 (1903).

[44] Brief for the Cherokee Nation, *Cherokee Nation v. Hitchcock* (No. 340), at 15.

[45] *Cherokee Nation*, 187 U.S. at 305.

[46] Id. at 308.

*Lone Wolf* involved a similar challenge by members of the Kiowa, Comanche, and Apache Tribes to a 1900 statute allotting tribal lands and releasing millions of acres of land to white settlers. The Medicine Lodge Treaty of 1867 had promised the lands in question to the tribes and stipulated that three-fourths of the adult male members of each tribe consent before the lands could be taken.[47] Lone Wolf, the chief of the Kiowa Tribe, challenged Congress's seizure of the lands without tribal consent on the ground that it overrode the tribe's Fifth Amendment rights. Once again, the Court ruled that Congress's control over tribal lands was beyond judicial review: "Plenary authority over the tribal relations of the Indians has been exercised by Congress from the beginning, and the power has always been deemed a political one, not subject to be controlled by the judicial department of the government."[48]

The decision in *Lone Wolf* was recognized at the time as momentous. On the floor of the Senate, Senator Matthew Quay of Pennsylvania called *Lone Wolf* "the *Dred Scott* decision No. 2, except that in this case the victim is red instead of black. It practically inculcates the doctrine that the red man has no rights which the white man is bound to respect, and that no treaty or contract made with him is binding."[49] Indian Commissioner Jones told the House Indian Affairs Committee that the *Lone Wolf* case "will enable you to dispose of [Indian] land without the consent of the Indians. If you wait for their consent in these matters, it will be fifty years before you can do away with the reservations."[50] Thereafter, the Indian Office ceased to negotiate purchases with Native Americans. Bypassing Native Americans more or less completely, it invited whites to enter lands and passed on payments to Native Americans. In the early twentieth century, the Burke Act codified the practice when it authorized the secretary of the interior to issue fee-simple titles to Native American allottees regardless of their consent.

In contrast to what transpired with Native Americans, there would no attempt to deny blacks' *jus soli* citizenship or to subject them to

---

[47] Medicine Lodge Treaty, U.S.-Kiowa and Comanche Tribes of Indians, October 21, 1867, 15 Stat. 581.
[48] *Lone Wolf*, 187 U.S. at 565.
[49] 36 Cong. Rec. 2028 (1903).
[50] Quoted in Frederick E. Hoxie, *A Final Promise: The Campaign to Assimilate the Indians, 1880–1920* (Lincoln: University of Nebraska Press, 1984), p. 155.

plenary power as immigrants were. Instead, blacks were rendered foreigners in a different way: through the opening of a gulf between formal and substantive citizenship.

During the 1860s, proposals to enfranchise blacks failed in upwards of fifteen northern states and territories. At least in part, the denial of the vote to blacks in the North was a kind of immigration law, driven by the fear that blacks would flood into Northern states upon emancipation. When Radical Republicans began to insist on impartial suffrage, the opposition to black enfranchisement revealed how whites could continue to represent blacks as foreigners. A group of Alabama conservatives sent a petition to Congress that pleaded: "Do not, we implore you, abdicate your own rule over us, by transferring us to the blighting, brutalizing and unnatural dominion of *an alien and inferior race.*"[51] In spite of such opposition, the Fifteenth Amendment, which sought to prohibit an abridgment of the right to vote "on account of race, color, or previous condition of servitude" became part of the U.S. Constitution in February 1870.[52]

As was the case with so many of the constitutional and statutory initiatives that came out of Radical Reconstruction, the Fifteenth Amendment's guarantee of impartial suffrage was defeated by a combination of political compromise, apathy, and judicial interpretation. By the end of the 1870s, Southern leaders had begun to call on Northerners to permit the New South to settle its "race problem" in its own way. What followed was a systematic program of disfranchisement. By the first decade of the twentieth century, through the application of measures such as registration rules, literacy and property qualifications, poll taxes, and grandfather clauses, blacks disappeared from the political arena and from juries. Courts repeatedly acquiesced in the fiction that voting restrictions were neutral measures that did not fall afoul of the Fifteenth Amendment. Blacks were expelled from Southern politics, a contemporary argued, "as absolutely as if the negroes had been deported to Liberia."[53]

As the old exclusion laws barring blacks from entering states and territories fell away, racial segregation and violence took their place.

---

[51] Cong. Globe, 40th Cong., 2d Sess. 1374 (1868) (emphasis added).
[52] U.S. Const., amend XV.
[53] Quoted in Leon F. Litwack, *Trouble in Mind: Black Southerners in the Age of Jim Crow* (New York: Alfred A. Knopf, 1998), p. 225.

Segregation expanded vastly when the U.S. Supreme Court ruled in *Plessy v. Ferguson* (1896) that legally mandated segregation on the railroads did not constitute a violation of the Fourteenth Amendment.[54] Southern whites also repeatedly used violence as a form of spatial control. Race riots destroyed the lives, property, and institutions of blacks. In the late 1880s, lynching began increasingly to be employed against blacks to suppress their demands for "social equality," a code for any behavior by blacks that transgressed boundaries of permissible behavior set by whites. In the 1890s, more than one hundred blacks on average suffered lynching every year.

Disfranchisement, segregation, violence, and harsh economic conditions drove blacks out of the South despite formal and informal efforts to hold black labor captive there. In the 1870s, approximately 40,000 blacks left the Deep South and moved to the North and the West, especially Kansas. But they abandoned the South in the thousands only to encounter potent forms of discrimination and violence in their new destinations. It occurred then to many rural and impoverished blacks that, notwithstanding their winning of citizenship in the aftermath of the Civil War, their only real hope lay in abandoning the United States. With the cruelest of ironies, the American Colonization Society, founded to rid the slave republic of its troublesome free blacks, came to enjoy a brief resurgence in the late nineteenth century. It began to receive requests from blacks for assistance in emigrating. In 1891, for example, a Georgia man wrote: "We have little or no voice here & our wages are so small we scarcely have enough means to subsist upon. Taxation is so pending that we cannot hold any real estate worth mentioning ... We feel like children away from home and are anxious to get home. We are quite sure that the U.S. of America is not the place for the colored man."[55] That same year, another described how blacks were trapped on plantations: "Down here on the Gulf Coast, La. & Miss., the negroes there isn't anything but slaves there and got them there and cant get out ... oh yes they run the negroes with Hound dogs now days and times as did before 1865. Oh may God help us to get out from here to Africa."[56] African Methodist Episcopal Church's

---

[54] *Plessy v. Ferguson*, 163 U.S. 537 (1896).
[55] Edwin S. Redkey, *Black Exodus: Black Nationalist and Back-to-Africa Movements, 1890–1910* (New Haven, CT: Yale University Press, 1969), p. 8.
[56] Id., p. 10.

bishop, Henry McNeal Turner, threw his weight behind the emigration movement on the ground that blacks could never be at home in the United States. Turner put it thus in 1883: "We were born here, raised here, fought, bled and died here, and have a thousand times more right here than hundreds of thousands of those who help to snub, proscribe, and persecute us, and that is one of the reasons I almost despise the land of my birth."[57]

In the 1890s, even as Southern growers sought to hold black labor captive, it remained thinkable for conservative Southern politicians to urge blacks to leave the country. In his December 1889 address to Congress, President Benjamin Harrison called for federal legislation to protect black Republicans from terror at the polls. Southern politicians interpreted Harrison's call as an attempt to wrest political control of the South. While the more effective long-term response was the disfranchisement of blacks, some Southern politicians also began to call for federal assistance for blacks seeking to emigrate to Africa. The most prominent of the proposed bills was that of Senator Mathew Butler of South Carolina. Butler's bill would have furnished transportation to every black individual who wished to leave the South provided that such individual became the citizen of another country. The bill did not explicitly invoke Africa, but was widely viewed as yet another African emigration scheme. Faced with vociferous Republican opposition and criticized by the Northern black press, the bill went nowhere. However, it remains revealing of what was still permissible political discourse at the heart of the nation's legislature.

Although the back-to-Africa movement won many adherents in the rural South, the number of those who actually left was minuscule. Between 1872 and 1890, just about a thousand blacks left the United States for Liberia. There were even fewer after that. The narrative of those who left was mostly unhappy. Rural emigrants sold properties at reduced prices, were cheated, stranded and abandoned before they boarded ships, and endured hardships on the way to Liberia. Many died there or decided to return. But blacks' decision to leave the United States exemplifies how, even after the grant of formal citizenship, they were made to feel as though they belonged elsewhere.

---

[57] Quoted in id., p. 32.

Chinese Americans experienced foreignness in a unique way: by being repeatedly assimilated with and treated like Chinese immigrants. The *Wong Kim Ark* case discussed earlier illustrates how, three full decades after the passage of the Fourteenth Amendment, the federal government could still engender uncertainty over the citizenship of the native-born children of Chinese immigrants and seek to have them classified as aliens. By requiring Chinese immigrants to carry proof of legal presence or face deportation, the 1892 Geary Act placed all persons of Chinese descent – citizens, lawful residents, and others – under suspicion of being in the country unlawfully. Beginning in 1909, every individual of Chinese descent had to be in possession of proof of legal presence in the country. As deportation increasingly became a tool of regulating Chinese presence in the early twentieth century, Chinese communities all over the United States were subjected to what has since become a tested method of ferreting out "illegal aliens" and of impressing upon certain kinds of citizens their lack of belonging: the immigration raid.

As a federal administrative apparatus emerged to police the country's borders, the principle of judicial deference to administrators also led to a repeated blurring of the distinction between Chinese Americans and Chinese immigrants. Of immediate concern to administrators was the strategy adopted by the attorneys of Chinese immigrants of taking admission applications of Chinese alleging to be native-born citizens directly to the courts – and thereby bypassing administrators – on the ground that the Chinese exclusion laws, and the administrative remedies they envisioned, were applicable only to aliens (and not to citizens).

The U.S. Supreme Court weighed in for the government. In *In re Sing Tuck* (1904), a case involving Chinese applicants for admission who claimed to be citizens, the Court ruled that such applicants had to exhaust their administrative remedies as provided by the exclusion laws before being able to turn to the courts. Although the Court refrained from deciding whether administrative officers had the jurisdiction to determine the fact of citizenship, the dissenters in the case recognized that the implication of the decision was to blur the distinction between citizen and alien, and that the decision ultimately rested upon a racialized notion of who might claim U.S. citizenship. Justice Brewer's dissent observed: "Must an American citizen, seeking to return to this, his native land, be compelled to bring with him two witnesses to prove the place of his birth, or else be denied his right to return, and all opportunity of establishing his citizenship in the courts of his country? No such rule is enforced against an American citizen of Anglo-Saxon descent."[58]

A year later, the Court went further. In *United States v. Ju Toy* (1905), it held that the administrative decision with respect to admission was final and conclusive despite the petitioner's claim of citizenship. Justice Holmes stated that, even though the Fifth Amendment protected the citizen, "with regard to him due process of law does not require judicial trial."[59] In subsequent years, in light of criticism of the Bureau of Immigration and its own decisions, the Court cut back on the *Ju Toy* decision by requiring in the case of a Chinese American applicant for admission who alleged citizenship that the administrative hearing meet certain minimum standards of fairness.[60] Nevertheless, Bureau of Immigration officials continued to view native-born Chinese as only "accidental" or "technical" citizens, as distinguished from "real" citizens. We have no way of knowing how many American citizens of Chinese descent were barred from entering the United States because they were denied adequate opportunities to make their case. But it is safe to conclude that, for such citizens, crossing the international border into the United States could be a fraught experience.

Chinese Americans were also mixed in with Chinese immigrants to the extent that both were routinely subjected to violence and destruction of property, which served as a kind of local border control. Although anti-Chinese violence went back to the 1850s, it peaked in the mid-1880s. In Washington, Oregon, and California, town meeting after meeting called for the expulsion of all Chinese, regardless of citizenship, from town limits. There were numerous incidents of mobs rounding up Chinese and driving them away. In September 1885, twenty-eight Chinese laborers were killed in Rock Springs, Wyoming. That same month, whites killed three residents of a Chinese campsite in Washington Territory.

Certain modes of racial segregation developed in the West to control the presence of the Chinese would migrate in the early twentieth century to other parts of the country and to other groups. On

[58] *United States v. Sing Tuck*, 194 U.S. 161, 178 (1904) (Brewer, J., dissenting).
[59] *United States v. Ju Toy*, 198 U.S. 253, 263 (1905).
[60] *Chin Yow v. United States*, 208 U.S. 8 (1908).

February 17, 1890, the San Francisco Board of Supervisors passed an ordinance mandating that the city's Chinese residents move to a prescribed area of the city within sixty days. The area was one earmarked for noxious trades such as slaughtering and tallow-rendering. Non-compliance was a misdemeanor punishable by six months' imprisonment. No American municipality had attempted to segregate residents on the basis of race prior to this time. In *In re Lee Sing et al.* (1890), a federal district court invalidated the ordinance on the ground that it violated the Fourteenth Amendment, the treaty with China, and civil rights statutes. The statute was not directed, Judge Sawyer put it, against any particular harm, but was intended "to forcibly drive out a whole community of twenty-odd thousand people, old and young, male and female, citizens of the United States, born on the soil, and foreigners of the Chinese race, moral and immoral, good, bad, and indifferent, and without respect to circumstances or conditions, from which a whole section of the city which they have inhabited, and in which they have carried on all kinds of business appropriate to a city, mercantile, manufacturing and otherwise, for more than 40 years."[61] The decision had little precedential effect. Cities in the South would pass laws to segregate neighborhoods a few decades later.

Late-nineteenth-century Californians also pioneered the use of racially restrictive covenants. The first American case regarding the legality of racially restrictive covenants, *Gandolfo v. Hartman* (1892), was decided in California. It involved a covenant intended to be binding on future owners that prohibited the purchaser from renting the premises "to a Chinaman or Chinamen." The covenant was struck down under the Fourteenth Amendment (on the ground that public enforcement of the private covenant would involve state action) and the 1880 Treaty with China.[62] As in the case of the *In re Lee Sing* decision, the decision had scant precedential effect. By the early twentieth century, racially restrictive covenants would spread all over the country and would be upheld by the U.S. Supreme Court.

The deeper meaning of such official and unofficial acts was hardly lost on Chinese Americans. In 1892, they formed the Chinese American Equal Rights League to protest the Geary Act, bolster the citizenship

---

[61] *In re Lee Sing et al.*, 43 F. 359, 361 (C.C.N.D. Cal. 1890).
[62] *Gandolfo v. Hartman*, 49 F. 181 (C.C.S.D. Cal. 1892).

claims of those barred from naturalizing, and defend the citizenship rights of Chinese Americans. The rhetoric of the League reveals the pressure on Chinese Americans and Chinese immigrants barred from naturalizing to prove their American-ness. Claiming to represent the "Americanized and American-born Chinese of the United States," the League disavowed "sympathy for those of our countrymen who persist in their own civilization and refuse to become Americanized." It insisted that every member "adopt American customs, ... cut off his queue, and wear the regulation clothing used in the United States." It proclaimed its "love ... for the home and country in which we live, but cannot legally call ... our own." At the same time, subscribing to a long tradition of immigrants' becoming American by distancing themselves from blacks, it sought to build its own case for citizenship by complaining about the grant of citizenship to blacks: "We feel grieved and humiliated every time we behold our colored brethren, even from the wilds of the African jungles, sit and eat from the National family table, while we, the descendants of the oldest race on earth, are not even allowed to pick up crumbs from under the table."[63]

Different yet was the peculiar kind of foreignness experienced by Mexican Americans. Mexican Americans were, of course, no strangers to the gap between formal and substantive citizenship experienced by blacks, Asian Americans, and others. Institutionalized inequality in schools, neighborhoods, and public employment, combined with exclusions from politics, spread across the Southwest in the 1880s and 1890s. What was unique was Congress's decision to delay statehood in Mexican majority territories such as New Mexico. There, Mexican Americans who had received federal citizenship under the Treaty of Guadalupe Hidalgo ended up with a lesser citizenship. Although Americans in general enjoyed federal *and* state citizenship, Congress refused to admit New Mexico as a state in the Union due in part to its majority Mexican and Indian population. Americans were not enthusiastic about having so-called "greasers" as fellow citizens. An 1882 *New York Times* article revealed their concerns in its headline: "Greasers as Citizens: What Sort of State New-Mexico Would

---

[63] All references to the Chinese American Equal Rights League from Lucy Salyer, "Wong Kim Ark: The Contest over Birthright Citizenship," in David A. Martin and Peter H. Schuck, eds., *Immigration Stories* (New York: Foundation Press, 2005), pp. 63–64.

Make; The origin and character of the so-called 'Mexicans' of that Territory – their hatred of Americans, their dense ignorance, and total unfitness for citizenship – the women of New-Mexico."[64] It was only after the demographic composition of the New Mexico Territory had shifted to the advantage of whites that Congress decided, in 1912, to admit New Mexico as a state, more than sixty years after the territory's acquisition.

The post–Civil War decades also did not witness any fundamental change in the lesser citizenship of American women. Women's rights activists were bitterly disappointed when the post–Civil War constitutional amendments were phrased narrowly in order to preserve patriarchal power. An early version of the Thirteenth Amendment had read: "All persons are equal before the law." Senators objected to such expansive language precisely on the ground that it would confer equality upon women. Republican Senator Jacob Howard of Michigan expressed the widely shared view that the proposed language would mean that "before the law a woman would be equal to a man, a woman would be as free as a man. A wife would be equal to her husband and as free as her husband before the law."[65] This kind of challenge to the proposed language was deemed formidable enough for Senator Charles Sumner to cease to endorse it. The Thirteenth Amendment was thus narrowly phrased to abolish only "slavery [and] involuntary servitude."[66]

To the extent that the post–Civil War constitutional amendments did embrace universalist language, such language failed to live up to its promise. In *Bradwell v. Illinois* (1873), the U.S. Supreme Court held that an Illinois law that barred women from the practice of law did not contravene the Fourteenth Amendment's injunction that states not abridge the "privileges and immunities" of citizens. As Justice Bradley's concurring opinion made clear, the Fourteenth Amendment was not intended to upset "natural" hierarchies: "The paramount destiny and mission of woman are to fulfill the noble and benign offices of wife and mother. This is the law of the Creator. And the rules of civil society must be adapted to the general constitution of things, and

[64] Laura E. Gómez, *Manifest Destinies: The Making of the Mexican American Race* (New York: New York University Press, 2007), pp. 63–64.
[65] Cong. Globe, 38th Cong., 1st Sess. 1488 (1864).
[66] U.S. Const., amend. XIII.

cannot be based upon exceptional cases … In the nature of things it is not every citizen of every age, sex, and condition that is qualified for every calling and position."[67] Women's demands for suffrage rights also met with defeat. An 1872 test case brought by Virginia Minor contended that a ban on women's suffrage fell afoul of the Fourteenth Amendment's Privileges and Immunities Clause. In 1874, the U.S. Supreme Court ruled against Minor on the ground that suffrage was not coextensive with citizenship and that states possessed the authority to decide which of their citizens could vote.[68]

As the *Bradwell* and *Minor* cases suggest, the post–Civil War women's movement came to focus prominently on suffrage and access to professions, but especially the former. Although no longer as significant in the women's rights agenda as it had once been, agitation for married women's property rights continued. With wide variation across the states, reforms tended to protect married women's separate property and earnings outside the home. Neither of these did much for the vast majority of married women.

However, there were also some changes of note. The denial of a federal constitutional right to vote did not mean that women were barred from voting at the state, county, or municipal level. In various places, women were granted the right to vote on particular issues such as education. In the West, offering women suffrage rights became a means of enticing female migrants and hence speeding up white settlement. As a result of lobbying, Illinois reversed its ban on female lawyers in 1872 and admitted the first woman to practice in 1873.

Despite such advances, however, the fundamental occlusion of women's political membership by that of their husbands' remained in place. Although American men had been able to confer citizenship upon their alien wives since 1855, American women could not do the same for their alien husbands. In the post–Civil War decades, notwithstanding Justice Story's understanding of the common law rule on the issue in *Shanks v. Dupont* (1830), there were scattered cases in which American women actually *lost* their American citizenship by virtue of marrying non-citizens. In 1883, a federal court in Michigan ruled that an American woman married to an alien, notwithstanding residence in

---

[67] *Bradwell v. Illinois*, 83 U.S. 130, 141–42 (1872) (Bradley, J.).
[68] *Minor v. Happersett*, 88 U.S. 162 (1874).

the United States, lost her American citizenship.[69] In 1874, President Ulysses S. Grant's daughter married an Englishman and moved to England to live with her husband. This act apparently also caused her to lose her American citizenship. In 1898, Congress passed a private naturalization act to restore American citizenship to the former president's daughter.

To these various kinds of foreignness and spatial controls imposed on Native Americans, blacks, Chinese Americans, Mexican Americans, and women, one must add the long-standing forms of lesser citizenship and restrictions on movement and residence experienced by the country's poor. After the federal assumption of control over immigration restriction, state poor laws that had played such an important role in the development of immigration regimes in the antebellum period no longer did the work of policing international borders. But this did not mean that they fell away. The laws of settlement survived the Civil War and, indeed, spread across the country. "Warning out," the colonial practice whereby towns delivered notice to newcomers to prevent them from acquiring a settlement, remained vital. Iowa's poor law provided, for example, that "[p]ersons coming into the state, or going from one county to another, who are county charges or are likely to become such, may be prevented from acquiring a settlement by the authorities ... warning them to depart therefrom."[70] Cities, towns, and counties routinely shipped individuals to their places of settlement. W. Almont Gates, secretary of the California Board of Charities, spoke at the 1912 National Conference of Charities and Correction of the "frequently followed" practice of "taking an insane person into another state and leaving him at a hotel, or on the street, or in fact dumping him."[71]

In many states, the poor were stripped of the franchise. If their children were bound out while they were receiving assistance, they might effectively lose custody of such children (even if the binding out took place without their consent). The poor had no legal right to demand relief that local governments were required to provide and could not even demand compensation for damage suffered. A 1911 case from Iowa suggests how the logic of settlement – and the impulse to get rid

---

[69] *Pequignot v. City of Detroit*, 16 F.Cas. 211 (C.C.E.D. Mich. 1883).
[70] Ann. Code 1897, Iowa, Ch. 1, Sec. 2226.
[71] Edith Abbott, *Public Assistance*, vol. I (Chicago: University of Chicago Press, 1940), p. 185.

of the needy – bore devastating consequences for Americans. A man examining timber in the Des Moines River broke through ice, got wet, and, unable to find lodging, spent the night in a straw stack. He awoke with frozen feet. When he arrived in Boone County, he was given first aid, but, following the practice of dealing with non-residents, was "shipped on" to Story County and from there to Cerro Gordo County. Both feet had to be amputated because of improper care in Boone County and the County's haste in removing him. When he sued Boone County for damages, sovereign immunity prevented recovery. The Court concluded its opinion by deploring "the practice of shifting foreign paupers from one county to another" as "a disgrace to our civilization."[72] Tellingly, the Court's use of the word "foreign paupers" did not refer to aliens, but to foreignness conceived in terms of the logic of settlement.

## Conclusion

In the late nineteenth century, once the country had resolved the long-standing problem of the internal foreignness of blacks, a federal immigration regime claiming exclusive power over immigration and naturalization finally emerged. As it became visible through the struggles of Chinese immigrants, the constitutional law governing this federal immigration regime vested in the federal government plenary power over the exclusion, deportation, and naturalization of immigrants. According to the U.S. Supreme Court, this meant that the federal government's actions vis-à-vis immigrants, subject to some exceptions, were virtually unchecked by the substantive provisions of the U.S. Constitution. Plenary power over immigrants thus inaugurated the widening of a gulf between a community of citizens who could claim the protections of the U.S. Constitution and a community of immigrants who could not. However, as this chapter has shown, notwithstanding the formal extension of citizenship among the native-born population in the aftermath of the Civil War, millions of Americans continued to be rendered foreigners in a variety of ways.

Chinese immigrants themselves were only a very small portion of the immigrant pool. In the late nineteenth century immigrants still came

---

[72] *Wood v. Boone County*, 133 N.W. 377, 381 (Iowa 1911).

overwhelmingly from Northwestern Europe. Of white immigration in the peak year of 1882, only slightly more than 10 percent originated in Eastern and Southern Europe. Immigration streams from Asian countries other than China, notably Japan, were vanishingly small.

Albeit small, the new immigration from Southern and Eastern Europe and from Asia was highly visible and evoked concerns that quickly pushed it to the fore of the policy debates of the 1880s and 1890s. In his presidential address to the American Economic Association in 1890, the economist Francis A. Walker warned that the immigration stream was beginning to draw from "great stagnant pools of population which no current of intellectual or moral activity has stirred for ages," people at "the very lowest stage of human degradation" who belonged to "races" who would not "for generations develop that capability of responding to the opportunities and incitements of their new life," which republican citizenship required.[73]

Late-nineteenth-century thinkers' solution to the problem of a degenerate immigration stream was a literacy test. In January 1891, former Harvard lecturer and Massachusetts representative (and later senator) Henry Cabot Lodge, who was an important figure in the East Coast elite-dominated Immigration Restriction League, argued for a literacy test as the best solution to the problem of unrestricted immigration. The literacy test would become one of the major battlegrounds in the immigration debates of the early twentieth century. At the state level, hostility toward immigrants began to mount. In the 1880s and 1890s, states that had granted aliens suffrage began to roll back such provisions.

Ideas about how to shape and regulate the immigrant stream could be put into action by a much more powerful, and ever larger, federal immigration regime. Undergirded by plenary power, the early-twentieth-century federal immigration regime would expand the purview of immigration restriction well beyond what it had been in the nineteenth century. At the same time, the experience of Chinese immigrants with blanket restriction would become the experience of other groups.

---

[73] F. A. Walker, "The Tide of Economic Thought: An Address to the Fourth Annual Meeting of the American Economic Association by the President, F. A. Walker, President of M.I.T., Washington, D.C." (December 26, 1890), in *Publications of the American Economic Association*, vol. VI, nos. 1 and 2 (Baltimore: Guggenheimer, Weil & Co., 1891), p. 37.

# 6

## Closing the Gates in the Early Twentieth Century

### Introduction

Almost 13 million immigrants entered the United States between 1900 and 1914, a number greater than the number that had entered over the previous three decades, a period twice as long. The sheer volume of early-twentieth-century immigration could not escape attention. Neither could the changes in its composition. On the eve of World War I, Southern and Eastern European countries outranked Northern and Western European ones as major sending countries. On the West Coast, there were smaller streams of immigrants from Asian countries, including Japan, Korea, India, and the Philippines. In the West and Southwest, there was a growing influx of Mexicans. Early-twentieth-century immigration was also inextricably intertwined with each of the massive and wrenching changes – industrialization, urbanization, capital–labor strife, imperialism, and entanglement in foreign affairs – that transformed the United States after 1900.

In light of immigration's scale, diversity, and significance in the early twentieth century, it is not surprising that Americans developed strong reactions to it. Concerns about race and national origin had always been part of immigration discourses. What is noteworthy in the early twentieth century, however, is the "scientific" cast that such discourses acquired. Between 1890 and 1920, prominent social scientists, many with prestigious university appointments, endorsed immigration restriction on the ground that native-born Americans were being drowned in a sea of racial inferiors. Their focus was heavily on Eastern and Southern European immigration. Madison Grant's influential eugenicist text, *The Passing of the Great Race; or the Racial Basis of European History* (1916), identified three European races – the Alpine, the Mediterranean, and the Nordic – that varied "intellectually and morally just as they do physically."[1] Authentic native-born Americans were Nordics, described as "a race of soldiers, sailors, adventurers and explorers, but above all, of rulers, organizers and aristocrats."[2] Unfortunately, according to Grant, Nordics were not reproducing in sufficient numbers and, to make matters worse, were annihilating themselves in internecine conflicts such as World War I. Ranged against this noble, enterprising, and tragically diminishing native stock were throngs of Southern and Eastern Europeans, Asians, and Mexicans pouring into the country. These were, as the social scientist Edward Ross described Eastern Europeans, "the beaten members of beaten breeds."[3]

Opposition to such scientific racial thinking existed, but was overwhelmed. Under the aegis of the new federal plenary power over immigration and naturalization, the federal government, together with the federal courts, was able to write the new sciences of race into immigration and naturalization law, building, as it were, upon its experience with Chinese immigrants. But there would be no easy translation of racial science into the messy politics of immigration and citizenship.

In the context of naturalization law, where immigrants had to demonstrate their "whiteness" as a prerequisite to obtaining citizenship, a series of early-twentieth-century legal challenges by immigrants from the Near East, South Asia, and East Asia drove courts to wrestle with the meaning of race. Courts soon discovered that racial science yielded confusing and undesirable results. "Whiteness" was judicially declared to inhere not in science, but in popular prejudice.

Inconsistency and compromise also beset the cause of immigration restrictionists pushing to exclude those they considered their

---

[1] Madison Grant, *The Passing of the Great Race; or the Racial Basis of European History*, rev. ed. (New York: Charles Scribner's Sons, 1918) (1916), p. 226.
[2] Id., p. 228.
[3] Edward A. Ross, *Foundations of Sociology*, 5th ed. (New York: Macmillan Co., 1917), p. 393.

racial inferiors. In 1917, blanket bans on practically all Asian immigration were instituted with relatively little opposition. During the
1920s, restrictionists finally also succeeded in instituting numerical
quotas based on national origins that sharply reduced the number of
entrants from Eastern and Southern Europe. This was a shift of enormous import. Instead of sifting out undesirables from the immigration
stream, as had been the case for centuries, the United States began for
the first time to limit the number who could enter in any given year
(with traditional grounds of exclusion retained as an additional barrier). The introduction of numerical quotas immediately gave rise to
the problem of undocumented migration. As in the case of naturalization, however, racial science proved unequal to the task of excluding perceived racial inferiors. The structuring of numerical national
origins quotas for European immigrants involved more guesswork
than anything else. Meanwhile, under pressure from southwestern
agricultural employers, immigration from Mexico remained open. The
United States' new colonial relationships also allowed immigration
from Puerto Rico and the Philippines.

The closure of political membership and territory was hardly the
only distinguishing feature of early-twentieth-century immigration
and citizenship law. In the early twentieth century, as the federal immigration order grew, there was an intensified focus on the relationship
of the state to the millions of immigrants *within* its borders. The status
of alien came to imply a number of specific legal disabilities, ranging
from older disabilities that denied aliens access to various jobs, trades,
professions, and economic entitlements to newer ones such as mounting vulnerability to deportation and denaturalization.

The consolidation of the federal immigration regime and the ratcheting upward of alien legal disabilities meant that the gulf between
citizen and alien grew wider than it had been at earlier periods in
American history. However, at the same time, the state actively assimilated many of its own to the status of aliens or otherwise rendered
them foreign. This took place in a variety of ways. First, when it came
to women, racial minorities, and the indigent, the possession of formal
citizenship did not liberate millions from legal disabilities comparable
to those suffered by immigrants or from subjection to an extensive
regime of territorial and spatial borders. Second, in the early twentieth
century, the federal government began to punish acts of native-born

citizens by stripping them of citizenship – that is, literally converting them into aliens. In 1907, Congress passed a law that involuntarily expatriated American women who married aliens. Third, when it came to certain groups – Mexican Americans, Japanese Americans, and others – the state indiscriminately mingled citizens and aliens, meting out to its citizens the same treatment it reserved for aliens. Finally, the United States' acquisition of overseas territories gave rise to a debate about whether residents of the Philippines and Puerto Rico were to be citizens notwithstanding their subjection to U.S. sovereign power. While Congress extended citizenship to Puerto Ricans by statute, it refused to do so for Filipinos, who were classified as "nationals" rather than citizens. Eventually, as nativist voices joined the decolonization debate, Filipinos found themselves transformed from "nationals" into excludable aliens.

The remainder of this chapter is organized into three sections. First, it explores the imbrication of racialist nativism with citizenship and immigration law, emphasizing the twists and turns of law and politics on the way to the institution of numerical quotas. Second, it examines the travails faced by resident immigrants as they became vulnerable to legal discrimination, Americanization efforts, deportation, and denaturalization. Finally, it details the multiple ways in which the state turned insiders into foreigners.

## Closing the Gates: Racial Science, Naturalization, and Immigration

Although Chinese immigrants had been barred from naturalizing on racial grounds since 1878, in the early twentieth century, as the immigration stream diversified, fresh questions arose about the "whiteness" – and hence the eligibility for citizenship – of naturalization applicants from different parts of Asia. Between the first ruling on Chinese naturalization applicants in 1878 and the end of formal racial bars to naturalization in 1952, federal and state courts heard more than fifty cases concerning the "whiteness" of aspiring citizens.

The early-twentieth-century racial prerequisite cases reveal the hollowness of the new racial science that undergirded the law. In the late nineteenth century, racial science and racial common knowledge had seemingly confirmed each other as courts ruled on naturalization applicants' "whiteness." For example, in *In re Ah Yup* (1878), the case that established Chinese immigrants' ineligibility for citizenship, the court held that the words "white persons" possessed a "well settled meaning in common popular speech," even as it invoked definitions of "white" in the theories of Blumenbach, Buffon, Cuvier, and Linnaeus.[4]

By the early twentieth century, however, this harmonious working together of racial science and racial common knowledge had begun to founder. As scientific and common knowledge understandings of "whiteness" pointed in different directions, courts began to confront the difficulties of determining "whiteness" in naturalization cases. As courts ruled this way and that, the results grew troublingly inconsistent. Complaining that "the statute as it stands is most uncertain, ambiguous, and difficult both of construction and application," a South Carolina federal court ruling on the naturalization petition of a Syrian applicant expressed its frustration with a rhetorical question: "Then, what is white?"[5]

In the contest between racial science and common knowledge, however, it was science that lost out. The judicial preference for common knowledge – as opposed to scientific – understandings of "whiteness" is revealed in two cases decided by the U.S. Supreme Court in the early 1920s. In *Ozawa v. United States* (1922), a Japanese immigrant, Takao Ozawa, argued that his skin tone, in conjunction with his assimilation into American society, should ensure his naturalization. But Ozawa's skin tone failed to win him judicial recognition as "white." The Court put it thus: "Manifestly the test afforded by the mere color of the skin of each individual is impracticable, as that differs greatly [even] among persons of the same race." What mattered instead was whether Ozawa could be classified, on the basis of racial science, as a member of the "Caucasian race." According to the Court, Ozawa was "clearly of a race which is not Caucasian and therefore belongs entirely outside the zone on the negative side."[6]

To the extent that the Court indicated in *Ozawa* that classification as "white" was a matter of membership of the "Caucasian race," its decision was welcome to immigrants from India, who *were* classified by racial science as "Caucasian." But in *United States v. Thind* (1923),

---

[4] *In re Ah Yup*, 1 F.Cas. 223 (C.D. Cal. 1878).
[5] *Ex parte Shahid*, 205 F. 812, 813 (E.D. S.C. 1913).
[6] *Ozawa v. United States*, 260 U.S. 178, 197–98 (1922).

a case involving an Indian applicant for naturalization decided just months after *Ozawa*, the Court balked at the implications of following racial science quite that far. It was not science, the Court insisted, but common knowledge that would govern: "It may be true that the blond Scandinavian and the brown Hindu have a common ancestor ... , but the average man knows perfectly well that there are unmistakable and profound differences between them to-day."[7] Thus, racial science, used effectively to exclude Japanese applicants for citizenship, was summarily abandoned in favor of the common knowledge of the "average man." In 1934, the U.S. Supreme Court made the determination of "whiteness" turn on sight, another proxy for common knowledge. Justice Cardozo put it thus: "In the vast majority of cases the race of a Japanese or a Chinaman will be known to anyone who looks at him ... The triers of the facts will look upon the defendant sitting in the courtroom, and will draw their own conclusions."[8]

If race barred membership in the polity, it also became a barrier to access to national territory. To be sure, early-twentieth-century immigration restriction was not only a matter of race. Federal plenary power had been sufficiently consolidated that the U.S. Supreme Court would proclaim that "over no conceivable subject is the legislative power of Congress more complete" than immigration.[9] General grounds of exclusion expanded. The exclusion of those "likely to become a public charge" (LPC) rapidly became the most important ground of barring entry into the United States, typically accounting for more than half of all exclusions during this period. The LPC provision was much more likely to be used against females than males. It was also used to exclude those whose identities fell outside heteronormative standards. Closely related to the LPC provision were laws restricting the admission of aliens with physical and mental defects, including epileptics and alcoholics, which led potential entrants to strive to conceal illnesses, limps, and coughs. Following the assassination of President McKinley in 1901, immigration laws also began to exclude aliens for their political beliefs.

[7] *United States v. Bhagat Singh Thind*, 261 U.S. 204, 209 (1923).
[8] *Morrison v. California*, 291 U.S. 82, 94 (1934).
[9] *Oceanic Steam Navigation Co. v. Stranahan*, 214 U.S. 320, 339 (1909).

By the early twentieth century, however, racial theories of immigration restrictionists had thoroughly infiltrated official discourses and practices. The massive report on immigration submitted to Congress by the Dillingham Commission (1910–11) included a *Dictionary of Races or Peoples* that exemplified the new scientific understanding of race in hierarchically organizing immigrants "according to their languages, their physical characteristics, and such other marks as would show their relationship to one another."[10] This racialization of immigration translated both into calls to make race a legal ground of exclusion and into the application of general immigration provisions in ways that affected certain immigrants more severely than others.

Predictably, Asian immigrants bore the brunt of the spread of racial thinking. By 1905, the Asiatic Exclusion League had been organized to bar immigration from Japan, Korea, and India. Attempts to segregate San Francisco schools (already segregated when it came to Chinese immigrants) sparked a diplomatic crisis between Japan and the United States, resulting in the Gentlemen's Agreement of 1907, according to which Japan agreed voluntarily to restrict the emigration of Japanese laborers. The Asiatic Exclusion League also lobbied fiercely for the exclusion of Indian immigrants, erroneously labeled "Hindoos."

In the absence of any statutory provision explicitly prohibiting the entry of Indian immigrants, zealous immigration officials began to interpret the general LPC provision to exclude them on the ground that strong anti-Indian prejudice in California would prevent them from getting jobs and thereby render them public charges. Prejudice thus built upon prejudice. When this discriminatory use of the LPC provision was challenged in federal court, it was upheld.[11] The discriminatory application of general exclusion provisions against Asians might be surmised from (admittedly imprecise) statistics. If about 1 percent of immigrants were excluded at New York's Ellis Island facility, where European immigrants landed, almost 20 percent were excluded at San Francisco's Angel Island facility, where Asian immigrants landed.

The context of suspicion fostered by World War I enabled nativists to score significant victories in the Immigration Act of 1917.

---

[10] Dillingham Commission Report, *Dictionary of Races or Peoples*, vol. 5, Senate Document 662, Session 61-3 (Washington, DC: U.S. Government Printing Office, 1911), p. 2.
[11] *In re Rhagat Singh*, 209 F. 700 (N.D. Cal. 1913).

Acquiescing to the West Coast's demand for the exclusion of Indian immigrants, and yet hesitant to single Indians out for exclusion, Congress created an "Asiatic Barred Zone" that stretched from the Arab world to Polynesia. Congress also gave nativists something they had pushed for since the late nineteenth century: the literacy test for adult immigrants that nativists hoped would keep out Southern and Eastern Europeans. In the end, it is unclear how much the literacy test affected immigration from Europe because of the spread of literacy there during the same years.

By 1920, the war boom economy had begun to collapse and immigration from Europe, depressed during the War, had revived, creating a propitious environment for even greater restriction. To be sure, there was vigorous opposition to restriction from immigrant groups and liberal voices. Immigrant groups had been protesting discriminatory laws for years. In 1921, the *Nation* deplored "the besotted Anglo-Saxons, who point with rapture to the Puritan tradition" and insisted that the country's "hopes lie rather in our fusion of many cultures."[12] Legislators from states with strong immigrant constituencies such as New York also opposed closing borders to European immigrants. Despite such opposition, however, the nativists won out. In 1921, the logic of immigration restriction that had been formally applicable to almost all Asian immigrants since 1917 – namely, exclusion – was extended to European immigrants, albeit in the form of numerical quotas rather than complete exclusion.

Thus, in the 1920s, for the first time in the history of immigration restriction, the basic theory of exclusion shifted from a matter of the shortcomings of the individual immigrant (poverty, criminal background, health, etc.) to a matter of numerical restriction. Older grounds of exclusion continued to apply. But the shift was momentous. The old presumption that one *could* immigrate to the United States switched to a presumption that one could *not* immigrate to the United States unless one fit within a set quota. The presumption of open borders became a presumption of closed ones.

The 1921 Act restricted immigration from each European country to 3 percent of the number of foreign-born people from that country residing in the United States in 1910. The goal was to tilt immigration

[12] Quoted in Zolberg, *Nation by Design*, p. 250.

toward Northern and Western Europe and away from Southern and
Eastern Europe. By 1923, the commissioner general of immigration
declared the Act a success. He revealed that the percentage of Southern
and Eastern European immigrants had decreased from 75.6 percent of
the total immigration in 1914 to 31.1 percent of the total immigration in 1923. For the same years, as a percentage of total immigration,
immigration from Northern and Western Europe had increased from
20.8 percent to 52.5 percent.

This change in the composition of the immigration stream failed to
satisfy nativists. The Immigration Act of 1924 was the result of negotiation. It reduced the percentage admitted from 3 to 2, with the base
population being the number of immigrants of each nationality present in the United States in 1890 instead of 1910. This aggravated the
discrimination against Southern and Eastern European immigrants. In
exchange for agreeing to these quotas, however, the Senate insisted that
a new "national origins" test be used beginning in 1927. But the new
"national origins" test hardly did away with the problem of discrimination. Capping the total number of annual admissions at 150,000, and
with the 1920 population as the base, it assigned quotas on the basis
of "national origins." However, instead of using only the foreign-born
1920 population, as was the case with the 1921 Act, it used the *entire*
1920 population, which once again tilted quotas in favor of Northern
and Western Europeans. Written into the "national origins" idea were
important exclusions. The Act excluded from consideration for purposes of calculating "national origins" immigrants from the New
World and their descendants; Asians or their descendants; descendants
of "slave immigrants"; and descendants of "American aborigines."[13]
Thus, the quotas basically worked only for whites (non-European
countries received nominal annual quotas of 100). The results were
dramatic: the quota for the United Kingdom went up from approximately 34,000 to more than 65,000; the quota for the Irish Free State
dropped from slightly more than 28,000 to less than 18,000; the quota
for Germany dropped from more than 50,000 to slightly more than
25,000. Demographic re-engineering was achieved.

But there was nothing clear or scientifically rigorous about how the
new quotas were calculated. A committee of experts, led by historian

---

[13] Immigration Act of 1924 (May 26, 1924), 43 Stat. 153.

Marcus Lee Hansen, claimed to have computed the "national stock" of the eligible 1920 population. The expert "estimate" was that persons whose ancestors were in the United States before the Revolution constituted approximately 45 percent of the eligible 1920 population and that later immigrants and their descendants constituted the rest. But how were "national stocks" to be determined after centuries of intermarriage, mobility, and name-changing? As in the case of determinations of "whiteness" in naturalization cases, racial nativism in the context of immigration restriction resulted in a murky and flawed calculus. The 1924 Act also definitively closed the door on Asian immigration. The law barred such aliens from entering the country as were, to use the euphemistic phrase of the time, "ineligible for citizenship." Because all other Asian immigration had already been prohibited at this point, the law's target was the Japanese.[14]

Fixed numerical immigrant quotas immediately gave rise to the figure of the "illegal alien," the non-citizen present in national territory without the state's authorization. This was not an entirely new phenomenon: Chinese immigrant smuggling networks had been around to subvert exclusion laws since the late nineteenth century. After the introduction of numerical quotas, however, "illegal aliens" became the most important immigration law violators. This in turn brought about further changes. The country's borders with Mexico and Canada, essentially open through the nineteenth century, had witnessed the beginnings of a rudimentary system of border control around the turn of the century. In 1925, Congress created a land border patrol to defend the country from unlawful entrants.

However, even as racial nativists won a victory in closing the borders, political and economic imperatives frustrated their hopes to close the borders to *all* non-white immigration. By the end of the nineteenth century, a range of transformations – the extension of railroad networks, the introduction of the refrigerated boxcar, the construction of irrigation projects, and so on – had laid the foundation for explosive economic growth in the American Southwest and fueled the region's seemingly limitless demand for agricultural labor. These changes took place just as conditions for Mexican peasants were worsening during the waning years of the nineteenth century. Mexicans began to pour

[14] Id.

into the Southwest. Although immigration statistics for the early twentieth century are notoriously inaccurate, at least 1 million, and possibly as many as a million and a half, Mexican immigrants entered the United States between 1890 and 1929.

At a time of rising nativism in the United States vis-à-vis European and Asian immigrants, southwestern employers' labor needs, combined with the neocolonial context of the Southwest, spared Mexican immigrants from becoming formal targets of U.S. citizenship and immigration laws. Given the history of the acquisition of the Southwest, as discussed in the preceding chapter, Mexican immigrants were allowed to naturalize. They were also exempt from bars to immigration. Influential arguments promoted the idea that history had rendered Mexican immigrants familiar – yet happily, temporary – sojourners in the United States. Thus, for example, in 1926, Congressman Edward Taylor of Colorado offered assurances that Mexicans, familiar to Americans after a century of contact, sought only to make a bit of money before returning to their own country. As he put it: "[Mexicans] simply want work ... Generally speaking they are not immigrants at all. They do not try to buy or colonize our land, and they hope some day to be able to own a piece of land in their own country."[15] Such arguments were intended to assuage nativists' fears that Mexicans might settle permanently in the United States.

But Mexicans inconveniently stayed on in the communities where they labored. By the mid-1920s, hardcore restrictionists began to call for curbs on Mexican immigration. Rejecting blanket exclusions or quotas for Mexicans, Congress resorted to other means. United States consuls in Mexico began to enforce general immigration restrictions in order to refuse visas. At the same time, the U.S. Border Patrol began to curb Mexican illegal immigration. Over the course of the 1930s, Border Patrol officers began to concentrate their efforts on Mexican immigrants.

During the first half of the 1930s, as the Great Depression worsened, emigration exceeded immigration. If the 1930s are taken as a whole, the average annual immigration was less than 7,000, a drastic

---

[15] Quoted in David G. Gutiérrez, *Walls and Mirrors: Mexican Americans, Mexican Immigrants and the Politics of Ethnicity* (Berkeley: University of California Press, 1995), p. 49.

drop from the peak years of the pre–World War I period. But the drop also had to do with a more aggressive effort to exclude immigrants, especially through reliance on the LPC clause. State Department officials' harsher application of the LPC clause slashed Mexican admissions between 1929 and 1930 by almost 70 percent.

The most tragic effect of the numerical quota regime of the 1920s lay in the United States' response to the plight of European Jews and other victims of the Nazis. Although President Roosevelt was apprised of Nazi persecution, he did little to alter immigration policy. Meanwhile, prominent restrictionist Congressmen such as Martin Dies opposed a refugee policy for European Jews on the ground that it would open the United States up to Communist and Nazi subversion. There is also considerable evidence that State Department officials made it well-nigh impossible for most refugees in general – and Jewish refugees in particular – to obtain visas. Indeed, the German quota went unfilled for most years during the 1930s. The nativism that had led to the institution of country quotas thus condemned potential European Jewish immigrants to their deaths.

## Immigrants Inside the United States: The New Politics of Alienage

In the early twentieth century, the growth of the federal immigration regime intersected with the politics of race, labor, welfare, and war to transform resident immigrants into a special kind of underclass, their formal lack of citizenship given meaning through an increasing number of legal disabilities. Resident immigrants had long been subject to state-level legal discrimination. Now they also confronted an increasingly powerful federal state largely unfettered by the courts.

By the 1920s, resident immigrants who had declared their intention to naturalize had lost the ability to vote all over the country. However, even though no alien was a formal participant in the affairs of the polity, there were vast differences in the ways in which different groups of resident immigrants experienced alien legal disabilities. Barred from naturalizing, Asian immigrants were unable to escape alien legal disabilities their entire lives: they were a class of permanent non-citizens. By contrast, European and Mexican immigrants *were* able to shed alien legal disabilities by naturalizing. However, European and Mexican immigrants were incorporated into American society in sharply different ways. Europeans were seen as potential Americans. In the industrial cities of the Northeast and Midwest, where most European immigrants tended to live, dense networks of institutions – churches, schools, settlement houses, charities, ethnic organizations, labor unions, and political machines – worked to fold immigrants into the body politic. In the Southwest and the West, where Mexican immigrants were concentrated, immigrants were afforded far fewer points of entry. These different forms and levels of incorporation translated not just into differences in rates of naturalization, but also into very different kinds of treatment.

In this section, I discuss three aspects of increased state power deployed vis-à-vis resident immigrants in the early twentieth century.

### Alien Legal Disabilities Relating to Economic Activities and Entitlements

Over the course of the nineteenth century, many states had lifted alien legal disabilities relating to landownership, but not those relating to many civil service positions. The growth of anti-immigrant sentiment in the late nineteenth and early twentieth centuries gave rise to a fresh burst of state and local anti-immigrant legislation, much of which assumed the form of restricting immigrants' economic opportunities.

Immigrants were quick to challenge such discriminatory laws. They were able to do so because, with the federal assumption of control over immigration, the legal landscape had changed. Federal courts now asked whether state legal discrimination against immigrants interfered with immigrants' constitutional rights to non-discrimination under the Fourteenth Amendment and with the federal government's now exclusive power over immigration. With some important exceptions, discriminatory state and local legislation withstood challenges.

According to a late-nineteenth-century U.S. Supreme Court ruling, states were entitled to deny non-state citizens access to state citizens' "common property," a term that historically referred to natural resources such as forests and fisheries. The exclusion could legally extend to *all* non-state citizens, not just aliens.[16] By the early twentieth century, however, the "common property" doctrine was invoked principally to uphold state-level anti-immigrant legislation. In 1914, for example, the U.S. Supreme Court upheld a Pennsylvania law that prohibited aliens from

---

[16] *McCready v. Virginia*, 94 U.S. 391, 396 (1876).

killing wild birds or animals (except in self-defense) and that made it illegal, therefore, for aliens to own shotguns or rifles. The Court ruled that Pennsylvania could "preserve [wild game] for its own citizens if it pleases."[17]

The "common property" idea soon expanded well beyond the traditional focus on a state's natural resources to encompass valuable economic benefits such as employment on public works, holding civil service jobs, and entering regulated trades and professions. If such restrictions had existed in earlier periods, they now received constitutional sanction as the U.S. Supreme Court attempted to demarcate the lines of division between federal and state powers. In 1915, the Court upheld New York laws that barred aliens from being employed on public works.[18] In 1927, it sustained against a Fourteenth Amendment challenge a Cincinnati ordinance that prohibited aliens from operating pool and billiard rooms.[19] In *Truax v. Raich* (1915), however, the Court overturned an Arizona law that prohibited employers of more than five workers from having less than 80 percent of their workforce consist of native-born citizens or qualified electors. According to the Court, Arizona's ability to make reasonable distinctions under the Fourteenth Amendment did not allow it to deny individuals "because of their race or nationality, the ordinary means of earning a livelihood." In enacting such a law, furthermore, Arizona was infringing on the exclusive federal immigration power.[20]

If the U.S. Supreme Court occasionally checked some of the worst state-level xenophobic impulses, it upheld serious economic discrimination targeting Asian immigrants. In the early twentieth century, the success of Japanese immigrants in agriculture led California to pass the 1913 Alien Land Act. Couched in race-neutral language but singling out Asian immigrants (the Act applied to aliens ineligible to citizenship), the Act prohibited such immigrants from buying land in California. The Act's proponents were outspoken about the fact that they intended the Act to shrink the Japanese presence in California. In other words, this was an immigration law masquerading as an alienage law. Several states passed similar or more severe laws. Washington's

[17] *Patsone v. Pennsylvania*, 232 U.S. 138, 145–46 (1914).
[18] *Crane v. New York*, 239 U.S. 195 (1915).
[19] *Clarke v. Deckebach*, 274 U.S. 392 (1927).
[20] *Truax v. Raich*, 239 U.S. 33, 41, 42 (1915).

1921 alien land law prohibited aliens ineligible to citizenship even from leasing land for agricultural purposes. In *Terrace v. Thompson* (1923), the Court upheld it. Departing from *Truax v. Raich*, the Court did not find that Washington's law interfered with Asian immigrants' opportunity to earn a living or with Congress's exclusive authority over immigration. Instead, it invoked the old common law position that "each state ... has power to deny to aliens the right to own land within its borders." Furthermore, the Court ruled, the law was entirely in step with congressional policy preventing Asians from naturalizing.[21]

With the blessing of the courts, then, alien legal disabilities multiplied. With the explosion of nativism sparked by World War I and the recession that followed the war boom economy, there were many public and private efforts to close economic opportunities to non-citizens. A 1933 study by social scientist Harold Fields reported that "there is today a consistent attitude among business-men and law-makers alike, that has for its announced purpose the refusal to aliens of the right to engage in certain, and many, occupations." Fields catalogued dozens of professions, types of public employment, kinds of occupational licenses, and miscellaneous categories of activity that required either first papers (i.e., a declaration of intent to naturalize) or full citizenship pursuant to the statutes of various states and the District of Columbia. These ranged from architecture to pharmacy, operating a steam boiler to being a private detective, taxidermy to lobster fishing.[22] By the early 1940s, laws, licensing requirements for professions, and the attitudes of private employers rendered aliens ineligible for a majority of all jobs in the United States. Such disabilities had a greater impact on Asian and Mexican immigrants.

If the forces of nativism increasingly restricted aliens' access to jobs, trades, professions, union membership, and landownership, the same forces also gave rise to resentment of immigrants' claims on the public fisc in times of difficulty. Depending upon their race and national origin, immigrants had vastly different experiences. Social workers typically defended European immigrants' interests in the public sphere. By contrast, few in the West and Southwest advocated on behalf of

---

[21] *Terrace v. Thompson*, 263 U.S. 197, 217, 220 (1923).

[22] Harold Fields, "Where Shall the Alien Work?" *Social Forces* 12, no. 2 (December 1933): 213–21, 213.

Mexican immigrants. Indeed, officials in the West and Southwest openly acknowledged that the appeal of Mexican labor lay precisely in the fact that Mexicans could be removed when and if their demands on the community grew excessive. A Los Angeles Chamber of Commerce official put it thus: "[T]he Mexican may be deported; the Filipino, the American, and Porto Rican negroes are American citizens and could not be deported."[23]

During the New Deal, immigrants were eligible for benefits under various programs: Federal Emergency Relief, Social Security, Unemployment Insurance, and Aid to Dependent Children. However, the way programs were structured helped European immigrants and hurt Mexicans immigrants. For example, although the Social Security Act did not restrict benefits to citizens, because it excluded agricultural and domestic workers from coverage, it omitted from coverage sectors of the economy in which most Mexicans were employed. Local administration of welfare also resulted in the provision of lower levels of welfare to Mexican immigrants. In some important New Deal programs, however, citizenship did act as a barrier to important benefits. After repeated attempts, nativists succeeded in making citizenship a prerequisite in respect of the Works Progress Administration and Old Age Assistance. Such restrictions were often short-lived. Nevertheless, the growing linkage between citizenship and welfare explains the rise in naturalizations from 1934 on.

### Americanization: Making Immigrants Americans

If early-twentieth-century resident immigrants faced barriers to jobs, trades, and welfare, they also faced other kinds of pressures, public and private, subtle and threatening, to transform themselves and assimilate. Prominent early-twentieth-century politicians such as Theodore Roosevelt insisted upon, even as they celebrated, the United States' ability to fuse different immigrant groups into a single national identity. The naturalization law of 1906 made knowledge of the English language and the U.S. Constitution a requirement for the acquisition of U.S. citizenship. In 1907, the North American Civil League set as

---

[23] Cybelle Fox, *Three Worlds of Relief: Race, Immigration, and the American Welfare State from the Progressive Era to the New Deal* (Princeton, NJ: Princeton University Press, 2012), p. 41.

its goal "[t]o change the unskilled inefficient immigrant into the skilled worker and efficient citizen."[24] The focus of these different voices was typically the European immigrant, who – unlike Asians or Mexicans – was considered a potential American.

The beginnings of such attempts were benign. States established commissions and bureaus to deal with immigrant affairs, passing laws to protect immigrants from exploitation, whether from notaries public, steamship ticket agents, or immigrant financial institutions. Funded at the federal and state levels, language instruction became a major part of the effort to prepare immigrants for life in America.

After 1914, however, benign attempts to incorporate European immigrants grew tinged with suspicions of immigrants' allegedly divided loyalties. In an address to the Sixty-fourth Congress in 1915, President Woodrow Wilson raised the specter of disloyalty among naturalized immigrants. Cities all over the country organized Americanization committees. A pamphlet issued by the National Americanization Day Committee called for an abandoning of immigrant national identities and the creation of "an American race." With a striking absence of references to Asian and Mexican immigrants, the pamphlet's author put it thus: "The need now is not *more* work for the *Italian* or the *Jew* as such, not more interest in school facilities for the *Greek* or the *Finn*, ... not the *importation* of *more peasants* for farm hands, but the conscious effort to forge the people in this country into an American race that will stand together for America in times of peace or of war."[25]

However, the politics of Americanization, as organized labor was quick to observe, were frequently pro-capital and anti-labor. Charges of disloyalty were leveled when immigrant *and* American workers attempted to improve work conditions. In 1916, Samuel Gompers, head of the American Federation of Labor and himself an immigrant, observed: "Any serious attempt to Americanize the foreign-workers who have been crowded into our industrial centers and our mining districts must concern itself also with the problem of Americanizing employers, trusts, and corporations. Before the employes [*sic*] of the United States Steel Corporation can have an opportunity to understand

[24] Quoted in Edward G. Hartman, *The Movement to Americanize the Immigrant* (New York: Columbia University Press, 1948), p. 38.
[25] Frances A. Kellor, "Immigrants in America: A Domestic Policy," *Immigrants in America Review* 1, no. 1 (March 1915): 9–84, 15 (emphasis in original).

the ideal for which America stands, the United States Steel Corporation must first express that ideal in its dealings with its employes [*sic*]."[26]

Regardless of such challenges to the ideology of Americanization, the war years saw a mounting suspicion of "hyphenism" – the shorthand to describe divided loyalties – that fell especially heavily upon German Americans. The 1917 census revealed a statistic that alarmed many: between 4 and 5 million people residing in the United States had been born in one of the Central Powers countries. Postwar security fears gave rise to the passage of legislation to suppress disloyalty. There was also a noticeable increase in mob violence against immigrants and minorities, including well-publicized lynchings of German Americans. At the same time, "Americanization" became a form of active cultural suppression. State laws forbade the teaching of common branches of study in foreign languages. States made efforts to enact legislation prohibiting the use of the mails for sending publications in foreign languages. There were also petty changes: hamburgers were renamed "liberty sandwiches" and sauerkraut became "liberty cabbage."

Immigrants fought back. The immigrant press portrayed the most aggressive forms of "Americanization" as "flavor[ing] more of Hungary where the magyarization of several millions of people was attempted by means not consistent with American tradition, or of Russia of the Tzarist days with the persecution of the Jew and the denationalization of the Poles."[27] Around this time, as part of a more organized response, the American Civil Liberties Union also began to focus on the question of immigrant rights. As a result of such resistance, some of the more extreme "Americanization" initiatives were ruled unconstitutional. Between 1923 and 1926, the U.S. Supreme Court struck down a Nebraska law forbidding the teaching of foreign languages; an Oregon law targeting Catholic schools; and a Hawaii law that subjected private Japanese language schools to stringent public oversight.[28]

---

[26] Quoted in Hartman, *Movement to Americanize*, p. 141.

[27] Carol Aronovici, "Americanization," *Annals of the American Academy of Political and Social Science: Present-Day Immigration with Special Reference to the Japanese* (ed. Clyde L. King) 93 (January 1921): 134–38, 134.

[28] *Meyer v. Nebraska*, 262 U.S. 390 (1923); *Pierce v. Society of Sisters*, 268 U.S. 510 (1925); *Farrington v. Tokushige*, 273 U.S. 284 (1927).

When the United States entered World War II, two decades later, it relied upon the 1798 Enemy Aliens Act, which provided that all "natives, citizens, denizens, or subjects of the hostile government" were "liable to be apprehended, restrained, secured, and removed."[29] Over December 7–8, 1941, President Roosevelt issued orders pursuant to which Japanese, German, and Italian aliens were subject to arrest. The brunt of the restrictions appears to have been borne by Japanese immigrants. According to J. Edgar Hoover, approximately 70 percent of the "enemy aliens" arrested within the first twenty-four hours were Japanese.[30] "Enemy aliens" were then provided with hearings in which they had to demonstrate their loyalty. They were either released, placed on parole, or deported. The most egregious wartime treatment of aliens – namely, mass internment – was reserved for Japanese immigrants. Because it involved the indiscriminate mingling of Japanese aliens and Japanese Americans, it will be discussed later.

### Deportation and Denaturalization

The early twentieth century also witnessed a sharp increase in the federal government's deployment of deportation and denaturalization. When it came to deportation, the statistics are striking. The federal government officially deported fewer than 3,000 individuals in 1892, a number that is understandably low given that the federal immigration regime was in its infancy. That number shot up in the early twentieth century, oscillating between 25,000 and 40,000 annually before declining in the late 1930s and early 1940s. To the number of those formally deported must be added the number of those removed through less formal methods, such as those who accepted to return to their countries "voluntarily," whether upon being apprehended at the border or otherwise.

In the early twentieth century, federal removal practices also shifted from being principally an adjunct of initial exclusion (i.e., removing people who should have been excluded but were not) to functioning as an instrument of the government's general social policy vis-à-vis the resident immigrant population. Thus, immigrants came increasingly to

---

[29]　50 U.S.C. Sec. 21 (as amended in 1918).

[30]　J. Edgar Hoover, "Alien Enemy Control," *Iowa Law Review* 29 (1944): 396–408, 396, 401, 402.

be punished with removal from the United States for activities undertaken long *after* they had become a part of the lived community.

The early-twentieth-century rise of deportation as an instrument of social policy was undergirded by the nineteenth-century plenary power doctrine that had declared the deportation power to be inherent in sovereignty and had deemed deportation a civil (rather than criminal) penalty exempt from the constitutional restrictions applicable to crimes. In the 1920s, with the sanction of the courts, the federal government relied ever more heavily on the "civil" nature of the deportation penalty to deny immigrants protections available as a matter of course in criminal cases. There was no presumption of innocence, no right to refuse to speak to prosecutors, prohibitions on contacting counsel until after preliminary examination, and curtailment of judicial review. The U.S. Supreme Court confirmed the permissibility of retroactive deportation – that is, making an activity a deportable offense when it had not been so at the time it had been engaged in. Defending its view that such laws were not in violation of the *Ex Post Facto* Clause of the U.S. Constitution, the Court observed: "Congress ... was not increasing the punishment for the crimes ... It was ... only seeking to rid the country of persons who had shown by their career that their continued presence here would not make for the safety or welfare of society."[31]

The most commonly used portion of the deportation law was the LPC provision. The 1891 deportation law had rendered those deportable who became public charges within one year of entry for causes existing *prior* to landing. By 1917, this period was increased to five years with a legal presumption to be overcome by the immigrant that the cause of becoming a public charge had arisen prior to landing.[32] Thus, the law effectively moved from deporting those who might have been excluded as public charges at the time of initial entry to deporting those who sought relief well after they had entered the community.

Deportation on LPC grounds, combined with less formal removal practices, was deployed in breathtakingly strategic ways. In September 1930, with the country in the throes of the Great Depression, President Hoover announced his administration's campaign to tighten

[31] *Mahler v. Eby*, 264 U.S. 32, 39 (1924).
[32] Act of February 5, 1917, 39 Stat. 874.

immigration enforcement, deny immigrants financial assistance, and deport immigrants using the LPC provision. The consequences of this policy were especially harsh for Mexican immigrants. Through a variety of formal and informal methods, and with unprecedented levels of cooperation between local welfare authorities and federal immigration authorities, Mexican immigrants were removed en masse from the Southwest in what was the largest single instance of mass deportation out of the United States in the country's history. Perhaps between half a million and 1 million persons were removed south of the border – most from the Southwest, but perhaps 50,000 from the Midwest. Most of the so-called *repatriados* were alleged to have left "voluntarily" and hence do not feature in official deportation statistics. But there is plenty of evidence of coercion. For example, on February 26, 1931, U.S. immigration agents and Los Angeles police rounded up some 400 individuals in Los Angeles and then transported hundreds straight to Mexico without giving them even the opportunity to notify their families. Mexican immigrants accounted for close to half of the total number deported during the 1930s.

Immigrants were also deported for crimes they committed. As in the case of LPC deportations, criminal deportation law moved from punishing those with criminal backgrounds predating their entry or who had committed crimes within a few years after entry to punishing those who committed crimes long after entry. In 1917, criminal grounds of deportation expanded. Furthermore, criminal grounds of deportation – especially those involving vague terms such as a "crime involving moral turpitude" – gave rise to considerable uncertainty. What constituted a deportable offense varied widely from jurisdiction to jurisdiction.

Finally, in the early twentieth century, in a practice that raised serious concerns about the free speech rights of resident immigrants, the government began to deport immigrants on ideological grounds. Here, too, laws that began as an adjunct to exclusion became laws that punished immigrants who engaged in undesirable political activity inside the country. Between 1911 and 1919, the United States deported a scant fourteen anarchists. The Bolshevik Revolution, however, terrified the American public. In April and May 1919, newspapers were crowded with reports of bombs mailed to public figures. On June 3, 1919, a bomb went off outside the home of Attorney General Mitchell

Palmer. This was a catalyst for the "deportation delirium" of 1919–20. The infamous Palmer raids of 1919 gave rise to thousands of arrests, which in turn led to the deportations of approximately 1,100 immigrants. Some immigrants were held for months without being able to contact their families or lawyers; at least one committed suicide.

The harshness and scale of the deportation regime that emerged in the 1920s did not go unnoticed. Nor did commentators fail to observe that, as deportation law became an attempt to punish post-entry behavior, the United States' resort to deportation was an expulsion of its "own." In 1926, Judge Learned Hand described deportation as "deplorable" for a deportee who was "as much our product as though his mother had borne him on American soil. He knows no other language, no other people, no other habits, than ours; he will be as much a stranger in Poland as any one born of ancestors who immigrated in the seventeenth century. However heinous his crimes, deportation is to him exile, a dreadful punishment, abandoned by the common consent of all civilized peoples."[33]

In the early twentieth century, the federal government also began to resort to denaturalization in conjunction with deportation. Denaturalization was a new weapon: it had essentially not existed in the nineteenth century. In 1906, in the wake of a controversy regarding naturalization fraud in a St. Louis election, Congress enacted a denaturalization act that provided for the first time for the setting aside of naturalizations procured through fraud. Thereafter, the government moved to denaturalize individuals not only to set aside fraudulent naturalizations, but also to render deportable those it deemed undesirable.

At the height of wartime hostility toward "hyphenism," German Americans became vulnerable to denaturalization for expressing what looked like sympathy for their country of origin. In legal terms, such individuals were denaturalized for having lacked "complete renunciation of all foreign allegiance," a requirement of naturalization law, at the time citizenship was granted. The situations in which the government decided to act bordered on the absurd, but are revealing of the atmosphere of intimidation that immigrants lived through. On October 17, 1917, Carl August Darmer, a German immigrant naturalized in

---

[33] *United States ex rel. Klonis v. Davis*, 13 F.2d 630, 630 (2d Cir. 1926).

1888, refused to buy Liberty Bonds, adding that he "would rather throw all his property into the bay than buy one $50 Liberty Bond." Darmer was denaturalized by a federal district court on the ground that, because attachment to one's native country should weaken over time, Darmer's refusal to buy Liberty Bonds almost thirty years after naturalizing permitted the inference that his attachment to Germany at the time of his naturalization was strong enough to constitute a non-renunciation of German nationality. The decision was echoed in another denaturalization case in New Jersey, where a German immigrant who had been a citizen for almost forty years was denaturalized for refusing to support the American Red Cross or the YMCA fund and for saying that he did not want the United States to win the war.[34]

The government also resorted to denaturalization to get rid of politically troublesome individuals. In the early twentieth century, the anarchist leader Emma Goldman was among its most prominent victims. The government had tried to deport Goldman for years but had failed because she was a naturalized U.S. citizen. Ultimately, however, the government discovered her Achilles heel: the derivative citizenship of women. Goldman had become a citizen as a result of her husband's naturalization. In 1909, her husband was denaturalized after twenty-five years as a citizen. Thereafter, the government insisted that Goldman had also lost her citizenship. Reclassified as an alien, she became deportable. Goldman's case was not unique. Anarchists could find their naturalizations set aside on the ground that their anarchism implied a lack of allegiance to the United States and, consequently, that their naturalizations had been fraudulently procured. Once denaturalized, they could be deported.[35]

A particularly damning exercise of the denaturalization power was the federal government's attempt to set aside the naturalizations of those who were ruled, after having procured citizenship, not to be "white." In the 1920s, in the aftermath of the *Thind* decision, the federal government began to strip naturalized Asian Indians of their citizenship. At least sixty-five people were thus denaturalized. Arriving with his family in 1915, Vaishno Das Bagai had naturalized. In 1928,

---

[34] *United States v. Darmer*, 249 F. 989, 990 (D.D.C. 1918); *United States v. Wursterbarth*, 249 Fed. 908 (D.N.J. 1918).

[35] *United States v. Swelgin*, 254 F. 884 (D. Or. 1918).

stripped of his citizenship, he committed suicide. In the note he left behind, Bagai wrote: "But now they come to me and say, I am no longer an American citizen ... What have I made of myself and my children? We cannot exercise our rights, we cannot leave this country. Humility and insults, who are responsible for all this? ... Obstacles this way, blockades that way, and the bridges burnt behind."[36]

Denaturalization peaked between the mid-1920s and the beginning of World War II. Thousands lost their citizenship during this period. Naturalization, it turned out, could not protect immigrants from being reclassified as aliens.

## Strategies of Disowning: Making Americans Foreigners

If early-twentieth-century immigrants were excluded and expelled from polity and territory on grounds of race, poverty, and political opinion, stripped of the vote, and subjected to pervasive legal discrimination when it came to employment and welfare, so were large segments of those inside the community. Those who were lesser members of the polity could find themselves rendered foreign in a variety of ways.

### *Disfranchisement, Economic Discrimination, and Internal Borders*
Formal participation in the polity increased dramatically during the first half of the twentieth century as a consequence of the ratification in 1920 of the Nineteenth Amendment, which granted the suffrage to women. Despite increases in the extension of the franchise, however, on the eve of World War II, millions of Americans remained unable to vote. In 1940, an article in the *New Republic* reported that American citizens could be barred from voting for more than fifty reasons, ranging from conviction as a felon to pauperism to adultery to miscegenation. When one added to these formal bars to voting "the terrorism which prevents Negroes and unpopular minorities from voting," the article's author speculated, "the wonder is that anyone is left to go to the polls."[37] Moreover, in the case of women, the right to vote did not automatically imply the right to hold public office. Several states had to pass special legislation to confer the latter upon women.

---

[36] Takaki, *Strangers from a Different Shore*, p. 300.
[37] Quoted in Keyssar, *Right to Vote*, p. 180.

The country's qualified record on opening up the franchise and public offices went along with a decidedly mixed record when it came to women's and racial minorities' employment opportunities. Sex and race proved no less effective as barriers to employment than alienage. Women were barred from many trades and professions, or were engaged on unequal terms, even as their workforce participation grew. The country's racial minorities, especially blacks, endured working conditions that were typically worse than those of European immigrants.

The same was true when it came to public entitlements. Women's historians have shown how women were systematically excluded from enjoying many New Deal benefits. The original Social Security legislation, by excluding many female-dominated areas of employment from coverage, denied benefits to more than half of all employed women. When it was revised, the Social Security Act sent mixed messages, rewarding widows who stayed at home and penalizing women who earned their living. This was also the case for the country's racial minorities. Blacks had been largely excluded from much public relief prior to the New Deal. The structure of major New Deal programs, with their exclusion of agricultural workers, furthered this trend. The Social Security Act excluded the majority of black workers. Furthermore, once the New Deal was under way, local administrators of federal programs discriminated openly. An investigator of relief practices reported hearing from a local welfare official: "'If it's a choice between a white man and a Negro, we're taking the white man ... We're taking the white applications first and turning away just as many Negroes as we can. We've got to, because of the mental attitude of the whites. We've been threatened with riots here.'"[38]

Early-twentieth-century Americans also encountered an extensive regime of internal borders that rendered them foreigners – even "illegal aliens" – in their own country. For many, negotiating territories and spaces during the first half of the twentieth century could be a perilous affair, carrying with it the risk of violence and even death.

When it came to indigent Americans, the nineteenth-century settlement laws remained largely in effect. During the Great Depression,

---

[38] Quoted in Fox, *Three Worlds of Relief*, p. 194.

millions of Americans left their communities and set out across the country in search of better opportunities. Just as the United States sought to get rid of poor immigrants during the 1930s, the Depression-induced internal migration led to an intensification of internal territorial restrictions grounded in the concept of legal settlement. Young travelers were especially vulnerable to being ordered to "move on." It was common knowledge among travelers that certain destinations were hostile to outsiders and would exclude or remove them. For example, during his travels through Florida in the early 1930s, eighteen-year-old Washington, DC native Robert Shaw Smith learned from others that Miami city authorities were likely to take him to the county line and leave him there if they learned that he was from out of town. This made Smith stay away from Miami, because "it is pretty tough being left at the county limits of towns in Florida[,] where there is nothing but swamps and bugs."[39]

As great numbers of migrants poured in, states and municipalities petitioned the federal government for assistance. In response, the federal government created two federal programs, the Federal Transient Program (FTP) and the Civilian Conservation Corps, both of which created networks of camps and shelters. It is revealing of how entrenched ideas of local belonging were in the 1930s that FTP officials launched a public relations campaign to combat local hostility to internal migrants. Federal officials urged Americans to "begin to think in terms of our national responsibility for all our fellows."[40]

However, despite an infusion of federal funds, many communities refused to be swayed by appeals to a sense of "national responsibility" for internal economic migrants. Consequences were especially harsh for black migrants. In September 1935, a representative of the Tampa Urban League complained to the Federal Emergency Relief Association director that the FTP had accomplished little for black transients in Florida: "Little or no consideration was given to the Negro transients by your local supervisors ... [E]ven when there was an inclination to turn Negroes back North, only a small fee was allowed for service

[39] All references to Smith in Elisa Alvarez Minoff, "Free to Move? The Law and Politics of Internal Migration in Twentieth-Century America" (PhD diss., Harvard University, 2013), p. 21.

[40] Quoted in Margot Canaday, *The Straight State: Sexuality and Citizenship in Twentieth-Century America* (Princeton, NJ: Princeton University Press, 2009), p. 103.

at private lodging houses, so much so, that they could not keep their places open, and Negro transients have walked until they were completely exhausted, some having collapsed on the porches of Negro parsonages."[41]

The end of the FTP in 1935 brought about a reinvigoration of local territorial controls. In November 1935, a committee reporting to the Los Angeles chief of police, James E. Davis, deliberated on how it might best prevent "indigent alien transients" from entering the city (revealingly, the word "alien" did not here refer to non-citizens but to any "person entering the state without visible means of support whose legal residence is foreign to the State of California").[42] In February 1936, Davis set up a force to patrol the state's borders. Eventually, because it was determined to be in violation of the California Constitution, the Los Angeles border guard withdrew. By this time, however, Florida and Colorado had created their own border patrols to guard their territories from indigent out-of-state migrants.

As the experience of black transients suggests, territorial and spatial restrictions and controls were employed in a pervasive way, and to devastating effect, against racial and national minorities. If it intersected with the poor laws, the overall logic was part of a larger structure of racial control and subordination.

Despite statutory grants of citizenship to Native Americans in the 1920s, most Americans in the early twentieth century deemed Native Americans, especially if they lived on reservations, incapable of participating in the affairs of a modern polity. But Native Americans who took up residence outside reservations immediately confronted racial segregation. In the West and Southwest, they shared the fates of Asian and Mexican immigrants and their descendants. In 1924, the California Supreme Court declared that it was "not in violation of the organic law of the state or nation ... to require Indian children or others in whom racial differences exist, to attend separate schools, provided such schools are equal ... with those furnished for children of the white race."[43] De facto school segregation of children of Native American, Asian, and Mexican descent was thus widespread in the

---

[41] Quoted in Minoff, "Free to Move?" p. 110.

[42] Id., pp. 123–24.

[43] *Piper et al. v. Big Pine School District of Inyo County et al.*, 226 P. 926, 929 (Cal. 1924).

West and Southwest. Racially restrictive covenants were used as well against those of Asian and Mexican descent.

Blacks experienced far more thoroughgoing segregation. For them, even as they embarked on their Great Migration northward beginning around 1910, the early-twentieth-century United States was a country of intricate borders enforced by law, custom, social convention, humiliation, and violence. The forms segregation took emerged through an ongoing battle between white segregationists and black resisters.

In 1910, the City of Baltimore passed a residential segregation ordinance that barred blacks from buying property on blocks where the majority of occupants were white, and vice versa. Several cities followed Baltimore's lead. These laws were challenged in state courts, where, unlike other Jim Crow laws, they met a mixed reaction. Eventually, in *Buchanan v. Warley* (1917), the U.S. Supreme Court struck down a Louisville, Kentucky, residential segregation ordinance.[44] The case was an important early victory for the National Association for the Advancement of Colored People.

Undeterred, restrictionists looked for other means of keeping blacks out of white neighborhoods. They came upon the racially restrictive covenant, according to which private parties bound themselves and their successors not to sell to blacks. After the U.S. Supreme Court upheld racially restrictive covenants in 1926, they spread like wildfire.[45] However, restrictionists also resorted to violence and other discriminatory real estate practices. In the early twentieth century, blacks' homes could be bombed or burned to deter them from moving into white neighborhoods. Between 1917 and 1921, dozens of black homes were bombed in Chicago. In 1924, the National Association of Real Estate Boards modified its "code of ethics" to read: "A Realtor should never be instrumental in introducing into a neighborhood a character of property or occupancy, members of any race or nationality, or any individuals whose presence will clearly be detrimental to property values in that neighborhood."[46] Critical support for segregation came as well from the federal government. The Federal Housing Administration's 1936 *Underwriting Manual* informed appraisers that

[44] *Buchanan v. Warley*, 245 U.S. 60 (1917).
[45] *Corrigan v. Buckley*, 271 U.S. 323 (1926).
[46] Quoted in Michael Jones-Correa, "The Origins and Diffusion of Racial Restrictive Covenants," *Political Science Quarterly* 115, no. 4 (Winter 2000–2001): 541–68, 564.

"if a neighborhood is to retain stability it is necessary that properties shall continue to be occupied by the same social and racial classes." Appraisers were to predict changes in racial composition and
instructed to respect and encourage racially restrictive covenants.[47]
The beneficiaries of these restrictive practices were native-born whites,
to be sure, but also Eastern and Southern European immigrants who
were acceding to "whiteness" and an American identity through the
ritual of homeownership.

As reflected in these patterns of spatial discrimination, for many
whites, the black presence in the country, because it could no longer
be expunged, had to be managed and kept at bay. It is not surprising,
then, that the 1920s witnessed yet another "back to Africa" movement, this time sponsored by the Jamaican immigrant Marcus Garvey.
Garvey's United Negro Improvement Association enjoyed great pop-
ularity with blacks in the United States and the Caribbean before it
became mired in fraud. From the perspective of immigration officials,
however, Garvey's radical message of black empowerment was the
problem. In 1917, J. Edgar Hoover, who had overseen many of the
Palmer era deportations, began an initial investigation into Garvey's
activities. In 1923, Garvey was convicted of mail fraud in connection
with his business. He was deported in 1927.

### Involuntary Expatriation

At the same time it set about denaturalizing naturalized immigrants,
Congress also began the involuntary expatriation of U.S. citizens –
that is, the conversion of naturalized and native-born citizens into
aliens against their will for having committed certain acts. In 1907,
Congress passed a law that established the loss of U.S. nationality
upon an individual's naturalization in a foreign country, taking an
oath of allegiance to a foreign state, or (in the case of a naturalized
citizen) return to a residence in his former homeland for more than
two years. Patrick Weil writes that the 1907 expatriation act "began
a period of fear and paranoia that would greatly expand by 1940."[48]

---

[47] Federal Housing Administration, *Underwriting Manual: Underwriting and Valuation
Procedure Under Title II of the National Housing Act* (Washington, DC: U.S.
Government Printing Office, 1936), sec. 233.

[48] Patrick Weil, *The Sovereign Citizen: Denaturalization and the Origins of the
American Republic* (Philadelphia: University of Pennsylvania Press, 2012), p. 55.

Revealingly, the 1907 expatriation law also provided that "any American woman who marries a foreigner shall take the nationality of her husband."[49]

The United States was by no means unique in expatriating women who married foreigners. Various countries, including Great Britain, did so as well. Nevertheless, the timing of the expatriation law, which essentially codified women's second-class citizenship as a matter of nationality law, was especially inopportune because it coincided with a period in which American women were, precisely, agitating for full political membership.

In 1915, the U.S. Supreme Court rejected a challenge to the 1907 expatriation law on the basis of the "ancient principle" of "the identity of husband and wife."[50] Thereafter, thousands of American women were denationalized – literally converted into aliens – for marrying foreign citizens. Historian Candice Bredbenner writes that, in the nativist political culture of the early twentieth century, "a citizen woman's marriage to a foreigner became vulnerable to interpretation as a brazenly un-American act and to the apposite punishment of expatriation."[51] In popular discourse, American women who married non-citizens were accused of being dazzled by the lure of a European title. In 1908, Representative Charles McGavin of Illinois accused such women of having made a "mockery of the most sacred relations of life"; he wanted to honor "those true American women who spurned the wiles of earls, lords, and counts for the love of His Majesty, an American citizen."[52]

The overwhelming majority of American women married to aliens had not, of course, married wealthy European aristocrats. Suddenly rendered aliens, such women found that they could be excluded or removed from the country, barred from occupations and professions reserved for citizens, and denied access to public relief. The impact was severe at a time when the forces of nativism were increasing alien legal disabilities. The situation of Florence Bain Gual in the early 1920s exemplifies the predicament of many women. After fifteen years as a

---

[49] Act of March 2, 1907, 34 Stat. 1228.
[50] *Mackenzie v. Hare*, 239 U.S. 299, 311 (1915).
[51] Candice L. Bredbenner, *A Nationality of Her Own: Women, Marriage, and the Law of Citizenship* (Berkeley: University of California Press, 1998), p. 6.
[52] Quoted in id., p. 63.

public school teacher in New York City, Gual discovered that marrying a Cuban man had jeopardized her employment. Furthermore, her husband had deserted her and their child. Gual put it thus: "I am the daughter of an American citizen and the mother of an American citizen, yet I am to be deprived of my livelihood in my own country because of the citizenship of a man."[53] During World War I, women married to citizens of the Central Powers discovered that, as a result of involuntary expatriation, they had become "enemy aliens." The Alien Property Custodian confiscated from such women property that amounted to 25 million dollars.

Once women won the vote in 1920, it became much harder to argue that women's political membership was derivative of that of their husbands and that their nationality should therefore follow that of their husbands. Under considerable pressure from women's groups, in the 1922 Cable Act, Congress partially repealed the 1907 expatriation act and at the same time ended the automatic naturalization of women married to male U.S. citizens. However, the Cable Act still mandated the involuntary expatriation of women who married aliens racially barred from citizenship, declaring that "any woman citizen who marries an alien ineligible to citizenship shall cease to be a citizen."[54] Therefore, native-born Asian American female citizens married to Asian men lost their citizenship. As aliens, they found themselves racially ineligible to citizenship. This provision was repealed only in 1931. It was only in 1934, furthermore, that American women achieved equality with men when it came to the transmission of their nationality to their foreign-born children.

### Mingling Citizens and Immigrants

Public and private acts directed against immigrants bore devastating consequences for U.S. citizens. Citizens suffered from having immigrant members of their families excluded, deported, denaturalized, and subjected to violence, intimidation, and humiliation; they lost out when immigrant breadwinners were denied economic opportunities; and they experienced the impoverishment of public discourse as immigrant political activity and speech were suppressed.

---

[53] All references to Gual in id., p. 83.
[54] Act of September 22, 1922, 42 Stat. 1021.

In many instances, however, citizens were also compelled in a far more direct fashion to share the fates of their immigrant relatives. When citizens thus shared the fates of immigrants, they experienced their own enforced foreignness vis-à-vis the polity, a non-belonging imposed upon them by their own government. According to scholarly estimates, as many as half of the *repatriados* in the mass deportation of Mexican immigrants in the early 1930s might have been U.S. citizens.

As discussed previously, the federal government had repeatedly treated citizens of Asian descent like foreigners insofar as it subjected Asian American communities to immigration raids, required all individuals of Asian descent to carry papers to prove their legal status, and refused individuals of Asian descent due process rights at the border even when they claimed to be birthright citizens of the United States. Such non-belonging continued to be imposed on Asian Americans through the first half of the twentieth century. Especially after the creation of the U.S. Border Patrol, Mexican Americans in the U.S.-Mexico borderlands had a similar experience: they were routinely taken for and treated like Mexican immigrants.

The most egregious instance of impressing non-belonging upon Asian American citizens came during World War II. On February 19, 1942, in Executive Order 9066, President Roosevelt authorized the U.S. Army to seize control of parts of California, Oregon, Washington, and Arizona and to exclude and remove therefrom all persons as military commanders deemed appropriate. Pursuant to the president's order, General John DeWitt issued "Civilian Exclusion Orders" that applied to "all persons of Japanese ancestry, *both alien and non-alien.*"[55] The use of the term "non-alien" conveys, more clearly than anything else, how American citizens of Japanese ancestry were viewed at the time.

During World War II, Japanese Americans were considered foreign in a way that Italian Americans and German Americans were not. General DeWitt wrote: "The Japanese race is an *enemy race* and while many second and third generation Japanese born on United States soil, possessed of United States citizenship, have become 'Americanized,' the racial

---

[55] See, e.g., Civilian Exclusion Order No. 34, 7 Fed. Reg. 3967 (May 28, 1942) (emphasis added).

strains are undiluted."[56] He also testified in 1943: "It makes no difference whether [a person of Japanese descent] is an American citizen, he is still a Japanese. American citizenship does not necessarily determine loyalty."[57] Even at the time, however, the egregiousness of what was attempted was widely recognized. Carey McWilliams observed: "A precedent of the gravest possible significance has been established in ordering the removal and internment of this one racial minority."[58] Nevertheless, the U.S. Supreme Court approved internment in *Hirabayashi v. United States* (1943) and *Korematsu v. United States* (1944).[59] Between 110,000 and 120,000 individuals, two-thirds of whom were native-born American citizens, were relocated to internment camps.

In July 1944, Congress passed the Denationalization Act, which authorized U.S. citizens to renounce their citizenship. During the winter of 1944–45, approximately 5,500 Japanese American internees attempted to renounce their U.S. citizenship. The motives behind renunciation were various, including avoidance of the draft. But at least some sought to give up their U.S. citizenship because of the way they had been treated. A Japanese American woman observed that the U.S. government had treated her U.S. citizenship as "but scrap-papers that gave us no privileges what so ever ... Therefore thousands of us rose decisively to clarify our status by fulfilling our duties for a true sovereign [Japan]."[60] The saga of the renunciants was complex. Eventually, many would claim that they had been pressured into renouncing their citizenship and sought to rescind their decisions. After a protracted

---

[56] "Final Report of General DeWitt," quoted in Jacobus tenBroek, Edward N. Barnhart, and Floyd W. Matson, *Prejudice, War, and the Constitution: Causes and Consequences of the Evacuation of the Japanese Americans in World War II* (Berkeley: University of California Press, 1954), p. 110 (emphasis added).

[57] Testimony of Lt. General John L. DeWitt, Commanding General of Western Defense Command, *Investigation of Congested Areas, Hearings Before a Subcommittee of Naval Affairs, House of Representatives. Seventy-eighth Congress, First Session Pursuant to H. Res. 30, A Resolution authorizing and Directing an Investigation of the Progress of the War Effort*, pt. III (Washington, DC: U.S. Government Printing Office, 1943), pp. 739–40.

[58] Quoted in Daniel Kanstroom, *Deportation Nation: Outsiders in American History* (Cambridge, MA: Harvard University Press, 2007), p. 209.

[59] *Hirabayashi v. United States*, 320 U.S. 81 (1943); *Korematsu v. United States*, 323 U.S. 214 (1944).

[60] Quoted in Mae Ngai, *Impossible Subjects: Illegal Aliens and the Making of Modern America* (Princeton, NJ: Princeton University Press, 2004), p. 190.

legal struggle, some 5,000 Japanese American renunciants reclaimed their citizenship.

### Colonialism: Granting and Refusing Citizenship to the Colonized

In the early twentieth century, in a reprise of a pre–Civil War position, race became once again a barrier to the formal citizenship of those unambiguously subject to American sovereign power. This time, colonized subjects were involved.

Questions arose over the citizenship of the residents of the United States' newly acquired colonies of Puerto Rico and the Philippines. The 1898 Treaty of Paris, which concluded the Spanish-American War, gave "natives of the Peninsula" – in other words, the Iberian Peninsula – the option of adopting U.S. citizenship or remaining Spanish nationals. When it came to the "civil rights and political status of the native inhabitants of the territories," however, the Treaty stated that these would be "determined by Congress."[61] It was as if the United States had learned from the "mistake" of extending U.S. citizenship to the non-white inhabitants of the territories acquired from Mexico in 1848.

The ambiguities created by the Treaty of Paris quickly transmogrified into questions regarding the applicability of the U.S. Constitution to the newly acquired territories. If the U.S. Constitution had extended to the Philippines and Puerto Rico, children born to residents of the islands would have been birthright citizens under the Fourteenth Amendment. Between 1901 and 1904, however, in a series of cases known as the *Insular Cases*, the U.S. Supreme court ruled that the U.S. Constitution did *not* automatically extend to the territories. Among the concerns expressed to justify these rulings was the "extremely serious" consequence that, had the U.S. Constitution applied automatically, children born of natives of these territories, "whether savages or civilized," would be birthright citizens of the United States.[62] As a result, after the cession of the Philippines and Puerto Rico to the United States, their residents ceased to be aliens vis-à-vis the United States, but were also not birthright citizens under the Fourteenth Amendment. At a minimum, not being an alien meant, as the U.S. Supreme Court clarified in *Gonzales v. Williams* (1904), that Puerto

[61] Treaty of Paris, 30 Stat. 1754, art. IX.
[62] *Downes v. Bidwell*, 182 U.S. 244, 279 (1901) (opinion of Brown, J.).

Ricans and Filipinos could not be excluded from the mainland United States as alien immigrants.[63]

If residents of the Philippines and Puerto Rico wished to become U.S. citizens, they would have to naturalize. Race would determine their eligibility to naturalize. In *In re Alverto* (1912), a federal district court in Pennsylvania was asked to rule upon the naturalization petition of an individual of mixed Spanish and Filipino descent. Conceding that "[c]itizens of the Philippine Islands or of Porto Rico, while not citizens of the United States, are not aliens," the Court decided that the applicant was ineligible for U.S. citizenship on the ground that he was not a "white" person.[64] "Whites" from the Philippines and Puerto Rico could, however, naturalize.

With respect to Puerto Rico, the position on citizenship was statutorily reversed. In the Jones Act of 1917, Congress enacted a bill of rights for Puerto Rico and extended U.S. citizenship to Puerto Ricans. Despite the statutory extension of citizenship to Puerto Ricans, the U.S. Supreme Court insisted that, because Puerto Rico was an unincorporated territory, only "fundamental" – as opposed to all – constitutional rights applied there, thereby reinscribing the idea of Puerto Ricans as lesser citizens.[65] The case of the Philippines was more complicated. If American territorial acquisitions in earlier periods had been premised upon territories' eventual admission to statehood once white majorities were achieved, admitting the Philippine islands to statehood was inconceivable to many Americans. Nevertheless, they were constrained by the discourse of "benevolent" imperialism. If Filipinos were not U.S. citizens at birth and were barred from naturalizing on grounds of race, they were nevertheless designated as American "nationals." Because they were free from the racial bars that applied to other Asians, Filipino immigrants came largely to replace excluded Chinese and Japanese labor.

Despite their status as "nationals," however, Filipinos soon fell victim to racial violence. Anti-Filipino racial violence at the grassroots level undergirded the national nativist lobby's efforts to pass legislation excluding Filipinos. In the late 1920s, the California Joint Immigration

---

[63] *Gonzales v. Williams*, 192 U.S. 1 (1904).
[64] *In re Alverto*, 198 F. 688, 690 (1912).
[65] *Balzac v. Porto Rico*, 258 U.S. 298 (1922).

Committee, American Federation of Labor, and the American Legion all endorsed Filipino exclusion. Congressman Richard Welch of California introduced legislation that would reclassify Filipinos from "nationals" into "aliens" so that they could be excluded from the United States. At the hearing on Welch's proposed bill, an irate Samuel Dickstein, chair of the House Immigration Committee, dubbed the bill "the first bill of its character, which deals with a race of people under the American flag, that I have ever seen before."[66] Congress initially dragged its heels. Eventually, however, the desire to exclude Filipinos mounted to the point that exclusionists allied themselves with Filipino nationalists. They finally proved successful. The Tydings-McDuffie Act of 1934 granted the Philippines independence and simultaneously transformed Filipinos from American "nationals" into aliens. As aliens, Filipinos were subject to the national origins quota legislation. Simultaneously, there was an official attempt to expel resident Filipinos. The 1935 Repatriation Act paid Filipinos' transportation back to the Philippines provided they abandoned rights of reentry into the country. Between 1936 and 1941, under the auspices of repatriation legislation, more than 2,000 Filipino nationals returned to the Philippines.

## Conclusion

By the beginning of World War II, as a result of decades of growing federal power over immigrants, immigrants could be excluded and removed from both territory and polity on grounds of race, poverty, criminal background, and political opinion. They experienced potent forms of economic discrimination while in the country and underwent intimidation, denunciation, denaturalization, and relocation in times of war. Not every immigrant group experienced these difficulties the same way. The European immigrant experience differed markedly from the Asian and Mexican. But even European immigrants were not immune to the shadow of overweening federal power.

All of this suggests that the gulf between citizen and alien had become considerably wider than in previous decades. But millions of

---

[66] "Exclusion of Immigration from the Philippine Islands," Hearings, House Immigration Committee, April 10, 1930, 71st Cong., 2d Sess., 6.

native-born citizens and nationals suffered disabilities similar to those suffered by immigrants. Women, racial minorities, and the indigent were barred from employment and public entitlements and subjected to a pervasive regime of internal borders as a means of ensuring their subordination. Women who married non-citizens could be turned into aliens; Mexican Americans and Asian Americans repatriated or interned along with Mexican and Asian immigrants; American "nationals" of Filipino descent reclassified as excludable immigrants. If immigrants were increasingly becoming a unique underclass, many Americans not only found it hard to claim full membership of the polity, but even risked being transformed into aliens in their own country.

# 7

# A Rights Revolution?

## Introduction

In the aftermath of World War II, the United States emerged as the world's leading power. As the country plunged into the Cold War, the emergence of a vast military-industrial complex, combined with the expansion of consumer culture, resulted in a quarter century of robust economic growth. During this heyday of American capitalism, both Republicans and Democrats, but especially the latter, were open to state intervention in the economy and the funding of social programs.

During this period, newly emboldened by the United States' victory over Fascism and its ideological struggle with the Soviet Union, the country's historically marginalized and subordinated groups demanded that it make good on its stated liberal and egalitarian commitments. The resulting "rights revolution" had the effect of strengthening individual rights, proscribing formal legal racism and sexism, and injecting a measure of equality into the polity. Various spaces – public and private, educational and residential, professional and recreational, political and civic – that had once been closed to blacks, Native Americans, Latinos, Asians, women, and others opened up through force of law. The constitutionalization of a "right to travel" throughout national territory dismantled the internal borders that states, counties, and localities had long set in place to control the influx and presence of the native-born poor. Between 1950 and 1980, the U.S. Supreme Court also made it much harder for the U.S. government to expatriate

American citizens against their will and thereby to convert citizens into aliens. These developments did not by any means bring older hierarchies to an end, but they did much to diminish domestic groups' enforced foreignness vis-à-vis the polity.

From the perspective of immigration and citizenship law, the post–World War II period was one of decidedly mixed consequences. One change that took place – a consequence of the country's Cold War commitments and its rights revolution – was both important and enduring. After 1965, race, ethnicity, and national origin were no longer formal bars to immigration and naturalization. If formal racial classifications fell away, however, critical features of the late-nineteenth- and early-twentieth-century immigration regime became entrenched. In the post–World War II period, there would be no questioning of closed national borders, numerical restrictions, country quotas, and long waiting times. When combined with the country's desire for cheap labor and the complicity of the state, numerical restrictions would result in a vast expansion of the population of exploitable undocumented immigrants.

Furthermore, even as it played a crucial role in engineering a rights revolution for citizens, the U.S. Supreme Court repeatedly affirmed the federal government's plenary power over the exclusion, deportation, and naturalization of aliens. Whether in the context of gender discrimination, free speech, political affiliation, or welfare rights, the Court declared that Congress could make rules vis-à-vis immigrants that would be constitutionally impermissible if made vis-à-vis citizens. Some of this strengthening of federal power came at the expense of the states, whose ability to craft alienage law was curtailed during the same period. But judicial deference to the federal government's power over immigrants – which at its height was perhaps greater than during the Chinese exclusion era – ultimately enabled the emergence of an immensely powerful federal machinery that acted with relative impunity against both documented and undocumented immigrants.

Thus, it is fair to say that, with some exceptions (such as the end of formal racial barriers to immigration and naturalization and the erosion of the states' authority over immigrants), the post–World War II rights revolution for citizens largely did not redound to the benefit of immigrants. The power of the postwar immigration state, and the devastation it could wreak on immigrants' lives, would manifest itself over and over again, climaxing in the mass deportations of the very end of the twentieth century. When the rights revolution for citizens is juxtaposed against the simultaneous affirmation of plenary power vis-à-vis aliens, what becomes clear in the post–World War II era is a greatly widened gap between citizen and alien. During the second half of the twentieth century, among the country's most vulnerable internal foreigners were resident immigrants, documented and especially undocumented.

None of this is to suggest that the promise of the rights revolution was fully realized for American citizens. This was especially the case as, during the last two decades of the twentieth century, the country changed course. Globalization and de-industrialization meant that American workers experienced declining real wages and stagnant family incomes. After the election of Ronald Reagan in 1980 and Republicans' seizure of control of Congress, there was a cutting back of federal programs and a delegation of power to the states. In legislatures, on the bench, and in the public sphere, conservatives sought to slow progress toward social equality and reverse the rights revolution. The consequences were harsh. Economic inequalities, always mapped onto racial and gender difference, worsened. The promise of individual rights was blunted. If certain ways of restricting the movement and presence of American citizens were taken off the table during the civil rights era, others took their place. Particularly in the post-1980 period, then, parallels between the fates of poor, racialized citizens and poor, racialized resident aliens were striking. The rendering foreign of insiders was particularly acute when citizens found themselves trapped in the dragnet of immigration law enforcement and literally treated like aliens.

The remainder of this chapter is organized as follows. First, it discusses the rights revolution and the concomitant internal invigoration of citizenship that followed World War II. Second, it explores the development of immigration and citizenship law between World War II and the early twenty-first century, covering the relationship between plenary power and the rights revolution, shifts in immigration policy, the evolving career of nativism, and the state's creation and treatment of internal foreigners. Finally, the conclusion catalogues briefly the various ways U.S. citizens continued to be rendered foreign vis-à-vis the polity in the post-1980 period.

## A New Citizenship for Americans: The Postwar Rights Revolution

The causes of the post–World War II rights revolution are varied. The victory over Fascism, the propaganda war with the Soviet Union, the spread of international human rights norms, decolonization in Asia and Africa, changes in personnel on the bench, party conflict, and, most important, the various campaigns of racial minorities, women's groups, and labor groups all played a part. Scholars disagree on what exactly the rights revolution consisted of, when it began and ended, and how transformative it really was. There is no doubt that its trajectory was twisting, its victories mixed, its results frustrated. Some groups – notably, American Communists – were decidedly not beneficiaries and, indeed, experienced more intense repression after World War II than they had before. Nevertheless, it is reasonable to assert that a post–World War II rights revolution occurred.

Three aspects of the rights revolution will be discussed here, each relevant because it altered past practices: first, the dismantling of formal barriers of race and sex, which played a significant role in incorporating racial minorities and women into the polity and opening up public and private spaces to them; second, the judicial invigoration of a domestic "right to travel" that ended centuries-old restrictions on the mobility and presence of America's poor; and finally, new limitations on the power of the U.S. government to expatriate Americans against their will.

### *Dismantling Barriers and Desegregating Spaces*

Most racial minorities had experienced some form of exclusion from the suffrage during the first half of the twentieth century. Beginning in the 1920s with attacks on the white primary, blacks' long struggle to win the vote scored piecemeal victories in the courts before registering a major victory with the passage of the Voting Rights Act of 1965. Initially intended to last for only a short period, the Act suspended restrictive voting practices in states and counties where it was determined that less than 50 percent of adults had voted in 1964. Suspensions were to last for five years; voter registration practices were subject to federal scrutiny; and governments of areas placed under federal scrutiny were to obtain federal approval before altering voting procedures. The increases in black voter registration in the

South were nothing short of dramatic. By the 1980s, with the major exception of convict exclusions, universal adult suffrage had largely become a reality in the United States. Those classified as citizens would no longer suffer a classic alien legal disability.

For blacks, the constitutional decisions that began the long process of dismantling racial segregation, both public and private, were also crucial to reducing their outsider status. In *Shelley v. Kraemer* (1948), the U.S. Supreme Court struck down racially restrictive covenants as unconstitutional.[1] In *Brown v. Board of Education* (1954), the Court declared unconstitutional the segregation of public schools and with it the "separate but equal" regime of *Plessy v. Ferguson* (1896).[2] The civil rights legislation of the 1960s targeted public and private discrimination in a range of contexts, from schools to public accommodations to employment to housing. By the 1970s, efforts were underfoot to hasten the incorporation of racial minorities through affirmative action programs.

For American women, who were waging their own distinct battle against gender hierarchies, the rights revolution meant that they were more able than in earlier periods to step out from the shadow of men. The U.S. Supreme Court's privacy decisions in the context of contraception and abortion proved enormously important.[3] In the 1970s, the Court also extended the Equal Protection Clause to laws that discriminated on the basis of gender.[4] That same decade, feminists began a long struggle to criminalize marital rape. Although the results were admittedly mixed (in some states, marital rape is still treated differently from rape), they succeeded in chipping away at the core of common law coverture: the husband's control of the physical body of his wife. Legal rules that made women's domicile derive from that of her husband also faded by the 1990s.

Native Americans, the country's oldest foreigners, were also beneficiaries of the anti-discrimination impulses of the rights revolution. However, their post–World War II experience was distinct. During the 1950s termination era, various tribes lost legal recognition as tribes pursuant to the government's initiative to accelerate assimilation.

---

[1] *Shelley v. Kraemer,* 334 U.S. 1 (1948).
[2] *Brown v. Board of Education,* 347 U.S. 483 (1954).
[3] *Griswold v. Connecticut,* 381 U.S. 479 (1965); *Roe v. Wade,* 410 U.S. 113 (1973).
[4] *Frontiero v. Richardson,* 411 U.S. 677 (1973); *Reed v. Reed,* 404 U.S. 71 (1971).

Concurrently, there began a complex experiment in recognizing and restoring Native American sovereignty. Much of this took the form of redrawing jurisdictional lines. Thus, in the key case of *Williams v. Lee* (1959), the U.S. Supreme Court held that a state court had no jurisdiction in a case brought against Native Americans by a non–Native American merchant operating a general store on a reservation.[5] In *United States v. Mazurie* (1975), the Court declared that "Indian tribes are unique aggregations possessing attributes of sovereignty over both their members and their territory."[6] Despite such recognitions, however, congressional plenary power over Native Americans loomed in the background. Of postwar Indian sovereignty, legal scholar T. Alexander Aleinikoff writes: "Tribal sovereignty ... is generally more limited than state sovereignty ... [W]hile Congress has authority to establish and alter reservation boundaries and regulate tribal civil and criminal jurisdiction, state borders and governmental processes are largely immune from direct federal control. But tribes also possess authority not recognized in the states, such as the power to determine membership rules (which deny political participation to non-tribal residents of a reservation) and to regulate access to reservation territory."[7]

It is important to underscore that, for racial minorities, especially blacks, the postwar civil rights struggle was very much a struggle to break down internal territorial and spatial borders that whites all over the country defended vigorously, even violently, in the 1950s, 1960s, and 1970s. Although there are multiple sites of study when it comes to the struggles around desegregation, both North and South, historian Kevin Kruse's important study of Atlanta details especially well the range of territorial and spatial strategies to which whites resorted, even as they represented blacks as invading foreigners.

The initial territorial strategies Atlanta's white political class devised in the 1940s were designed to keep the city majority white. In the 1940s, the city's celebrated mayor, William Hartsfield, urged annexation of surrounding white communities, revealing in the process that he saw the in-migration of blacks in terms of attack and defense. As he

[5] *Williams v. Lee*, 358 U.S. 217 (1959).
[6] *United States v. Mazurie*, 419 U.S. 544, 557 (1975) (citations omitted).
[7] T. Alexander Aleinikoff, *Semblances of Sovereignty: The Constitution, the State, and American Citizenship* (Cambridge, MA: Harvard University Press, 2002), p. 98.

put it: "[Negroes] stay right in the city limits and grow *by taking more white territory inside Atlanta* ... With the federal government insisting on political recognition of negroes in local affairs, the time is not far distant when they will become a potent force in Atlanta *if our white citizens are just going to move out and give it to them.*" To combat this development, the city promulgated an annexation plan that went into effect in 1952: Atlanta's black population dropped from 41 percent of the total to 33 percent.[8]

However, annexation proved not to be a lasting solution. The forces of segregation had long compelled blacks to live crammed into neighborhoods with substandard housing, infrastructure, and services. As desegregation gathered strength, blacks with the means sought, not surprisingly, to escape these confines.

The responses of whites ranged widely, from hostility to outright violence. As Atlanta's battle for the integration of neighborhoods played out street by street and block by block, whites policed the borders of their neighborhoods. They formed neighborhood associations that sought to dissuade or even reverse sales to blacks. Klansmen threatened to destroy homes advertised for sale to blacks. Black-owned homes in white neighborhoods fell prey to arson and bombings. In a faint echo of the efforts of the American Colonization Society, White Citizens Councils in Southern cities even spoke of subsidizing the passage of black families who wanted to move north.

Such strategies failed. Over the course of the 1950s, 1960s, and 1970s, many spaces formally and informally closed to blacks for decades were opened up to them. These included not just neighborhoods, but schools, parks, and golf courses, as well as privately owned restaurants, diners, and department stores. Desegregation enabled blacks not just to enter, but to be present in, spaces and territories on terms more equal to those enjoyed by whites, to shrug off their foreignness vis-à-vis such spaces, and to reclaim a social citizenship.

As spatial and territorial barriers fell, what one white Atlantan labeled "the Congolese infiltration" (the phrase itself equating Atlanta's blacks to foreigners) was met by reterritorialization, a reestablishment

---

[8] Quoted in Kevin M. Kruse, *White Flight: Atlanta and the Making of Modern Conservatism* (Princeton, NJ: Princeton University Press, 2005), pp. 37–38 (emphasis added).

of borders.[9] As public spaces and institutions were integrated, whites abandoned them for private ones. As cities became increasingly black, white suburbs expanded. This was not just a Southern phenomenon, but a national one. A Northerner warned of the consequences of deseg- regating Atlanta's bus system in ways that captured the logic: "As of today, Detroit, Chicago, Cleveland public transportation systems are mere shells of their former place in public utility. They are almost aban- doned to the private car – bumper to bumper, one man to a vehicle – definitely to avoid Integration."[10] For a complex of reasons, including the difficulties of obtaining financing and having to pay inflated prices for houses whites abandoned, urban neighborhoods occupied by blacks took on the aspect of decline. So did public institutions exclu- sively patronized by blacks. This was because, as public spaces opened to blacks, cities underfunded them. The long-term consequences of white flight were urban blight and degradation.

### *A New Right to Travel for America's Poor*

The 1960s and 1970s witnessed a vigorous welfare rights movement that, at least relative to the past, resulted in some concrete victories for America's poor. As part of the larger revolution in voting rights jurisprudence, pauper disfranchisement was largely abolished by the early 1970s. Meanwhile, there was a judicial recognition that welfare entitlements were not mere favors bestowed by the state, but property interests to which constitutional due process protections attached.[11] Race and welfare were intimately tied together. In a 1965 speech at Howard University, President Lyndon Johnson recognized that dis- mantling barriers of racial segregation was insufficient and that more needed to be done for America's underclasses. As he put it, it was "not enough just to open the gates of opportunity. All our citizens must have the ability to walk through those gates."[12] "Great Society" pro- grams in areas such as education, health, urban issues, transportation, and economic opportunity were designed to accomplish this.

---

[9] Id., p. 150.
[10] Id., p. 115.
[11] *Goldberg v. Kelly*, 397 U.S. 254 (1970).
[12] Lyndon B. Johnson, "Commencement Address at Howard University: To Fulfill These Rights," June 4, 1965, *Public Papers of the Presidents of the United States: Lyndon B. Johnson, 1965* (Washington, DC: U.S. Government Printing Office, 1966), p. 636.

Along with such developments came much stronger judicial recognition of the citizen's "right to travel," something that the country's poor had been unable to invoke for centuries. Midcentury critics of the settlement laws objected to them on the ground that they illegitimately blurred the distinction between citizen and alien. As citizens, they argued, Americans should have the right to travel to and live in every part of national territory. Denying them this right rendered them akin to aliens. In a speech to the Annual Meeting of Travelers Aid workers in 1940, D.C. Circuit Judge Justin Miller observed that Depression era migrants were angered by laws restricting their movement because, in contradistinction to immigrants, "many of the migrants today are native born, thoroughly conditioned to the philosophy of individual rights, privileges and immunities, so long recognized in this country."[13]

The first major successful challenge to the poor law regime was the landmark case of *Edwards v. California* (1941).[14] In December 1939, Fred Edwards left his home in California for Texas, with the intention of picking up his brother-in-law, Frank Duncan, and bringing him to California. When Edwards arrived in Texas, he learned that Duncan was an indigent person, having last been employed by the Works Progress Administration. When Edwards drove Duncan back to California, he was charged under Section 2615 of the state's Welfare and Institutions Code, which made guilty of a misdemeanor "every person ... that brings ... into the State any indigent person who is not a resident of the State, knowing him to be an indigent person." Edwards was convicted and sentenced to six months' imprisonment in the county jail, although the sentence was suspended.[15]

When the case reached the U.S. Supreme Court, the majority acknowledged that "the spectacle of large segments of our population constantly on the move has given rise to urgent demands upon the ingenuity of government."[16] California's attorney general asserted in his brief that the massive influx of migrants into California had "resulted in problems of health, morals, and especially finance, the proportions of which are staggering."[17] But the state's arguments

[13] Quoted in Minoff, "Free to Move?" p. 198.
[14] *Edwards v. California*, 314 U.S. 160 (1941).
[15] Id. at 171.
[16] Id. at 173.
[17] Id.

proved unavailing. Even though it recognized the problems posed by the influx of migrants into California, the Court struck down the California law as a violation of Congress's interstate commerce powers under Article I, Section 8 of the U.S. Constitution. A state's police power would no longer encompass the right to restrict out-of-state indigents' access to its territory.

In support of the law, California urged that "the concept which underlies [the statute] enjoys a firm basis in English and American history."[18] As previous chapters have suggested, the state could not have been more correct. The U.S. Supreme Court itself had held as much in *New York v. Miln* (1837). In *Edwards*, however, the Court's response was simply and categorically that it no longer considered itself bound by *Miln*. An emerging substantive *national* citizenship, instantiated in New Deal welfare programs, had undermined internal territorial borders. The Court put it thus: "We ... suggest that the theory of the Elizabethan poor laws no longer fits the facts. Recent years, and particularly the past decade, have been marked by a growing recognition that, in an industrial society, the task of providing assistance to the needy has ceased to be local in character."[19]

If the majority in *Edwards* struck down the California law on the ground that it interfered with Congress's constitutional authority over interstate commerce, two concurring opinions – those of Justices Douglas and Jackson – put forth another theory. Justice Douglas expressed the theory thus: "The right to move freely from State to State is an incident of *national* citizenship protected by the privileges and immunities clause of the Fourteenth Amendment."[20] To tolerate state legislation excluding and removing paupers "would ... introduce a caste system utterly incompatible with the spirit of our system of government. It would permit those who were stigmatized as indigents, paupers, or vagabonds to be relegated to an inferior class of citizenship."[21]

Although some states abolished their settlement laws in the aftermath of the *Edwards* decision, many did not. Meanwhile, the discourse linking citizenship to movement, now recognized in concurring

---

[18] Id. at 174.
[19] Id. at 174–75.
[20] Id. at 178 (Douglas, J.) (emphasis in original).
[21] Id. at 181 (Douglas, J.).

opinions in *Edwards*, gathered strength. In a 1955 speech entitled "The Constitution and the Right of Free Movement," the legal scholar and activist Jacobus tenBroek argued that the Commerce Clause afforded inadequate protection to the "right of free movement." That right was a "basic right" and was "presupposed by the system of personal rights which the document [the U.S. Constitution] is designed to protect."[22] TenBroek disaggregated the right to free movement into three distinct rights: the right to be present, the right to leave one's community and to move elsewhere, and the right to non-discrimination in a new community when it came to essential rights and services. Although *Edwards* had made it difficult to bar citizens altogether, this third component of the right to free movement, tenBroek argued, needed considerable invigoration. All over the country, new residents were subject to residence requirements before they could exercise basic rights to vote, use the courts, enter professions, and apply for public assistance. Such requirements, tenBroek argued, were a "vestigial remainder of notions of locality and community dominant in an earlier period of history and geography" and were inconsistent with new conceptions of aid as social insurance.[23] Striking a similar note, social workers underscored that those hurt by settlement laws were "Americans" and "citizens of the United States." The AFL-CIO even denounced state settlement laws as "un-American" because they denied the "fact that, say a Kansan or Virginian or Oregonian are Americans too."[24]

During the second half of the 1960s, lawyers had begun challenging settlement laws everywhere. TenBroek's arguments ended up winning the endorsement of the U.S. Supreme Court. In *Shapiro v. Thompson* (1969), the Court struck down state laws that imposed residence requirements of up to a year before out-of-state citizens could claim assistance under the federal Aid to Families with Dependent Children program. The Court asserted:

> The constitutional right to travel from one State to another ... occupies a position fundamental to the concept of our Federal Union ... The right finds no explicit mention in the Constitution. The reason ... is that a right so elementary was conceived from the beginning to be a necessary concomitant of the stronger Union

[22] Jacobus tenBroek, *The Constitution and the Right of Free Movement* (New York: National Travelers Aid Association, 1955), p. 14.

[23] Id., p. 13.

[24] Quotes in the last two sentences of this paragraph from Minoff, "Free to Move?" p. 333.

the Constitution created. In any event, freedom to travel throughout the United States has long been recognized as a basic right under the Constitution.[25]

If they wished to burden citizens' constitutional right to travel, states would be required to show a "compelling governmental interest" in distinguishing between in-state and out-of-state residents, which the Court found they were unable to do.[26]

The "right to travel" as an incident of citizenship received powerful re-endorsement at the very end of the twentieth century in *Saenz v. Roe* (1999), a case in which the U.S. Supreme Court struck down a portion of California's Welfare and Institutions Code that stipulated that newly arrived residents who had lived in California for less than twelve months would be restricted to welfare payments at the levels established by the state they had left. The constitutional right to travel, the Court insisted, was "firmly embedded in our jurisprudence" and was "a virtually unconditional personal right, guaranteed by the Constitution to us all."[27] It consisted of three components: "the right of a citizen of one State to enter and leave another State; the right to be treated as a welcome visitor rather than an unfriendly alien when temporarily present in the second State; and, for those travelers who elect to become permanent residents, the right to be treated like other citizens of that State."[28] Poor Americans would no longer be "unfriendly aliens" as they traveled across their country.[29]

[25] *Shapiro v. Thompson*, 394 U.S. 618, 630–31 (1969) (quoting *United States v. Guest*, 383 U.S. 745, 757–58 (1966)).

[26] Id. at 634.

[27] *Saenz v. Roe*, 526 U.S. 489, 498 (1999) (quoting *United States v. Guest*, 383 U.S. 745, 757 (1966) and *Shapiro v. Thompson*, 394 U.S. 618, 643 (1969)).

[28] Id. at 500.

[29] It is important to emphasize, however, that the new "right to travel" extended only to domestic travel. Consistent with a conception of sovereignty going back to medieval times, the post-World War II United States continued to arrogate to itself the right to restrict its citizens' right to travel internationally. This typically took the form of refusing to issue passports to, or canceling the passports of, individuals deemed politically troublesome. In 1981, the U.S. Supreme Court upheld the government's right to restrict the international travel of its citizens in the following terms: "Revocation of a passport undeniably curtails travel, but the freedom to travel abroad with a "letter of introduction" in the form of a passport issued by the sovereign is subordinate to national security and foreign policy considerations; as such, it is subject to reasonable governmental regulation. The Court has made it plain that the *freedom* to travel outside the United States must be distinguished from the *right* to travel within the United States." *Haig v. Agee*, 453 U.S. 280, 306 (1981) (emphasis in original).

*Curtailing the State's Power of Involuntary Expatriation*

The post–World War II U.S. Supreme Court also made it harder for the government to strip Americans of citizenship and to convert them into aliens. In *Mackenzie v. Hare* (1915), discussed in the preceding chapter, the Court had located the expatriation power in Congress's inherent sovereign power over foreign relations – that is, in a source similar to the plenary power that undergirded the federal immigration power. Although the Court had observed in that case that expatriation could not be "arbitrarily imposed … without the concurrence of the citizen," it had inferred consent from the fact that the expatriating act – in that case, an American woman's marrying an alien – had been "voluntarily entered into, with notice of the consequences."[30] In so doing, the Court dispensed with any requirement that there be *specific* intent on the part of the citizen to expatriate herself.

For all practical purposes, then, the *Mackenzie* Court signed off on Congress's ability to strip Americans of their citizenship if they engaged in acts of which Congress disapproved. Taking its cue from this decision, in the Nationality Act of 1940 Congress expanded the early-twentieth-century grounds of expatriation to include service in foreign armed forces, working for a foreign state in conjunction with nationality of that state, desertion from the U.S. armed forces, remaining outside the United States in order to avoid wartime military service, residing in a foreign country for an extended period of time if a naturalized citizen, and voting in a political election in a foreign state. Any of these acts might suffice to transform a U.S. citizen into an alien. In the two decades following the end of World War II, more than 100,000 Americans, most of whom were native-born, would be stripped of their citizenship.

Clemente Martínez Pérez had been born in Texas in 1909, moved to Mexico with his parents, and resided there until 1943. When faced with deportation from the United States, he claimed to be a U.S. citizen on the basis of his birthplace. In response, the government asserted that Pérez's voting in the Mexican presidential election of 1946 caused his involuntary expatriation under the Nationality Act of 1940. In *Perez v. Brownell* (1958), the Court upheld Pérez's expatriation. According to Justice Frankfurter's majority opinion, voting in a foreign election

---

[30] *Mackenzie v. Hare*, 239 U.S. 299, 311–12 (1915).

implied "allegiance to another country in some measure, at least, inconsistent with American citizenship"; because this act was "potentially embarrassing to the American Government," Congress could resolve the problem by terminating citizenship.[31]

The decision in *Perez* sparked a forceful dissent from Chief Justice Warren. According to Warren, because governmental power was a creature of the citizenry, government was "without power to sever the relationship that gives rise to its existence." Furthermore, the consequences of expatriation for the citizen were severe: "Citizenship *is* man's basic right for it is nothing less than the right to have rights."[32] Warren would have allowed for loss of citizenship only when the citizen "manifests allegiance to a foreign state [in a manner] so inconsistent with the retention of [American] citizenship as to result in loss of that status"; he rejected the idea that mere voting in a foreign election was such an act.[33]

In 1960s, the Court began slowly to erode the government's expatriation power. The decisive blow came in 1967. Beys Afroyim had been a naturalized U.S. citizen since 1926. In 1949, he left the United States and settled in Israel. In 1960, when Afroyim sought to renew his U.S. passport, he was issued instead a Certificate of Loss of Nationality on the ground that his voting in an Israeli national election in 1951 resulted in his involuntary expatriation. When the case came before the U.S. Supreme Court, the Court adopted the arguments set forth in Chief Justice Warren's dissent in *Perez*. In an opinion by Justice Black, the Court refused to accept that "Congress has any general power, express or implied, to take away an American citizen's citizenship without his assent."[34] Justice Black discerned in the Fourteenth Amendment "no indication ... of a fleeting citizenship, good at the moment it is acquired but subject to destruction by the Government at any time."[35] Indeed, the government's ability to strip American citizens of their citizenship was now represented as entirely inconsistent with free government: "The very nature of our free government makes it completely incongruous to have a rule of law under which a group of

---

[31] *Perez v. Brownell*, 356 U.S. 44, 60–61 (1958).
[32] Id. at 64 (Warren, C. J., dissenting) (emphasis in original).
[33] Id. at 68, 75 (Warren, C. J., dissenting).
[34] *Afroyim v. Rusk*, 387 U.S. 253, 257 (1967).
[35] Id. at 262.

citizens temporarily in office can deprive another group of citizens of their citizenship."[36]

Although *Afroyim*'s language appeared to preclude involuntary expatriation altogether, it would take decades for the idea to take hold. In 1986, Congress amended the Immigration and Nationality Act, providing that statutorily listed expatriating acts be undertaken "with the *intention* of relinquishing United States nationality" in order for there to be a loss of citizenship.[37] In 1990, the Department of State adopted new guidelines that greatly reduced the risk of involuntary expatriation. The government pledged to work from "the premise that U.S. citizens intend to retain U.S. citizenship when they obtain naturalization in a foreign state, subscribe to routine declarations of allegiance to a foreign state, or accept non-policy level employment with a foreign government."[38] Thus, the government arrested the early-twentieth-century trend of turning its own citizens into aliens for acts it frowned upon.

### Citizenship, Immigration, and Internal Foreigners: 1950–2000

In 1944, when Earl G. Harrison resigned as the U.S. commissioner of immigration and naturalization, he observed pointedly that the United States and Nazi Germany were the only countries that made race a factor in naturalization law. He added: "[A]ll will agree that this is not very desirable company."[39] It was painfully evident that the racism the United States claimed to be combating in World War II was potent in the way the country treated outsiders. Incremental changes came during the War itself. Between 1943 and 1946, in a gesture to wartime allies, Congress abolished immigration and naturalization bars for China, India, and the Philippines.

Immigration flows created by World War II placed considerable pressure on the 1920s quota system, chipping away at it bit by bit.

---

[36] Id. at 268.

[37] Pub. L. No. 99-653, 100 Stat. 3655, 3658 (1986), amending INA Sec. 349(a), 8 U.S.C. 1481(a) (emphasis added).

[38] Telegram from U.S. Department of State, April 16, 1990, Office of the Legal Advisor, *Digest of United States Practice in International Law, 1989–1990* (Washington, DC: International Law Institute, 1998), p. 4.

[39] Quoted in Milton R. Konvitz, *The Alien and the Asiatic in American Law* (Ithaca, NY: Cornell University Press, 1946), pp. 80–81.

During the War, the federal government had generally turned its back on war refugees. In 1945, however, President Truman issued an executive order admitting 40,000 refugees. Toward the end of 1946, there was a push for special legislation to bring displaced persons from Europe to the United States. However, when Congress passed legislation to deal with refugees – the Displaced Persons Act of 1948 – it insisted on "quota mortgaging," such that refugee admissions were met out of established country quotas, in many cases "mortgaging" them well into the future. Although widely recognized as a breach of the quota system, the policy came under heavy criticism. Accordingly, in 1953, Congress passed the Refugee Relief Act, which provided for 205,000 non-quota refugee visas. There were other breaches of the quota system. In passing the War Brides Act of 1945, Congress enabled alien wives, husbands, and children of armed services members to enter the United States regardless of quotas.

Despite such inroads, the 1920s quota system was preserved in the first major piece of postwar immigration legislation. In 1952, overriding President Truman's veto, Congress passed the McCarran-Walter Act. Although the Act allowed immediate relatives of U.S. citizens to enter free of numerical restriction, it subjected all other immigrants to the 1920s quota structure, giving Northern and Western European nations 85 percent of annual admissions. There was a numerical cap of 150,000 slots for the Eastern Hemisphere. Immigration from the Western Hemisphere was kept, as was the tradition, free from numerical limits, except that residents of European colonies in the Western Hemisphere were charged to the quotas of their respective metropoles and were limited to one hundred annual admissions per colony. This measure was designed to keep Caribbean blacks from immigrating to the United States in large numbers. Within each country quota, there were preferences for skilled immigrants and relatives of U.S. citizens.

In crucial respects, however, the McCarran-Walter Act broke from older models. It formally lifted race as a barrier to naturalization. Culminating the trend begun by the wartime acts ending Chinese, Indian, and Filipino exclusion, the Act ended the ban on immigration from Asian countries. Asian countries now received nominal quotas. These were Cold War measures designed to combat overseas perceptions of American racism and win allies in the contest with the Soviet Union. Thanks to this limited opening, the number of immigrants from

Asia grew during the 1950s. During the 1940s, virtually all immigration to the United States had been from Europe and Latin America. When it came to immigration between 1953 and 1965, however, Europeans no longer constituted an absolute majority.

The Cold War origins of the McCarran-Walter Act are also revealed in the pressure it placed on those suspected of Communist affiliation. The Act prohibited the naturalization and immigration, and provided for the deportation, of members of various "subversive" groups. "Subversives" found it difficult to obtain even short-term entry visas. As a result, celebrated leftist intellectuals such as Jean-Paul Sartre were unable to lecture in the United States. The Act also introduced a special ground of exclusion and deportation for aliens afflicted with a psychopathic personality, an imprecise way of keeping out homosexuals.[40]

In the middle decades of the twentieth century, even as the rights revolution was under way for American citizens, a combination of closed borders, numerical quotas, and mounting labor needs saw the rise to prominence of a specific population of internal foreigners, namely temporary foreign workers and undocumented aliens, two categories that bled into one another. It was precisely the rights revolution that led to the creation of this new type of internal foreigner. As U.S. citizens became less exploitable, exploitable immigrant labor became more attractive.

During World War II, severe labor shortages had prompted southwestern employers to look south of the border. What emerged was a binational "guest worker" program called the *bracero* program (*bracero* corresponds to "manual laborer" in Spanish). The Mexican government, unhappy about the mass "voluntary" repatriations and deportations of the 1930s and the widespread maltreatment of Mexican workers in the United States, insisted on bilateral negotiations to establish the wages, working conditions, and terms of transportation under which its citizens would labor in the United States. Because of virulent anti-Mexican discrimination in Texas, it refused to let Texas growers benefit under the program.

Initially set up by executive agreement in 1942, the program was formally approved by Congress in 1943. By the time it ended in 1964, it had supplied millions of Mexican (but also Canadian and

[40] The ban on homosexual aliens was formally removed from immigration law in 1990.

Caribbean) workers to growers and ranchers across the country. A separate non-immigrant visa program would continue to supply temporary agricultural laborers into the late twentieth century. Certain states were especially dependent on *bracero* labor. In 1945, for example, California farms employed more than 60 percent of the total number of *braceros*. *Bracero* labor had a direct impact on farm wages, which remained stagnant in areas dependent on it, even as they registered a rise elsewhere.

Corruption was a problem from the outset. *Braceros* protested that they were cheated when it came to wages and working conditions. Investigating authorities discovered that growers had violated employment contracts in approximately half the cases of complaint registered in the mid-1950s. As part of the original agreement, Mexico and the United States established an obligatory "savings fund" into which a percentage of the wages of Mexican workers was to be paid and released to them upon their return to Mexico. Many (perhaps most) *braceros* never received these withheld wages. In 2008, following a protracted lawsuit, a California judge ruled that former *braceros* had been cheated and that they should receive $3,500 per worker.[41]

But an entirely different problem was the U.S. government's complicity in subverting the official *bracero* program and facilitating the growth of undocumented immigration to meet the demands of U.S. employers. Growers addicted to cheap, exploitable labor complained that going through the Mexican government made Mexican labor too expensive. In support of growers' preferences, the Immigration and Naturalization Service (INS) invoked the attorney general's administrative discretion to admit inadmissible aliens into the country. This provision allowed employers to recruit Mexican workers directly at the border instead of deeper within Mexico. Those recruited would be admitted by the INS and would thus bypass the Mexican recruitment process. Border recruitment also gave Texas growers access to *bracero* labor in contravention of the terms of the official program.

However, the INS also played a direct role in legalizing undocumented immigrants already inside the United States. In a practice it cynically referred to as "a walk around the statute," undocumented immigrants were marched across the border and then admitted as

---

[41] *Cruz v. United States*, Case No. 3:01-CV-00892 (October 10, 2008).

*braceros*. In another practice referred to as "drying out wetbacks," undocumented immigrants were legalized without even the charade of a march across the border. Both of these questionable practices served to satisfy the needs of western and southwestern growers and circumvented the official *bracero* program. Indeed, the number of undocumented workers that the INS thus made available to growers far outstripped the number recruited through the formal program. Between 1947 and 1949, around 75,000 *braceros* were recruited from Mexico, while almost twice that number of undocumented workers were legalized and contracted to growers. In 1950, while fewer than 20,000 *braceros* were recruited from Mexico, close to 100,000 undocumented workers were legalized. The official *bracero* program had required workers to leave, but the INS looked the other way when workers stayed on. By 1952, estimates put the number of undocumented workers in the United States at 1.5 million.

If the line between undocumented aliens and temporary foreign workers thus proved highly porous, it did not mean that undocumented aliens became less vulnerable. The opposite was true. Even as the INS was turning a blind eye toward undocumented immigration when it came to satisfying the needs of growers, the McCarran-Walter Act made apprehension and deportation of undocumented aliens easier by empowering immigration agents to conduct, without warrant, searches of "any railway car, aircraft, conveyance or vehicle" within a "reasonable distance" of the border and searches of private lands up to "twenty-five miles" from the border. It also made harboring undocumented aliens a felony punishable by as much as five years' imprisonment and a $2,000 fine. However, bowing to growers, the Act spared U.S. employers from legal penalties. Employers who employed undocumented aliens using "usual and normal practices incident to employment" would face no legal penalties.[42]

In the 1950s, politicians in the West and Southwest complained angrily about unauthorized migration and demonized undocumented immigrants. California governor Earl Warren argued that a "wetback invasion" was a serious drain on his state's resources. "Wetbacks" were charged with depressing farm wages, endangering public health, and engaging in criminal activities. Organized labor as well as

---

[42] Act of June 27, 1952, 66 Stat. 163.

Mexican American groups stepped up attacks. A cresting wave of anti-"wetback" sentiment – including Senator McCarran's assertion that as many as 5 million aliens were in the United States, including "militant Communists, Sicilian bandits and other criminals" – led to calls for a crackdown.[43] In June 1954, the attorney general began an enforcement drive with the code name "Operation Wetback." Between 1 and 2 million Mexicans were repatriated in 1954 alone. Undocumented aliens could thus have their residence cut short unceremoniously whenever it became politically opportune to do so. This made those who remained a compliant, exploitable workforce, which is precisely why they were attractive to employers.

The country's tolerance of an expanding, exploitable population of undocumented workers as a significant rights revolution was under way for citizens was an important part of the widening gap between citizen and alien in the postwar decades. But the gap widened not just between citizens and undocumented immigrants, but also between citizens and legal immigrants. Nowhere was this discrepancy clearer than in the schizophrenic jurisprudence of the postwar Court, which revealed a strong commitment to racial equality and individual rights for citizens, on the one hand, even as it repeatedly affirmed the plenary power doctrine vis-à-vis aliens, on the other. As the postwar Court protected the rights of citizens and disregarded those of aliens, the postwar state discovered that it could accomplish with immigrants what it could no longer accomplish with citizens.

By midcentury, the Court had recognized that outsiders present in the United States slowly became insiders and that, accordingly, the levels of substantive and procedural protections constitutionally owing to them increased. In *Johnson v. Eisentrager* (1950), for example, the Court observed that an alien "has been accorded a generous and ascending scale of rights as he increases his identity with our society."[44] During the 1940s, this view had meant a raising of the evidentiary bar when the government tried to denaturalize immigrants suspected of Communist affiliations.[45] However, with the splintering of the U.S.-Soviet alliance and growing paranoia about Communism

---

[43] Kitty Calavita, *Inside the State: The Bracero Program, Immigration, and the INS* (New York: Routledge, 1992), p. 49.
[44] *Johnson v. Eisentrager*, 339 U.S. 763, 770 (1950).
[45] *Schneiderman v. United States*, 320 U.S. 118 (1943).

in the United States in the early 1950s, the emphasis on the constitutional weight accorded an immigrant's stake in American society fell away.

In the 1950s, the Court became far more deferential to the government's efforts to deport former Communists and failed to give appropriate constitutional weight to long-term immigrants' stake in American society. In the landmark case of *Harisiades v. Shaughnessy* (1952), the immigrant in question, Peter Harisiades, a former member of the Communist Party, had been a legal resident of the United States for more than three decades. The government sought to deport Harisiades under a deportation statute that had been enacted *after* he had ended his party membership. In other words, membership in the Communist Party had *not* been a ground of deportation when Harisiades had been a party member. Those defending Harisiades hoped that the First Amendment might limit the government's power to deport aliens for past Communist Party memberships. They were bitterly disappointed. The Court upheld Harisiades's deportation in the name of plenary power, finding no violation of the Due Process Clause, the *Ex Post Facto* Clause, or the First Amendment.[46] Justice Jackson's opinion emphasized that legal permanent residents' "domicile here is held by a precarious tenure."[47] On November 12, 1952, Harisiades, his wife, Esther, and their two children were deported to Poland. He never returned to the United States.

What this meant, of course, was that long-term resident immigrants could not exercise expressional freedoms free of the risk of deportation. The harshness of deportation on political grounds for immigrants and their U.S. citizen families was widely recognized. A National Lawyers Guild study of political deportation cases found that more than three-fourths of the deportees were more than forty years old and that half had children who were U.S. citizens, suggesting significant ties to the United States. In *Galvan v. Press* (1954), Justice Frankfurter himself observed that deportation would "deprive a man of all that makes life worth living" and may be "at times the equivalent of banishment or exile."[48]

---

[46] *Harisiades v. Shaughnessy,* 342 U.S. 580 (1952).
[47] Id. at 587.
[48] *Galvan v. Press,* 347 U.S. 522, 530 (1954) (citations omitted).

Since the late nineteenth century, procedural protections had been an established way of softening the harshness of plenary power. However, the postwar Court failed to give immigrants adequate procedural protections as well. Indeed, in the 1950s, the Court's pronouncements on the procedural protections due to aliens subject to exclusion were perhaps harsher than they had been at the height of the Chinese exclusion era.

*United States ex. rel. Knauff v. Shaughnessy* (1950) involved an alien seeking admission as a war bride who was excluded and denied a hearing before a board of inquiry on the ground that her exclusion was based on confidential security information. The Court declined to find a constitutional problem. As the Court put it: "Whatever the procedure authorized by Congress is, it is due process as far as an alien denied entry is concerned."[49] This severe position in the context of a first-time entrant was extended seamlessly to that of a returning long-term resident immigrant. In the case of *Shaughnessy v. United States ex. rel. Mezei* (1953), Ignatz Mezei found himself excluded when he tried to return home to the United States. Mezei had lived in the United States from 1923 to 1948, but then left for nineteen months to visit his dying mother in Romania. The Court reaffirmed its ruling in *Knauff*, treating Mezei – notwithstanding his quarter-century-long period of permanent residence – no differently from an alien seeking admission for the first time. The situation was worse still. Mezei was potentially subject to indefinite exclusion in New York Harbor: the United States would not admit him and no other country would take him back. The Court remained unmoved: "[W]e do not think that respondent's continued exclusion deprives him of any statutory or constitutional right."[50]

If the foregoing suggests that the plenary power doctrine allowed the state to ride roughshod over the substantive and procedural rights of immigrants even as a rights revolution was under way for citizens, the rights revolution did have an osmotic impact. By 1960, with the Civil Rights movement in high gear and with the Cold War ideological struggle in mind, the Democratic Party platform for the first time criticized the national origins quota system as "a policy of

---

[49] *United States ex. rel. Knauff v. Shaughnessy*, 338 U.S. 537, 544 (1950).
[50] *Shaughnessy v. United States ex. rel. Mezei*, 345 U.S. 206, 215 (1953). Congressional and public pressure eventually secured the release of both Knauff and Mezei.

deliberate discrimination" that "contradict[ed] the founding principles of this nation" and that was "inconsistent with our belief in the rights of man."[51]

Passed during the Johnson administration, the Hart-Celler Act of 1965 did away with blatantly discriminatory national origins quotas. It was widely represented as part of the larger transformation in federal law that included the passage of the Civil Rights Act of 1964, the Voting Rights Act of 1965, and the laws creating Medicare/Medicaid. As one congressman stated: "Just as we sought to eliminate discrimination in our land through the Civil Rights Act, today we seek by phasing out the national origins quota system to eliminate discrimination in immigration to this nation."[52]

But for all that, the Hart-Celler Act retained quotas. The Act allotted 170,000 slots to countries in the Eastern Hemisphere (with equal country quotas) and, for the first time, 120,000 slots to countries in the Western Hemisphere (without country quotas). In 1976, new legislation established the same per-country ceilings for both hemispheres. In 1978, the Eastern and Western Hemispheres were subjected to a single worldwide cap. The traditional preference given to Western Hemisphere countries, long a source of "backdoor" agricultural labor, was removed. Within this quota structure, immigration into the United States was to take place under two broad heads: family ties and labor (immediate family members of U.S. citizens could enter free of restriction).[53]

---

[51] Kirk H. Porter and Donald Johnson, *National Party Platforms, 1840–1964* (Urbana: University of Illinois Press, 1966), p. 577.

[52] 111 Cong. Rec. 21783 (August 25, 1965).

[53] A distinct and important component of the post–World War II immigration regime, one that cannot be treated here for reasons of length, involved the admission of refugees. Until 1980, refugee admissions typically tracked Cold War politics. After the passage of the Refugee Act of 1980, a systematic and permanent procedure for the resettlement of refugees emerged. The Act provided for 50,000 annual admissions, but authorized the president to raise that number after consultation with Congress. The Act defined a "refugee" as "any person who is outside any country of such person's nationality … and who is unable or unwilling to avail himself or herself of the protection of that country because of persecution or a well-founded fear of persecution on account of race, religion, nationality, membership in a particular social group, or political opinion." Act of March 17, 1980 (Refugee Act of 1980), 94 Stat. 102. Apart from the context of refugee and asylum law, I would argue that postwar international legal norms have not had a major direct impact on U.S. immigration and citizenship law. For reasons of length, I have elected not to discuss them in this book.

Furthermore, for all the rhetoric about ending discrimination, the Act was not intended in the first instance to benefit Asian, Latin American, or African immigrants. Instead, as a measure of redress for the wrongs done to Southern and Eastern European immigrants in 1924 and 1952, it was calculated to win the support of white ethnics. In 1964, making the case for the act, Attorney General Robert Kennedy stated that the problem with existing immigration law was that it implied that "a man or woman born in Italy, or Greece, or Poland, or Portugal, or Czechoslovakia, or the Ukraine, is not as good as someone born in Ireland, or England, or Germany, or Sweden."[54] The Act was not supposed to alter the country's existing demography at all. Indeed, when President Johnson signed the bill into law in a ceremony on Liberty Island in New York Harbor, he stated: "This bill that we sign today is not a revolutionary bill. It does not affect the lives of millions. It will not reshape the structure of our daily lives, or really add importantly to our wealth or our power."[55]

But politics and economics in post–World War II Europe meant that out-migration from that continent would be small. By 1970, Spanish had surpassed Italian as the country's second language. In 1970s, the leading sending countries were Mexico, the Philippines, Korea, Cuba, and India. European and Canadian migration accounted for an ever smaller part of the immigration stream.

The end of the *bracero* program in 1964, combined with the introduction of quotas for immigrants from the Western Hemisphere in the Hart-Celler Act, established the conditions under which illegal immigration mounted. In the 1970s, the stereotypical undocumented alien was a poorly educated, unskilled young male from Mexico, Central America, or the Caribbean (neither the public imagination nor the authorities paid sufficient attention to undocumented immigration from European countries such as Ireland). Throughout the 1970s and 1980s, although INS raids were sporadic, America's ever larger population of undocumented internal foreigners came to live with the

---

[54] *Hearings Before Subcommittee No. 1 of the Committee on the Judiciary, House of Representatives, Eighty-Eighth Congress, Second Session on H.R. 7700 and 55, Identical Bills to Amend the Immigration and Nationality Act, and for Other Purposes* (Washington, DC: U.S. Government Printing Office, 1964), p. 412.

[55] Lyndon B. Johnson, "Remarks at the Signing of the Immigration Bill, Liberty Island, New York (October 3, 1965)," *Public Papers*, p. 1038.

perpetual threat of discovery, detention, and deportation. This could mean an unwillingness to venture forth in the community. An undocumented immigrant in Maryland confessed to a journalist: "I live with the constant fear that they might find me someplace and deport me, send me away. Wherever I go, I have that constant fear. Before, I used to play soccer. I used to go to the Spanish theaters and restaurants. Now I have no place to go. I watch TV."[56] But it could also translate into an inability to resist exploitation at home, at work, or in the community; a fear of seeking out law enforcement officials; and a reluctance to avail of basic social services.

After years of public debate about undocumented immigration, in 1986 Congress passed the Immigration Reform and Control Act (IRCA), an attempt to mitigate the problem of illegal immigration by offering undocumented immigrants an opportunity to legalize their status. Some 3 million undocumented immigrants, almost three-fourths of whom were from Mexico, sought legalization. Most lived in California and Texas. As a consequence of legalization, the number of immigrants officially admitted to permanent residence spiked in 1990 and 1991. Under IRCA, as under earlier statutes, it was relatively difficult to prosecute U.S. employers and the penalties imposed on them remained light.

However, as long as closed borders, numerical restrictions, country quotas, and the desire for cheap exploitable labor continued, IRCA's legalization would not stem the flow of undocumented aliens into the country. Illegal immigration continued after the passage of IRCA, with undocumented immigrants remaining a highly vulnerable group of internal foreigners. In significant part, this vulnerability was exacerbated by law. In *Hoffman Plastic Compounds, Inc. v. NLRB* (2002), for example, the U.S. Supreme Court held that certain labor protections did not apply to undocumented workers.[57]

After the 1965 reform, the U.S. Supreme Court's basic commitment to the plenary power doctrine remained firm in the exclusion, deportation, and naturalization contexts, notwithstanding clear evidence of ideological or gender discrimination that would be impermissible in

---

[56] David M. Reimers, *Still the Golden Door: The Third World Comes to America* (New York: Columbia University Press, 1985), pp. 223–24.
[57] *Hoffman Plastic Compounds, Inc. v. NLRB*, 535 U.S. 137 (2002).

the domestic context. When the well-known Belgian Marxist scholar
Ernest Mandel was denied a non-immigrant visa to the United States
on ideological grounds, the Court upheld the exclusion: "[O]ver no
conceivable subject is the legislative power of Congress more complete than it is over the admission of aliens."[58] In *Fiallo v. Bell* (1977),
individuals challenged a provision of the Immigration and Nationality
Act that defined the word "child" to exclude illegitimate children of
natural fathers, but not illegitimate children of natural mothers. The
result was that illegitimate children of natural fathers could neither be
sponsored as immigrants nor sponsor their natural fathers as immigrants. Were such a law to have existed in a domestic context, it would
very likely have been struck down for gender discrimination. Because
it related to immigrants, however, it was sustained.[59]

Plenary power in such contexts was in turn invoked to uphold
the federal government's discrimination against resident aliens. In
*Mathews v. Diaz* (1976), the Court explicitly grounded the constitutional permissibility of Congress's decision to deny immigrants welfare
benefits in Congress's plenary power over immigration and naturalization. It captured succinctly the logic of the postwar gulf between citizen
and alien: "In the exercise of its broad power over naturalization and
immigration, Congress regularly makes rules that would be unaccept-
able if applied to citizens. The exclusion of aliens and the reservation
of the power to deport have no permissible counterpart in the Federal
Government's power to regulate the conduct of its own citizenry. The
fact that an Act of Congress treats aliens differently from citizens does
not in itself imply that such disparate treatment is 'invidious.' "[60]

More recently, in what might be a subtle way of limiting federal plenary power, the Court has attempted to establish a relationship of sorts
between plenary power and equal protection jurisprudence. In *Nguyen
v. INS* (2001), the Court was asked to consider the constitutionality of
a law that discriminated on the basis of gender (against men) when it
came to the law of citizenship *jure sanguinis*, or citizenship transmitted
by blood. The federal government invoked plenary power in defense of
the law. But the Court did not reach the government's plenary power

---

58 *Kleindienst v. Mandel*, 408 U.S. 753, 766 (1972) (citations omitted). Ideological
   grounds of exclusion were reduced considerably in the Immigration Act of 1990.
59 *Fiallo v. Bell*, 430 U.S. 787 (1977).
60 *Mathews v. Diaz*, 426 U.S. 67, 79–80 (1976) (citations omitted).

argument, finding instead that the law met the constitutional standard applied to gender-based discrimination.[61] At least implicitly, in
other words, the Court extended its equal protection jurisprudence to
citizenship law. The Burger and Rehnquist Courts also mitigated the
harshness of plenary power by being more solicitous of immigrants'
procedural rights.[62] Despite such subtle hints and procedural ploys,
however, federal plenary power over exclusion, deportation, and naturalization was never explicitly overruled.

If federal plenary power was mostly upheld, the Burger and
Rehnquist Courts actively wielded federal preemption doctrines and
equal protection theories to strike down *state* alienage laws. The Court
thereby arrested a trend toward upholding state-level alien legal disabilities that had been building since the early twentieth century, effectively concentrating power over aliens in the federal government.

In *Takahashi v. Fish & Game Commission* (1948), the Court had
invalidated a 1943 California statute that barred the issuance of a
commercial fishing license to any "alien Japanese" (later amended to
bar any "person ineligible to citizenship").[63] Shortly thereafter, the
Court also struck down the alien land laws targeting Asian immigrants
that had been instituted in the early twentieth century.[64] Both of these
rulings were part of the mid-twentieth-century process of ridding
immigration law of its formal racist trappings.

In 1971, however, the Burger Court went much further, preventing state discrimination against aliens in the important area of welfare rights. In *Graham v. Richardson* (1971), the Court struck down
Arizona and Pennsylvania welfare statutes that made citizenship a prerequisite to receiving state welfare.[65] In these cases, the Court openly
asserted its post–New Deal role as protector of minorities. Aliens were
a "discrete and insular minority" within the meaning of *United States
v. Carolene Products* (1934), the Court asserted, and therefore alienage classifications were "inherently suspect and subject to close judicial scrutiny" under the Equal Protection Clause.[66] This was the first

---

[61] *Nguyen v. INS*, 533 U.S. 53 (2001).
[62] *Landon v. Plasencia*, 459 U.S. 21 (1982); *Reno v. Flores*, 507 U.S. 292 (1993).
[63] *Takahashi v. Fish & Game Comm'n*, 334 U.S. 410, 413 (1948).
[64] *Oyama v. California*, 332 U.S. 633 (1948).
[65] *Graham v. Richardson*, 403 U.S. 365 (1971).
[66] The phrase "discrete and insular minorities" comes from *United States v. Carolene Products Co.*, 304 U.S. 144, 152–53, n. 4 (1938).

time that alienage was added to the list of constitutionally "suspect" classifications under the Fourteenth Amendment's Equal Protection Clause. Thereafter, the Court proceeded to strike down a number of state alienage laws that restricted aliens' access to state civil services, the legal profession, the engineering profession, and state educational benefits.[67]

The Court's most important attack on state alien legal disabilities came in the early 1980s. In the celebrated case of *Plyler v. Doe* (1982), the Court held that the Equal Protection Clause prohibited Texas from withholding public education from the foreign-born children of undocumented aliens. The decision was far more controversial than *Graham v. Richardson* because the Court could not rely unambiguously on federal preemption theories. Congress *had* expressed a strong policy of dissuading undocumented immigration, and Texas's law, if anything, bolstered this effort. Nevertheless, according to Justice Brennan, Texas's law could withstand constitutional scrutiny only if it furthered "some substantial state interest": the state was unable to make such a showing. What was troubling about the law, said the Court, was that it "raise[d] the specter of a permanent caste of undocumented resident aliens, encouraged by some to remain here as a source of cheap labor, but nevertheless denied the benefits that our society makes available to citizens and lawful residents. The existence of such an underclass presents most difficult problems for a Nation that prides itself on adherence to principles of equality under law."[68] *Plyler v. Doe* thus made very concrete the argument that undocumented aliens should *not* be a class of permanent internal foreigners and that school education should be made available to them to facilitate their assimilation into the mainstream.

Simultaneously, there began a scaling back. In the late 1970s, the Court upheld state laws that reserved for citizens employment as state police officers and public schoolteachers.[69] In *Cabell v. Chavez-Salido* (1982), the Court provided a theoretical grounding. Although the era of the "special public interest" doctrine was over, this did not mean that all state discrimination on the basis of alienage was impermissible.

---

[67] *Sugarman v. Dougall*, 413 U.S. 634 (1973); *In re Griffiths*, 413 U.S. 717 (1973); *Examining Board v. Flores de Otero*, 426 U.S. 572 (1976); *Nyquist v. Mauclet*, 432 U.S. 1 (1977).

[68] *Plyler v. Doe*, 457 U.S. 202, 230, 218–19 (1982).

[69] *Foley v. Connelie*, 435 U.S. 291 (1978); *Ambach v. Norwick*, 441 U.S. 68 (1979).

The Court distinguished between economic and sovereign functions of government. Discrimination against aliens was permissible in the case of the latter. The Court put it thus: "The exclusion of aliens from basic governmental processes is not a deficiency in the democratic system but a necessary consequence of the community's process of political self-definition ... Judicial incursions in this area may interfere with those aspects of democratic self-government that are most essential to it."[70]

By the late 1970s, nervousness about the change in the size and composition of post-1965 immigration, the rise in the undocumented immigrant population, and pro-immigrant advocacy that led to cases like *Plyler* gave rise to a nativist backlash paralleling that of the early twentieth century. Founded in 1979 by Dr. John Tanton, a retired physician from rural Michigan, the Federation for American Immigration Reform rapidly became one of the country's most influential anti-immigrant organizations. Prominent politicians openly expressed reservations about the cultural assimilability of the new streams of immigrants. In 1981, Senator Alan Simpson of Wyoming, a major figure in immigration reform until his retirement, worried: "[I]f language and cultural separation rise above a certain level, the unity and political stability of our nation will – in time – be seriously eroded."[71] By the early 1990s, nativism assumed an economistic cast, focusing on the impact of immigration on the labor market, the welfare system, and the environment, but never without an unmistakable racial/cultural component. The best-known racist salvo came from the period's "new Madison Grant," Peter Brimelow, himself a British immigrant. Brimelow's *Alien Nation: Common Sense about America's Immigration Disaster* (1992) insisted that "[r]ace and ethnicity are destiny in American politics" and characterized post-1965 immigration policy as "Adolf Hitler's posthumous revenge on America." The 1965 legislation threatened, Brimelow argued, "to transform – and ultimately, perhaps, even to destroy" – America.[72] His polemic sold more than 60,000 copies.

---

[70] *Cabell v. Chavez-Salido*, 454 U.S. 432, 439–40 (1982).

[71] Quoted in Roger Daniels, *Guarding the Golden Door: American Immigration Policy and Immigrants Since 1882* (New York: Hill & Wang, 2004), p. 222.

[72] Peter Brimelow, *Alien Nation: Common Sense About America's Immigration Disaster* (New York: Random House, 1995), pp. xvii, xv.

Congress responded by giving European immigrants a preferential route of entry. In response to complaints that Irish immigrants faced "reduced" immigration opportunities, it enacted an amendment to IRCA that created a new visa category labeled, with no irony, the "diversity visa" category. At a time when general immigration was restricted to family and employment visas, Irish immigrants obtained legal permanent residence on the basis of nothing more than the "diversity" that their Irishness allegedly contributed to America's demographic mix. After trying various formulas, Congress settled on a permanent "diversity" lottery system, available only to those immigrants from "underrepresented" countries and regions (which excluded all immigrants from major sending countries). Initially tilted toward Europe (and especially Ireland), the "diversity visa" category opened up in subsequent years to Europeans and Africans.

Another congressional response to late-twentieth-century nativism was an emphasis on border protection. In 1994, the Clinton administration requested appropriations of an additional $172.5 million "to protect our borders, remove criminal aliens, reduce work incentives for illegal immigration, stop asylum abuse, reinvent and revitalize INS, and encourage legal immigrants to become naturalized."[73] The administration's border control plan involved the deployment of many more U.S. Border Patrol agents and the erection of physical barriers at the southern border. The massive investment in immigration enforcement made traditional routes of entry unavailable. Beginning in the mid-1990s, those seeking to cross the border illegally were driven to take more precarious paths. As a result, thousands of would-be entrants died over the next decade and a half.

At the same time, however, Congress bowed to U.S. employers' demands for highly skilled immigrants. Since the passage of the Immigration Act of 1990, which raised legal immigration levels by 40 percent, Congress has divided immigrants into three broad groups: family-based immigrants; employment-based immigrants; and so-called diversity immigrants. Relative to earlier legislation, the second of these categories (together with non-immigrant visa categories that feed into it) was expanded to facilitate the migration of

---

[73] William J. Clinton, *Accepting the Immigration Challenge: The President's Report on Immigration* (Washington, DC.: U.S. Government Printing Office, 1994), p. iv.

highly skilled professionals thought to enhance the country's global competitiveness. Opening the gates to the highly skilled was perfectly consistent with late-twentieth-century nativism. What nativists most strenuously objected to was family-based immigration, which formed the largest portion of the immigration stream and allowed people in regardless of their skills, property, or ability to contribute.

Meanwhile, the push for stronger action on immigration was suddenly made much more urgent by developments in California. Governor Pete Wilson proclaimed that the use of public schools and hospitals by undocumented immigrants constituted a heavy burden for the state, with costs running into the billions. The result was Proposition 187, a multipronged initiative to deny undocumented immigrants public services and benefits and to compel public services and benefits providers to verify applicants' immigration status. Proposition 187 carried by a 59–41 percent margin and Wilson won a second term as governor. While parts of it were struck down by a federal district court on the ground that it conflicted with *Plyler v. Doe* and Congress's exclusive power over immigration, Proposition 187's real effect was pushing Congress to enact major immigration legislation in 1996.[74]

In 1996, Congress passed three immigration statutes: the Antiterrorism and Effective Death Penalty Act (AEDPA); the Personal Responsibility and Work Opportunity Reconciliation Act (PRWORA); and the Illegal Immigration Reform and Immigrant Responsibility Act (IIRAIRA). In different ways, the Acts demonstrated how the non-citizenship of resident immigrants (documented and undocumented) could be used opportunistically against them and how, under the plenary power doctrine, the gap between citizen and alien could be widened at will in ways that immigrants were powerless to contest.

A sweeping welfare reform statute, the PRWORA confirmed the ineligibility of undocumented and non-immigrant aliens for most welfare benefits. When it came to legal immigrants, who *had* been eligible to participate in many welfare programs as the American welfare state reconstituted itself in the 1970s, the statute imposed stricter standards of eligibility and authorized states to deny certain kinds of assistance. Approximately 45 percent of the savings from welfare reform between

---

[74] *See League of United Latin American Citizens v. Wilson*, 908 F. Supp. 755 (C.D. Cal. 1995) (invalidating California's Proposition 187).

1997 and 2002 came from cutting immigrant welfare, although many of the excessive cuts were restored a few years after being instituted. Taken together, AEDPA and IIRAIRA made it much easier for the government to deport aliens with criminal convictions by expanding grounds of deportation, curbing judicial review, and eliminating various forms of legal relief.

Not surprisingly, the number of formal removals shot up dramatically after 1996. In fiscal year 1990, there were 30,000 non-citizens removed; in fiscal year 2005, there were 246,000; and in fiscal year 2010, there were 383,000. When the number of voluntary returns is factored in, immigration scholar Daniel Kanstroom estimates, almost 12 million individuals were sent out of the United States between 2000 and 2010.[75] The majority of criminal deportees had committed drug-related crimes, although there were also tens of thousands of deportations for drunk driving and even lesser traffic offenses. The bulk of the deportations were to Latin America and the Caribbean. Alongside the deportation system, a vast federal detention system emerged.

The greatest perversity is that many of these immigrants came to the United States as children, grew up and acquired their identities and habits in the United States, and knew no other country. They were effectively Americans but for the fortuity of never having naturalized, Americans without American passports. When the United States deported them to "their" countries, it was often ridding itself of its "own," just as clearly as Great Britain had done with the convict trade of the eighteenth century. Such individuals were internal foreigners par excellence, products of the community that could be removed from it when the occasion arose.

Since 2001, as might be expected, a major focus of immigration law has also been terrorism. The USA Patriot Act (2001) and the Enhanced Border Security and Visa Entry Reform Act (2002) expanded the definition of "terrorist" for purposes of exclusion and deportation, tightened requirements for obtaining a visa to enter the United States, and authorized the attorney general to detain and incarcerate non-citizens if there are "reasonable grounds to believe" they pose a threat to

---

[75] Daniel Kanstroom, *Aftermath: Deportation Law and the New American Diaspora* (New York: Oxford University Press, 2012), p. 12.

national security. In the post-9/11 period, the government and the courts have invoked plenary power in order to justify the selective detention of non-citizens of particular national backgrounds.[76]

## Conclusion: Making Citizens Foreigners after the Rights Revolution

The rights revolution of the second half of the twentieth century made it significantly more difficult for the state to sanction the exclusion of large portions of its citizenry from the suffrage; the exclusion and removal of its citizens from territories and spaces on the grounds of race and poverty; and the stripping of citizens of their citizenship. As citizens won these crucial rights and protections, they ceased to suffer from legal disabilities they had shared with aliens for centuries. In the postwar period, the gulf between citizen and alien had never been wider.

However, to say that the gulf between citizen and alien had never been wider is not to assert that the promise of the rights revolution for the country's subordinated populations was fully realized, that formal rights accorded citizens translated into substantive ones, that older hierarchies vanished, or that substantive equality was achieved. As in earlier periods, as certain strategies of exclusion and rejection were taken off the table when it came to rendering insiders foreigners, others took their place.

Although the backlash against the rights revolution had begun decades earlier, serious retrenchment set in with the election of Ronald Reagan in 1980. The burst of support for racial and gender equality represented by the constitutional jurisprudence and legislation of the 1960s and 1970s faded as the Rehnquist Court scaled back on affirmative action and individual rights.[77] Industrial and manufacturing jobs began to disappear. Economic inequalities began to increase. As a result, millions of citizens came to share the fates of aliens all over again, but in substantive rather than in formal ways.

---

[76] *Arar v. Ashcroft*, 585 F.3d 559 (2d Cir. 2009); *al-Marri v. Wright*, 487 F.3d 160 (4th Cir. 2007); *Al Maqaleh v. Gates*, 605 F.3d 94 (D.C. Cir. 2010); *Kiyemba v. Obama*, 555 F.3d 1022 (D.C. Cir. 2009; judgment vacated in 2010).

[77] *City of Richmond v. J. A. Croson Co.*, 488 U.S. 469 (1989); *Adarand Constructors, Inc. v. Pena*, 515 U.S. 200 (1995).

This is revealed by the parallels between the fates of poor, racialized citizens and poor, racialized immigrants in the context of welfare. The last decades of the twentieth century were marked by a vigorous attack on welfare and a demonization of welfare recipients. Beginning in the 1970s, the benefits offered by major welfare programs shrank in real terms. The welfare reform of 1996 was an attack on immigrants *and* the country's poor, although immigrants paid a disproportionate price.

The same parallels existed when it came to the new punitive attitude toward crime. The post-1996 crackdown on immigrants with criminal backgrounds had an analogue in the extended crackdown on racial minorities that was part of the post-1980 "War on Drugs." Unlike millions of "Americans" with non-U.S. passports, who were deported to countries in Latin America and the Caribbean, native-born blacks and Latinos were "removed" from society by being imprisoned at astonishing rates. During the last two decades of the twentieth century, while higher education and housing accounted for ever lower shares of public budgets, federal, state, and local expenditures on corrections went up exponentially and prison populations rose dramatically. Labeling the incarceration phenomenon the "new Jim Crow," legal scholar Michelle Alexander reports that black males in Chicago with a felony record constitute 55 percent of the black adult male population and an astounding 80 percent of the adult black male workforce.[78] The disappearance of these men from society is compounded by the fact that convict disfranchisement remains one of the few permissible grounds of exclusion from the suffrage. Nationwide, large numbers of black males are barred from voting because they are in prison or have been convicted of felonies. Rehabilitation is impeded because individuals with criminal convictions might also be barred from many professions and even from living in certain places.

Spatial and territorial restrictions for U.S. citizens have also made a comeback. Late-twentieth-century America was in some respects a more racially and economically segregated society in terms of residence and schooling than it was during the civil rights era, although the segregation was de facto rather than de jure. The last decades of the twentieth century and the first decade of the twenty-first were

---

[78] Michelle Alexander, *The New Jim Crow: Mass Incarceration in the Age of Color Blindness* (New York: New Press, 2010), p. 184.

crowded with instances of the consequences faced by blacks who crossed spatial and territorial borders, ranging from humiliating treatment in retail establishments to regular police harassment to outright violence or death when they entered white neighborhoods.

Yet another way of making U.S. citizens foreign in their own country involved the ripple effects of the immigration regime itself. The impact of apprehending, detaining, and removing millions of non-citizens after 1996 was devastating for American citizens and communities, who experienced their foreignness vis-à-vis the country as a result. The toll on immigrants' children was especially grave. Millions of Americans with immigrant parents saw their families split or experienced deportation as entire families relocated to foreign countries.

Equally (if not more) disturbing was a different phenomenon. With the ratcheting upward of immigration law enforcement starting in the late 1990s, despite the hundreds of millions of dollars poured into immigration enforcement, American citizens found themselves trapped in the dragnet of immigration authorities. Racial profiling of Americans of Latino descent and indigenous peoples along the Mexican border became common and led to widespread abuses of human rights. But the problem went beyond intimidation, harassment, or abusive treatment. The political scientist Jacqueline Stevens estimates that, between 2003 and 2010, as many as 20,000 U.S. citizens might have experienced detention and/or deportation from the United States because of their skin color, foreign birth, or Hispanic last names. Summarizing her research, Stevens reports: "US citizens who previously had been housed and self-sufficient or cared for by their families have been found bathing in the Tijuana River and eating garbage; drifting among Latin American shelters and obtaining nourishment and liquid from roadside soda cans in El Salvador; and, in a somewhat surreal reversal, eking out livings as day laborers in Mexico or telemarketing in the Dominican Republic."[79]

The Kafkaesque experience of Mark Lyttle is unfortunately not exceptional. Lyttle, a U.S. citizen born in North Carolina, was deported in December 2008. Lyttle was slated for release from criminal custody

[79] Jacqueline Stevens, "U.S. Government Unlawfully Detaining and Deporting U.S. Citizens as Aliens," *Virginia Journal of Social Policy and Law* 18, no. 3 (2011): 607–720, 608.

after serving a sentence for a misdemeanor. Instead, an Immigration and Customs Enforcement (ICE) official told Lyttle that his real name was Jose Thomas, that he was from Mexico, and that he was going to be deported there. Lyttle reported:

The prison gave me my release papers and the next thing I know, I'm in a white minivan and they drive me all the way to Raleigh. Then after that they fly me [to a detention center] and I stayed there for a month. They were calling me Jose Thomas. They were trying to say that's my real name. I told them my name is Mark Daniel Lyttle, I was born in North Carolina ... My mother's Jeanne Lyttle, here's my social security number, my brother's in the army, please call someone!

Although Lyttle repeated his story to other ICE agents and then to Immigration Judge William Cassidy, it did not stop his being deported to Mexico. In Mexico, Lyttle wandered around until he was taken in by some missionaries. Some two months later, Lyttle ran into the Mexican police, who took away his only identity document, his deportation order, and shipped him to Honduras. When Lyttle could not produce an identity document for Honduran border guards, they drove him to San Pedro and put him in jail. After more than a month in a Honduran jail, Lyttle was transported to Guatemala, where the U.S. Embassy was finally persuaded that he was a U.S. citizen.[80]

Things might be even worse for some U.S. citizens. In the context of prosecuting the "War on Terror" in the first decade of the twenty-first century, the United States has sanctioned, planned, and completed the targeted extrajudicial killing of one of its own citizens. In April 2010, the Obama administration placed a native-born citizen, Anwar al-Awlaki, on a list of individuals the Central Intelligence Agency was authorized to kill for terrorist activities. On September 30, 2011, a drone strike killed Al-Awlaki in Yemen. Two weeks after that, a second drone strike killed Al-Awlaki's sixteen-year-old Denver-born son. The American Civil Liberties Union and the Center for Constitutional Rights have sued the federal government, arguing that the killings constitute a violation of due process owing to American citizens.[81]

---

[80] Paragraph drawn from Kanstroom, *Aftermath*, pp. 101–102.
[81] For a history of the *Nasser Al-Aulaqui v. Panetta* litigation, see https://www.aclu.org/national-security/al-aulaqi-v-panetta.

# 8

# Conclusion and Coda

The history of U.S. immigration and citizenship law recounted in this book brings together the histories of immigrants with those of Native Americans, blacks, women, the poor, Asian Americans, and Latino Americans. It does so with a view to sparking a rethinking of U.S. citizenship history, on the one hand, and U.S. immigration history, on the other.

The history of U.S. citizenship has conventionally been recounted as a story of those on the territorial "inside." From this perspective, subordinated groups on the "inside" – women, the poor, Native Americans, blacks, Latino Americans, and Asian Americans – are viewed as citizens-in-the-making. This has allowed for a relative lack of interest in interrogating the core citizen–alien distinction and in connecting insiders' histories to those of immigrants. Exploring another side of the same coin, the history of U.S. immigration has conventionally been recounted as a story of those coming from the territorial "outside." Immigrants' travails are the quintessential struggles of foreigners: bars to entry, barriers to political and social incorporation, and the threat of expulsion. There is often not enough interest in the fact that those on the territorial "inside" have been subjected to the same travails, which results in a related lack of interest in historicizing the core citizen–alien distinction. Such conventional accounts of U.S. citizenship and immigration history have been transformed by much recent scholarship. But they still hold, not just in prominent works of scholarship, but also in popular understandings.

I have attempted in this book to rework the conventional historiographical traditions of U.S. citizenship history and immigration history by taking seriously the multiple strategies of what I have called "rendering insiders foreign": formally designating domestic groups as alien; transforming citizens into aliens for performing prohibited acts; subjecting domestic groups to extensive barriers to movement and residence; mingling citizens with immigrants; and otherwise subjecting groups to the classic legal disabilities suffered by aliens. In this book, such strategies of rendering insiders foreign are joined to strategies of absorbing and rejecting outsiders.

There are sound historical reasons for recounting the history of U.S. citizenship and immigration this way. From the first English settlement of North America until the Civil War, immigrants entered highly decentralized (albeit centralizing) polities that were crowded with native-born citizens *and* native-born aliens. Even as native-born white males acceded to important rights of citizenship, native-born aliens proliferated. A long politico-legal tradition labeled Native Americans aliens despite the fact that Americans claimed sovereignty over them. In certain Southern states, free blacks from outside the state could be labeled aliens and subjected to alien legal disabilities. The complete occlusion of women's legal personalities led some, including female activists, to liken women to aliens. Immigrants were also hardly the only ones to face restrictions on mobility and residence. In a world in which immigration restriction was local, states, counties, and towns routinely excluded and removed citizens *and* aliens. Derived from the eighteenth-century poor laws, antebellum immigration restriction focused more and more on immigrants, but targeted those from beyond *and* within the country's limits.

This world changed dramatically after the Civil War as a result of the extension of formal citizenship to native-born blacks. No longer impeded by the claims of slave states insistent upon excluding free blacks, a federal immigration order, its gaze turned outward upon immigrants, finally emerged. With the blessing of the U.S. Supreme Court, and as hammered out in extensive litigation by Chinese immigrants, the federal immigration power came to be cloaked in plenary power, a power grounded in sovereignty and essentially unchecked by substantive provisions of the U.S. Constitution. The constitutionalization of *jus soli* citizenship among the native-born population, combined with the emergence of a federal immigration order possessed of plenary power, resulted in a widening of the gulf between citizen and alien, insider and outsider. However, numerous strategies, old and new, continued to render insiders foreigners: segregation, the extension of plenary power to Native Americans, territorial restrictions on the poor, the occlusion of women's citizenship, and the mingling of citizens and aliens for administrative and other purposes.

In the early twentieth century, under the aegis of plenary power, the federal government further increased its powers over immigrants. Grounds of exclusion and deportation multiplied. Deportation exploded as a means of punishing and oppressing immigrants. State alienage laws barring access to jobs and professions, public entitlements, and landownership expanded. Moreover, with the institution of numerical quotas in the 1920s, a population of even more vulnerable undocumented immigrants – those present in the country in violation of law – began to grow. This strengthening of the federal immigration and citizenship regime did not mean, however, that America's entrenched patterns of rendering its own foreign disappeared. In addition to established patterns of rendering the poor, blacks, and Native Americans foreign, the state indiscriminately mingled citizens with aliens in the case of Asians and Latinos and began an unprecedented use of involuntary expatriation that converted citizens into aliens against their will. After 1907, American women married to non-American men suddenly found themselves aliens in their own country regardless of whether they had actually intended to give up their American citizenship. The passage of the Nineteenth Amendment in 1920 did a great deal to extinguish the view that women were derivative citizens. The expatriation of women married to aliens was partially reversed in 1922.

After World War II, a momentous rights revolution in the areas of race, gender, welfare, criminal procedure, free speech, and so on transformed the United States. Formal discrimination on grounds of race and gender eroded. A "right to travel," declared to be an incident of national citizenship, ended centuries-old barriers to the movement and residence of America's poor. In a process beginning in the 1950s, the

U.S. Supreme Court curtailed Congress's power to strip Americans of their citizenship against their will. Millions of Americans' experience of being rendered foreign in their own country began to ebb.

Even as the rights revolution was transforming the lives of Americans, however, the federal government's plenary power over immigrants was affirmed. As a result, the gulf between citizen and alien grew wider than it had been at any previous time. In a range of areas, from free speech to gender discrimination to denial of procedural protections, the U.S. Supreme Court upheld the federal government's actions vis-à-vis immigrants where it would almost certainly have struck them down had they been undertaken vis-à-vis citizens.

To be sure, under the impact of the rights revolution, racial barriers to immigration and naturalization ended by the mid-1960s. But this undoubtedly salutary change went along with a massive explosion in the number of exploitable undocumented immigrants, whose presence in the United States was enabled by a combination of immigration quotas, public and private complicity, and the country's desire for cheap, exploitable labor. In the closing decades of the twentieth century, undocumented immigrants were among the country's most vulnerable populations. Living with the constant threat of apprehension and removal, they were unable to resist exploitation in the home, workplace, and community; unable to avail of many basic social services; and driven into the shadows.

As the promise of the rights revolution faded by 1980, however, the gap between citizen and alien, insider and outsider opened up by the rights revolution began to narrow. Both Americans and immigrants would suffer, albeit in different ways, from the country's late-twentieth-century drive to punish drug offenses. Even as the federal government stepped up its drive to deport immigrants with criminal backgrounds, large numbers of black men experienced imprisonment and disfranchisement, leading some to label the phenomenon the "new Jim Crow." Furthermore, it has proved impossible to separate out immigrants from citizens in the current deportation mania. In the early twenty-first century, scholars estimate, thousands of American citizens, caught in the dragnet of a powerful immigration enforcement machine, have been erroneously removed from the United States.

Notwithstanding the post-1980 ebbing of the promise of the rights revolution and the concomitant explosion of attempts to take away from Americans their hard-won rights, it is still the case today that aliens are more or less exclusively those from foreign countries who might be excluded and removed from national territory and legally subjected to many kinds of discrimination. Citizens are the entire native-born population, who by and large enjoy a panoply of many formal rights, including rights to political participation and movement and residence throughout national territory. If the gulf between aliens and citizens, foreign-born and native-born, outsider and insider was once not terribly wide, this book argues, it has grown wider over time. To recognize this historical trajectory is not to deny that it has been messy.

The object of tracing this historical trajectory has been to reveal the manipulability of the border between "citizen" and "alien," the relationship between subordination and foreignness, and the contingent emergence of a powerful national immigration order that now wields considerable authority over aliens. This historicization should spur rethinking. As we look over the long span of American history, we see the multiple uses to which the category of "alien" has been put, not as simple reflections of the "fact" that an individual is from elsewhere, but rather as active strategies of management, control, and subordination. Given the fact that those once aliens are now citizens, that "we" were once "them," might "we" identify differently with "them"? How might this lead us to rethink our responsibility to the immigrants in our midst and at our borders?

Engaging in such a rethinking does not imply a descent into chaos, or what some would see as a catastrophic doomsday scenario of open borders and tides of impoverished immigrants. It does, however, imply a recognition that the current situation might be undesirable and worth reimagining. As the legal scholar Daniel Kanstroom brilliantly puts it in the context of a discussion of undocumented immigration: "The basic legitimacy of the nation-state and its borders does not demand absolute, disproportionate or arbitrary power. The assertion that [an alien] has broken a law is the *beginning* of a conversation, not the end of one."[1] As I shall suggest in the coda, that conversation is beginning afresh – when had it ever stopped? – even as it reveals the bitter and ironic legacies of America's history.

---

[1] Kanstroom, *Aftermath*, p. 10 (emphasis in original; citations omitted).

## Coda: Immigration and Citizenship Law in the Early Twenty-First Century (as of November 2014)

In the first decade and a half of the twenty-first century, even as immigration and citizenship matters have rarely been off the front pages of newspapers, a number of concrete developments merit discussion. Possibly the most important is the exponential rise in the number of deportations since 1996 discussed in the preceding chapter. Many of those deported might legitimately be considered the country's own. As has been argued in this book, excluding and expelling one's own is hardly a new phenomenon. Indeed, it has been an integral part of the way communities have defined themselves – whether at the local, state, or national level – over the long span of American history.

There are also other phenomena in the field of immigration and citizenship law in which a distant past might be reappearing. Among the more interesting is a kind of "return to the local" when it comes to immigration restriction. Since 2000, there has been an upsurge in federal-state partnership in the area of immigration enforcement. But the return to the local in the realm of immigration law has gone well beyond federal-state partnership. States and cities swept up in anti-immigration fervor have enacted their own immigration laws. From 2006 to 2010, state legislators passed hundreds of laws relating to immigration issues. The focus of these laws tended to be on undocumented immigrants. States such as Alabama, Arizona, Georgia, Indiana, South Carolina, and Utah criminalized aliens' failure to carry appropriate immigration documents and attempts to secure unauthorized employment. State law enforcement officials were empowered to detain individuals they suspected of being present in the United States in violation of law. In some cases, state penalties went well beyond those that federal law might impose. Under the impact of such laws, commercial farmers in the states involved reported, Mexican laborers fled. Immigrant groups argued that such practices inevitably resulted in the racial profiling of Latinos.

Significantly, not all local authorities adopted harsh positions vis-à-vis immigrants. By 2005, millions of *matrículas consulares* issued by Mexican consulates to Mexican nationals in the United States were being accepted by local governments and police agencies.

Dozens of cities – from Los Angeles to Washington, DC, from Houston to Minneapolis – passed "sanctuary" laws proclaiming their non-cooperation with federal immigration authorities except in cases involving felony crimes.

In 2010, the United States brought suit to enjoin Arizona's undocumented alien law (known as S.B. 1070) on the ground that Arizona was encroaching upon the exclusive federal authority over immigration. In *Arizona v. United States*, a 5–3 decision issued in June 2012, the U.S. Supreme Court struck down those provisions of S.B. 1070 that criminalized aliens' failure to carry immigration documents and attempts to seek unauthorized employment. Arizona law enforcement officials could not detain those they suspected of deportable offenses. They could, however, seek to determine the immigration status of those they detained on other legitimate grounds.

In the immigrant rights advocacy community and in the press, *Arizona v. United States* was largely hailed as a triumph. I propose, however, to dwell briefly on Justice Scalia's blistering dissent in the case. Justice Scalia observed that "Arizona is *entitled* to have 'its own immigration policy' – including a more rigorous enforcement policy – so long as that does not conflict with federal law."[2] In support of his position, Justice Scalia returned, as he has so often done, to the Republic's founding. At the time of the founding, Justice Scalia observed, the federal government was given a naturalization power, but not an immigration power. Justice Scalia summarized the history thus: "[I]n the first 100 years of the Republic, the States enacted numerous laws restricting the immigration of certain classes of aliens, including convicted criminals, indigents, persons with contagious diseases, and (in Southern States) freed blacks."[3]

As this book makes clear, there is no question that Justice Scalia was correct as a matter of history. The U.S. Constitution provides no firm basis for a federal immigration power. Furthermore, for the first century or so of the country's history, the states *were* in control of regulating access to "their" territories and excluded criminals, indigents, persons with contagious diseases, and free blacks. What Justice

---

[2] *Arizona v. United States*, 132 S.Ct. 2492, 2516–17 (2012) (Scalia, J., concurring in part and dissenting in part) (emphasis in original).
[3] Id. at 2512.

Scalia left out, however, was that the United States before the Civil
War was a decentralized country with foreign-born *and* native-born
aliens, and in which formal membership in the polity carried few
of the rights we now casually associate with citizenship, including
the right to travel and reside throughout the country (which also
lacks a firm grounding in the constitutional text). State immigration
laws were directed against aliens *and* citizens, the native-born and
the foreign-born. If Arizona is to have "its own immigration policy,"
as Justice Scalia put it, we need to think far more seriously about
what that might entail. A politically conservative fantasy of federalism might reveal itself to be rather unappetizing when translated into
actual practice.

In the spring of 2014, the president of the National Council of La
Raza, Janet Murguía, labeled President Barack Obama the "deportation president" or the "deporter-in-chief" to draw attention to the
record number of deportations since President Obama took office and
to demand that the administration halt deportations. At stake was
nothing short of Latino voters' support for the president.[4] Murguía
was not wrong. After President Obama took office, the United States
expelled from its shores millions of non-citizens, documented and
undocumented, long-term residents, and short-term visitors.

The irony is that, ever since he took office, the "deportation president" has himself been assailed by allegations that he is a foreigner.
Article II of the U.S. Constitution requires, inter alia, that the president of the United States be a "natural born citizen."[5] So-called
birthers have insisted that President Obama does not qualify for his
post on the grounds that his published birth certificate is a forgery;
that he was born in Kenya; or that he lost his American citizenship
and acquired Indonesian citizenship. In response to such accusa-
tions, President Obama has made public his official birth certificate. Evidence has accomplished little. According to polls in 2010,
fully 25 percent of American adults remained skeptical of President
Obama's birth on U.S. soil. In May 2011, a Gallup poll reported that
more than 10 percent of American adults (and more than 20 percent

---

4 President Janet Murguía, interview by Melissa Block and Audie Cornish, *All Things
  Considered*, National Public Radio, March 5, 2014.
5 U.S. Const., art. II, § 1.

of Republicans) continued to adhere to this view.[6] What has attached itself to President Obama, one might speculate, is the reverberation of the United States' long history of rendering blacks foreigners in their own country.

Meanwhile, a new, vibrant, highly visible social movement – that of the so-called DREAMers – has transformed the immigration debate in the United States. Taking their name from the since failed Development, Relief and Education for Alien Minors (DREAM) Act, DREAMers have erupted into the public sphere in what is an unprecedented and powerful claim by the undocumented on the polity. The movement began as a movement of undocumented youth brought to the United States by their parents as children. Such youth could ground their claims in the fact that they were blameless in entering the United States in violation of law. In June 2012, in response to their successful mobilization, the Obama administration approved Deferred Action for Childhood Arrivals, in which the government agreed not to proceed against undocumented immigrants who arrived here as children and who also met other conditions. The DREAMer movement has since expanded to encompass the claims of undocumented immigrants more generally – that is, not just those who were "blameless" because they were brought here as minors.

It is not illegitimate to see the DREAMers as having provided a critical push to President Obama's November 20, 2014, announcement of executive action on immigration. In announcing a plan that could grant millions of undocumented immigrants the opportunity to regularize their status, the president specifically mentioned a young woman, Astrid Silva, who was brought to the United States illegally as a four-year-old, went to school as a result of the ruling in *Plyler v. Doe*, discovered that she could not return to Mexico for her grandmother's funeral without risk of being discovered and deported, and then came out of the shadows and began to advocate for change. The trajectory of President Obama's legalization plan is as yet unclear. One can also disagree about whether the president has overstepped the legitimate bounds of executive discretion. In his urging Americans to support his

---

[6] Gallup, Inc., "Obama's Birth Certificate Convinces Some, but Not All, Skeptics," May 13, 2011, accessed September 24, 2014, http://www.gallup.com/poll/147530/obama-birth-certificate-convinces-not-skeptics.aspx.

plan, however, comes a line that fits the argument of this book: "[W]e were strangers once, too."[7] Strangers, as I have tried to argue, can be made at home and at the border. The DREAMer movement is only the country's latest attempt to alter received meanings of "citizen" and "alien," insider and outsider. We might see it as the latest of a long series of struggles by those rendered foreign that have made America what it is.

---

[7] Barack Obama, "Remarks by the President in Address to the Nation on Immigration" (speech, Washington, DC, November 20, 2014), The White House, http://www.whitehouse .gov/the-press-office/2014/11/20/remarks-president-address-nation-immigration.

# Bibliographic Essay

## Introduction

This book covers four centuries of American immigration and citizenship law, from the early seventeenth century to the beginning of the twenty-first. Furthermore, in reorienting our understanding of immigration and citizenship law toward a more fluid understanding that juxtaposes the acceptance, rejection, and regulation of outsiders alongside processes of rendering insiders foreign, the book joins the histories of immigrants with those of Native Americans, blacks, Latino Americans, Asian Americans, women, and the poor. It also ranges across multiple disciplines: mainly history, law, and political science, but also anthropology and sociology.

Not surprisingly, then, the literature that informs this book is vast. In this bibliographic essay, therefore, no attempt has been made to canvass in their entirety the multiple historiographies and disciplines I drew upon. Instead, the essay serves a rather different purpose. I would like to set it forth briefly.

This book draws from and builds upon the work of a large number of scholars. It would simply not exist without the facts these scholars have uncovered and the interpretations they have advanced. The style and length constraints of this book, however, made it impossible for me to acknowledge within the text itself scholarly work upon which I relied heavily. Urged to keep footnotes to a bare minimum, I eliminated a great many footnotes from earlier drafts of the manuscript. For the final version, I adopted a rule-of-thumb according to which I used footnotes only for cases, direct quotations, and (in very few cases) arguments identified with particular scholars that I needed for purposes of my own argument. This bibliographic essay stands in lieu of the many footnotes I would have liked to include in the text but which I felt compelled to omit. It should be read as a charter of my many debts to other scholars. Where possible, I indicate in the essay those portions of the book where a particular scholar's work was especially influential.

## Sources

There is a rich literature on the history of American citizenship. For me, the indispensable starting point is still James H. Kettner's *The Development of American Citizenship, 1608–1870* (Chapel Hill: University of North Carolina Press, 1978). In my view, Kettner's elegant monograph remains the authoritative history of theories and laws of political membership from the colonial period until the Civil War. Chapters 2, 3, and 4 rely heavily on Kettner when it comes to discussions of theories of citizenship and subjecthood. Rogers M. Smith's *Civic Ideals: Conflicting Visions of Citizenship in American History* (New Haven, CT: Yale University Press, 1997) traces the history of citizenship from the colonial period to the beginning of the twentieth century, reading the unfolding of citizenship as a contest between the United States' liberal commitments and its ascriptive ones. I relied on Smith's book at various points throughout the text. Douglas Bradburn's *The Citizenship Revolution: Politics and the Creation of the American Union, 1774–1804* (Charlottesville: University of Virginia Press, 2009) emphasizes the significance of citizenship as a foundational category in the post-revolutionary and early Republican periods. William J. Novak's brilliant essay, "The Legal Transformation of Citizenship in Nineteenth-Century America," in Meg Jacobs, William J. Novak, and Julian Zelizer, eds., *The Democratic Experiment: New Directions in American Political History* (Princeton, NJ: Princeton University Press, 2003), pp. 85–119, shares the orientation of this book insofar as it emphasizes the importance of legal categories other than citizenship in shaping Americans' lives before the Civil War. Barbara Young Welke's compelling *Law and the Borders of Belonging in the Long Nineteenth Century United States* (New York: Cambridge University Press, 2010) explores the complex relationship between legal personhood and formal citizenship, emphasizing how the former is a necessary concomitant to the realization of the latter. Furthermore, in showing how the privilege of able white men was intertwined with the subject status of women, racial minorities, and the disabled, it follows a track parallel to my own.

There are many excellent works devoted to specific dimensions of citizenship. Alexander Keyssar's comprehensive *The Right to Vote: The Contested History of Democracy in the United States* (New York: Basic Books, 2000) remains the key work on questions of suffrage. The discussions of suffrage in every single chapter of this book draw upon Keyssar. On welfare, race, and citizenship (especially in Chapter 6), I relied upon Cybelle Fox, *Three Worlds of Relief: Race, Immigration and the American State from the Progressive Era to the New Deal* (Princeton, NJ: Princeton University Press, 2012). On women, welfare, and citizenship, I consulted Linda Gordon, *Pitied But Not Entitled: Single Mothers and the History of Welfare* (New York: Free Press, 1994), and Alice Kessler-Harris, *In Pursuit of Equity: Women, Men, and the Quest for Economic Citizenship in 20th Century America* (New York: Oxford University Press, 2001).

Scholars of citizenship do not always pay attention to rights of residence and mobility and their relationship to citizenship. As a result, much of the literature on rights of residence and mobility does not see itself as being "about" citizenship. Christopher L. Tomlins's essay "Law, Population, Labor," in Christopher L. Tomlins and Michael Grossberg, eds., *The Cambridge History of Law in America* (hereinafter *CHLA*), vol. 1 (New York: Cambridge University Press, 2008), pp. 211–252, outlines the various legal disabilities on movement and residence suffered by English subjects in the early modern period. Tomlins builds on the subject at much greater length in *Freedom Bound: Law, Labor, and Civic Identity in Colonizing English America* (New York: Cambridge University Press, 2010). Marilyn C. Baseler, *"Asylum for Mankind": America, 1607–1800* (Ithaca, NY: Cornell University Press, 1998), also contains valuable information on limitations on English subjects' rights to movement. Tomlins's and Baseler's work informs the discussions on residence and mobility rights in Chapters 2 and 3.

On the eighteenth-century New England poor laws, see Douglas Lamar Jones, *Village and Seaport: Migration and Society in Eighteenth Century Massachusetts* (Hanover, NH: University Press of New England, 1981); Ruth Wallis Herndon, *Unwelcome Americans: Living on the Margin in Early New England* (Philadelphia: University of Pennsylvania Press, 2001); and Cornelia H. Dayton and Sharon V. Salinger, *Robert Love's Warnings: Searching for Strangers in Colonial Boston* (Philadelphia: University of Pennsylvania Press, 2014). Herndon's work was especially helpful for Chapter 2. On the phenomenon of town-splitting in eighteenth-century Massachusetts, see Kunal M. Parker, "Thinking Space, Thinking Community: Lessons from Early American 'Immigration' History," in Marc S. Rodriguez, ed., *Repositioning North American History: New Directions in Continental Migration, Citizenship, and Community* (Rochester, NY: University of Rochester Press, 2004), pp. 284–301. Kunal M. Parker, "State, Citizenship, and Territory: The Legal Construction of Immigration in Antebellum Massachusetts," *Law and History Review* 19 (2001): 583–643, canvasses Massachusetts poor laws from the eighteenth century through the Civil War. However, far more comprehensive studies are needed for the nineteenth century.

My major sources for the late-nineteenth- and early-twentieth-century poor laws were the Progressive Era critiques thereof, a good representative of which is Edith Abbott, *Public Assistance* (Chicago: University of Chicago Press, 1940). For the twentieth century, the major work on the right to travel will be, when it is published as a monograph, Elisa Alvarez Minoff, "Free to Move? The Law and Politics of Internal Migration in Twentieth Century America" (PhD diss., Harvard University, 2013). Margot Canaday's *The Straight State: Sexuality and Citizenship in Twentieth Century America* (Princeton, NJ: Princeton University Press, 2009) was also useful on the regulation of mobility in early-twentieth-century America. I relied upon Minoff in Chapters 6 and 7.

When it comes to the way citizenship has functioned "negatively" vis-à-vis resident aliens, it is fair to conclude that much more work is needed. The authoritative account of the racial prerequisites to naturalization, and one I drew upon in Chapter 6, remains Ian Haney López, *White by Law: The Legal Construction of Race* (New York: New York University Press, 1996). We lack a solid history of alien legal disabilities over the long span of American history. In *The Development of American Citizenship*, Kettner discusses alien legal disabilities in the colonial period and early Republic. So does Baseler, *"Asylum for Mankind."* I relied upon Kettner and Baseler in Chapters 2 and 3. A summary of alien property disabilities in the nineteenth century that I found useful for Chapters 3, 4, and 5 is Polly J. Price, "Alien Land Restrictions in the American Common Law: Exploring the Relative Autonomy Paradigm," *American Journal of Legal History* 43 (1999): 152–208. For excellent overviews that I also relied on in Chapters 3, 4, and 5, see Allison Brownell Tirres, "Property Law as Immigration Law: The Creation of Non-Citizen Property Rights," *Michigan Journal of Race and Law* 19 (2013): 1–59 and "Property Outliers: Non-Citizens, Property Rights and State Power," *Georgetown Immigration Law Journal* 27 (2012): 77–134. Keyssar, *The Right to Vote,* discusses the granting and taking away of alien voting rights over the long span. Linda Bosniak's *The Citizen and the Alien: Dilemmas of Contemporary Membership* (Princeton, NJ: Princeton University Press, 2008) is a theoretical work that makes alien legal disabilities within the polity central to its problematic.

In recent years, scholars have paid increasing attention to the law of expatriation and denaturalization. I-Mien Tsang's *The Question of Expatriation in America Prior to 1907* (Baltimore: Johns Hopkins Press, 1942) is an early work for the revolutionary period and nineteenth century. Peter J. Spiro's excellent essay *"Afroyim:* Vaunting Citizenship, Presaging Transnationality," in David A. Martin and Peter H. Schuck, eds., *Immigration Stories* (New York: Foundation Press, 2005), pp. 147–68, was especially influential in guiding my thinking about the evolution of expatriation law in Chapter 7. The most recent monograph, Patrick Weil's *The Sovereign Citizen: Denaturalization and the Origins of the American Republic* (Philadelphia: University of Pennsylvania Press, 2012), was valuable for my discussions of the law of expatriation and denaturalization in Chapters 6 and 7.

On immigration law, I had the benefit of a number of important historical overviews. Aristide R. Zolberg's impressive and detailed *A Nation by Design: Immigration Policy in the Fashioning of America* (New York: Russell Sage Foundation, 2006) covers a historical span comparable to that of this book. While Zolberg's interpretation and emphasis differ from my own, his book is an indispensable comprehensive work. I had recourse to it for every chapter and relied especially on its excellent discussions of legislative history and its wealth of statistical information. Legal scholar Daniel Kanstroom's wonderful *Deportation Nation: Outsiders in American History* (Cambridge, MA: Harvard University Press, 2007) shares much more closely the orientation of my book and offers a masterful account of the law of deportation. I rely on Kanstroom at various points, but especially in Chapters 6 and 7. Roger Daniels, *Guarding the Golden Door: American Immigration Policy and Immigrants Since 1882* (New York: Hill & Wang, 2004) and *Coming to America: A History of Immigration and Ethnicity in American Life* (New York: Harper Collins, 1990), supplied much valuable information on late-nineteenth- and twentieth-century immigration, especially (but not only) when it came to statistics. Aziz Rana's *The Two Faces of American Freedom* (Cambridge, MA: Harvard University Press, 2010) represents the United States as a "settler society" and details various policies of absorption and rejection.

Other important overviews are Marion T. Bennett, *American Immigration Policies: A History* (Washington, DC: Public Affairs Press, 1963); Michael C. LeMay, *From Open Door to Dutch Door: An Analysis of U.S. Immigration Policy Since 1820* (New York: Praeger, 1987); Desmond King, *Making Americans: Immigration, Race, and the Origins of the Diverse Democracy* (Cambridge, MA: Harvard University Press, 2000); and Daniel J. Tichenor, *Dividing Lines: The Politics of Immigration Control in America* (Princeton, NJ: Princeton University Press, 2002). An invaluable guide to immigration legislation is E. P. Hutchinson, *Legislative History of American Immigration Policy, 1798–1965* (Philadelphia: University of Pennsylvania Press, 1981).

Many valuable histories of immigration focus on more discrete periods. For the eighteenth and early nineteenth centuries, I relied on Kettner's *Development of American Citizenship* and Baseler's *"Asylum for Mankind"* for discussions of British policies regarding the settlement of displaced European Protestants, paupers, and convicts in North America. An indispensable discussion of the Alien and Sedition Acts, from which my own derives, is James Morton Smith, *Freedom's Fetters: The Alien and Sedition Acts and American Civil Liberties* (Ithaca, NY: Cornell University Press, 1956). Also valuable were A. Roger Ekirch, *Bound for America: The Transportation of British Convicts to the Colonies, 1718–1775* (New York: Oxford University Press, 1987); Aaron S. Fogleman, "From Slaves, Convicts, and Servants to Free Passengers: The Transformation of Immigration in the Era of the American Revolution," *Journal of American History* 85 (1998): 43–76; Aaron S. Fogleman, *Hopeful Journeys: German Immigration, Settlement, and Political Culture in Colonial America, 1717–1775* (Philadelphia: University of Pennsylvania Press, 1996); Alison Games, *Migration and the Origins of the English Atlantic World* (Cambridge, MA: Harvard University Press, 1999); and Marianne S. Wokeck, *Trade in Strangers: The Beginnings of Mass Migration to North America* (University Park: Pennsylvania State University Press, 1999).

For antebellum immigration (Chapter 4), the literature I relied upon consists of a few important articles. Historians had long been aware of state-level immigration regimes in the antebellum period. Benjamin J. Klebaner, "State and Local Immigration Regulation in the United States Before 1882," *International Review of Social History* 3 (1958): 269–81. However, Gerald Neuman's important and thoroughly researched article, "The Lost Century of American Immigration Law," was the first in more recent years to draw legal scholars' attention to the plethora of regimes of territorial restriction – internal and external – that flourished in antebellum America. See Gerald L. Neuman, "The Lost Century of American Immigration Law, 1776–1875," *Columbia Law*

*Review* 93 (1993): 1833–1901; and *Strangers to the Constitution: Immigrants, Borders, and Fundamental Law* (Princeton, NJ: Princeton University Press, 1996). Mary Sarah Bilder, "The Struggle over Immigration: Indentured Servants, Slaves and Articles of Commerce," *Missouri Law Review* 61 (1996): 743–824, examines antebellum Commerce Clause jurisprudence and provides a thorough account of the connections between slavery and the trade in indentured persons. Building upon Neuman and Bilder, Parker, in "State, Citizenship, and Territory," focuses upon the experience of Massachusetts, tracing the shift from a local to a state-level immigration regime between 1780 and 1860. Hidetaka Hirota's work on antebellum immigration restriction is the most recent in the area. See Hidetaka Hirota, "Nativism, Citizenship, and the Deportation of Paupers in Massachusetts, 1837–1883" (PhD diss., Boston College, 2012); "The Great Entrepot for Mendicants: Foreign Poverty and Immigration Control in New York State to 1882," *Journal of American Ethnic History* 33 (2014): 5–22; and "The Moment of Transition: State Officials, the Federal Government, and the Formation of American Immigration Policy," 99 (2012): 1092–1108. While I relied upon all of Hirota's writings, I ought to mention that I drew statistics about Massachusetts pauper removals in Chapters 4 and 5 from Hirota's dissertation.

For the antebellum period, there is also a large literature on nativism. Classic works I consulted are Ray Allen Billington, *The Protestant Crusade, 1800–1860: A Study of the Origins of American Nativism* (New York: Rinehart & Co., 1938), and Kerby A. Miller, *Emigrants and Exiles: Ireland and the Irish Exodus to North America* (New York: Oxford University Press, 1985). There is also a substantial literature on the nativist Know-Nothing Party. Good introductions are John R. Mulkern, *The Know-Nothing Party in Massachusetts: The Rise and Fall of a People's Movement* (Boston: Northeastern University Press, 1990), and Tyler G. Anbinder, *Nativism and Slavery: The Northern Know Nothings and the Politics of the 1850s* (New York: Oxford University Press, 1992).

Most of the work on the legal history of immigration has focused on the activities of the post-1870 federal immigration regime. On the constitutional law of immigration and citizenship after 1870 (Chapters 5–7), including discussions of plenary power and alienage law, I found especially valuable T. Alexander Aleinikoff, *Semblances of Sovereignty: The Constitution, the State, and American Citizenship* (Cambridge, MA: Harvard University Press, 2002); Bosniak, *The Citizen and the Alien*; Hiroshi Motomura, "The Curious Evolution of Immigration Law: Procedural Surrogates for Substantive Constitutional Rights," *Columbia Law* Review 92 (1992): 1625–1704; Neuman, *Strangers to the Constitution*; Daniel Kanstroom, *Deportation Nation* and *Aftermath: Deportation Law and the New American Diaspora* (New York: Oxford University Press, 2012); and Peter H. Schuck, *Citizens, Strangers, and In-Betweens: Essays on Immigration and Citizenship* (Boulder, CO: Westview Press, 1998). I advance my own interpretation in Kunal M. Parker, *The Constitution, Immigration, and Citizenship in American History, 1790–2000* (Washington, DC: American Historical

Association, 2013). I also turned to Martin and Schuck, eds., *Immigration Stories*, for the "back stories" of some of the major U.S. Supreme Court cases on immigration and citizenship of the post-1870 period. In addition to the essay of Peter Spiro, mentioned earlier, I relied on the excellent essays of Lucy Salyer and Burt Neuborne for my discussions of the *Wong Kim Ark* and *Harisiades* cases, respectively.

There are also excellent thematically demarcated histories for the post-1870 period. Lucy E. Salyer's *Laws Harsh as Tigers: Chinese Immigrants and the Shaping of Modern Immigration Law* (Chapel Hill: University of North Carolina Press, 1995) is an important pioneering monograph that traces how the efforts of late-nineteenth-century Chinese immigrants to use the judicial system provided the impetus for concentrating power in the hands of immigration officials and curtailing judicial review; I relied upon Salyer's book in Chapters 5 and 6. Mae M. Ngai's monumental and deeply researched *Impossible Subjects: Illegal Aliens and the Making of Modern America* (Princeton, NJ: Princeton University Press, 2004) is the leading monograph on immigration history for the twentieth century. In Chapters 6 and 7, I turned to Ngai's work for multiple issues: the intertwining of race and nationality in the passage of the quota legislation of the 1920s; the emergence of the figure of the "illegal alien"; Japanese internment; Philippine decolonization; the *bracero* program; and the 1965 legislation. Kanstroom's *Deportation Nation* and *Aftermath* are excellent on the law of deportation. Two recent studies I consulted for valuable statistics and information that inform Chapters 6 and 7 are Dorothee Schneider, *Crossing Borders: Migration and Citizenship in the Twentieth Century United States* (Cambridge, MA: Harvard University Press, 2011), and Deirdre M. Moloney, *National Insecurities: Immigrants and U.S. Deportation Policy Since 1882* (Chapel Hill: University of North Carolina Press, 2012).

On the suppression of dissent in the twentieth century, I found useful William Preston, Jr., *Aliens and Dissenters: Federal Suppression of Radicals, 1903–1933* (Cambridge, MA: Harvard University Press, 1963). On Americanization movements, see Christopher Capozzola, *Uncle Sam Wants You: World War I and the Making of the Modern American Citizen* (New York: Oxford University Press, 2008); Edward George Hartmann, *The Movement to Americanize the Immigrant* (New York: Columbia University Press, 1948); and David M. Kennedy, *Over Here: The First World War and American Society* (New York: Oxford University Press, 1980). In Chapter 6, I relied especially on Hartmann. For the intersection of immigration law with questions of sexuality, see Canaday, *The Straight State*. On the early-twentieth-century medicalization of immigration restriction, see Amy L. Fairchild, *Science at the Borders: Immigrant Medical Inspection and the Shaping of the Modern Industrial Labor Force* (Baltimore: Johns Hopkins University Press, 2003). On immigration and labor history, see Kitty Calavita, *U.S. Immigration Law and the Control of Labor, 1820–1924* (London: Academic Press, 1984); Neil Foley, *The White Scourge: Mexicans, Blacks, and Poor Whites in Texas Cotton Culture* (Berkeley: University of California Press, 1998); Evelyn Nakano Glenn,

*Unequal Freedom: How Race and Gender Shaped American Citizenship and Labor* (Cambridge MA: Harvard University Press, 2002); and Gunther Peck, *Reinventing Free Labor: Padrones and Immigrant Workers in the North American West, 1880–1930* (New York: Cambridge University Press, 2000).

Scholars studying the mid-twentieth century have done impressive work on temporary labor. For my discussion of *bracero* labor in Chapter 7, I found Kitty Calavita, *Inside the State: The Bracero Program, Immigration, and the I.N.S.* (New York: Routledge, 1992) very useful. More recent work is Ngai, *Impossible Subjects* and Deborah Cohen, *Braceros: Migrant Workers and Transnational Subjects in the Postwar United States and Mexico* (Chapel Hill: University of North Carolina Press, 2011). Many of the statistics on *bracero* and undocumented labor in Chapter 7 come from Calavita, Ngai, and Cohen, but especially Calavita. Cindy Hahamovitch's wonderful recent monograph, *No Man's Land: Jamaican Guestworkers in America and the History of Deportable Labor* (Princeton, NJ: Princeton University Press 2011), focuses on temporary Jamaican labor.

For general histories of the post-1965 period (Chapter 7), see Zolberg, *A Nation by Design*; Daniels, *Guarding the Golden Door* and *Coming to America*; David M. Reimers, *Still the Golden Door: The Third World Comes to America* (New York: Columbia University Press, 1985) and *Other Immigrants: The Global Origins of the American People* (New York: New York University Press, 2005). On changes in U.S. immigration law since 1996, I relied especially upon Kanstroom, *Deportation Nation* and *Aftermath*. See also the collection of essays in Monica W. Varsanyi, ed., *Taking Local Control: Immigration Policy Activism in U.S. Cities and States* (Stanford, CA: Stanford University Press, 2010). On the DREAMers, there is already a growing literature. A good introduction is Walter J. Nicholls, *The DREAMers: How the Undocumented Youth Movement Transformed the Immigrant Rights Debate* (Stanford, CA: Stanford University Press, 2013).

There is an enormous, multidisciplinary literature on refugees, asylees, and undocumented immigrants in the post–World War II period far too voluminous to cite here. Zolberg, *Nation by Design*, , is especially good. An introduction to undocumented immigration is Cecilia Menjívar and Daniel Kanstroom, eds., *Constructing "Illegality": Critiques, Experiences, and Resistance* (New York: Cambridge University Press, 2014). *See also* the work of Susan Bibler Coutin, *The Culture of Protest: Religious Activism and the U.S. Sanctuary Movement* (Boulder, CO: Westview Press, 1993); *Legalizing Moves: Salvadoran Immigrants Struggle for U.S. Residency* (Ann Arbor: University of Michigan Press, 2000); *Nations of Emigrants: Shifting Boundaries of Citizenship in El Salvador and the United States* (Ithaca, NY: Cornell University Press, 2007); and María Cristina García, *Seeking Refuge: Central American Migration to Mexico, the United States, and Canada* (Berkeley: University of California Press, 2006).

Closely allied is an established literature on the U.S.-Mexico borderlands. Some of it covers the nineteenth century. See, e.g., David J. Weber, *The Mexican Frontier, 1821–1846* (Albuquerque: University of New Mexico Press, 1982);

and Andrés Reséndez, *Changing National Identities at the Frontier: Texas and New Mexico, 1800–1850* (Cambridge, MA: Harvard University Press, 2005). But much of it focuses on the twentieth century, including the post–World War II period. For Chapters 6 and 7, I consulted Geraldo L. Cadava, *Standing on Common Ground: The Making of a Sunbelt Borderland* (Cambridge, MA: Harvard University Press, 2013); Timothy J. Dunn, *The Militarization of the U.S. Mexico-Border, 1978–1992: Low Intensity Conflict Comes Home* (Austin: University of Texas Press, 1996); Kelly Lytle Hernandez, *Migra! A History of the U.S. Border Patrol* (Berkeley: University of California Press, 2010); Joseph Nevins, *Operation Gatekeeper and Beyond: The War on 'Illegals' and the Remaking of the U.S.-Mexico Boundary* (New York: Routledge, 2010); Rachel St. John, *A Line in the Sand: A History of the Western U.S.-Mexico Border* (Princeton, NJ: Princeton University Press, 2011); and Samuel Truett, *Fugitive Landscapes: The Forgotten History of the U.S.-Mexico Borderlands* (New Haven, CT: Yale University Press, 2006).

The reader should consult the vast literature on American nativism after 1870 inaugurated by John Higham's *Strangers in the Land: Patterns of American Nativism, 1860–1925* (New Brunswick, NJ: Rutgers University Press, 1955). I relied upon Gary Gerstle, *American Crucible: Race and Nation in the Twentieth Century* (Princeton, NJ: Princeton University Press, 2001); Thomas A. Guglielmo, *White on Arrival: Italians, Race, Color, and Power in Chicago, 1890–1945* (New York: Oxford University Press, 2003); Reginald Horsman, *Race and Manifest Destiny: The Origins of American Racial Anglo-Saxonism* (Cambridge, MA: Harvard University Press, 1981); Noel Ignatiev, *How the Irish Became White* (New York: Routledge, 1995); Matthew Frye Jacobson, *Whiteness of a Different Color: European Immigrants and the Alchemy of Race* (Cambridge, MA: Harvard University Press, 1998) and *Barbarian Virtues: The United States Encounters Foreign Peoples at Home and Abroad, 1876–1917* (New York: Hill & Wang, 2000); Ngai, *Impossible Subjects*; David M. Reimers, *Unwelcome Strangers: American Identity and the Turn Against Immigrants* (New York: Columbia University Press, 1998); Alexander Saxton, *The Indispensable Enemy: Labor and the Anti-Chinese Movement in California* (Berkeley: University of California Press, 1971); Barbara Miller Solomon, *Ancestors and Immigrants: A Changing New England Tradition* (Cambridge, MA: Harvard University Press, 1956); and Zolberg, *A Nation by Design*.

A large part of the discussion of the history of citizenship and immigration in this book has to do with the distinct historical experiences of different groups: women, Native Americans, African Americans, Asian Americans, Latino Americans, and the poor. The literature on immigration and citizenship canvassed in this essay also discusses the histories of subordinated groups. In what follows, therefore, I refer only to those books I have not already mentioned.

Women's history has long made questions of formal and substantive citizenship a central preoccupation. Indispensable to me in this regard were Linda K. Kerber's *Women of the Republic: Intellect and Ideology in Revolutionary*

*America* (Chapel Hill: University of North Carolina Press, 1980) and espe-
cially *No Constitutional Right to Be Ladies: Women and the Obligations of
Citizenship* (New York: Hill & Wang, 1998). I relied on Kerber's analyses
throughout the book. Nancy F. Cott's *Public Vows: A History of Marriage and
the Nation* (Cambridge, MA: Harvard University Press, 2002) and Martha
Gardner's *The Qualities of a Citizen: Women, Immigration and Citizenship*
(Princeton, NJ: Princeton University Press, 2005) were both very useful.
Candice Lewis Bredbenner's *A Nationality of Her Own: Women, Marriage,
and the Law of Citizenship* (Berkeley: University of California Press,
1998) offers perhaps the most tightly argued account of the contradictions
posed by the 1907 expatriation law as applied to women; my entire discus-
sion in Chapter 6 derives from Bredbenner's. Leti Volpp's article "Divesting
Citizenship: On Asian American History and the Loss of Citizenship Through
Marriage," *UCLA Law Review* 53 (2005): 405–83 is a valuable account of
how the law of expatriation had particularly harsh consequences for Asian
American women. For a recent discussion of the intersection of race, gen-
der, and nationality, see Kristin A. Collins, "Illegitimate Borders: *Jus Sanguinis*
Citizenship and the Legal Construction of Family, Race, and Nation," *Yale
Law Journal* 123 (2014): 2134–235.
   There is a vast related literature on the law of coverture and marriage. I found
especially useful Kerry Abrams, "The Hidden Dimension of Nineteenth-Century
Immigration Law," *Vanderbilt Law Review* 62 (2009): 1353–1418; Norma
Basch, *In the Eyes of the Law: Women, Marriage, and Property in Nineteenth
Century New York* (Ithaca, NY: Cornell University Press, 1982); Richard
H. Chused, "Married Women's Property Law: 1800–1850," *Georgetown Law
Journal* 71 (1983): 1359–1425; "Late Nineteenth Century Married Women's
Property Law: Reception of the Early Married Women's Property Acts by
Courts and Legislatures," *American Journal of Legal History* 29 (1985): 3–35;
Michael Grossberg, *Governing the Hearth: Law and the Family in Nineteenth
Century America* (Chapel Hill: University of North Carolina Press, 1985);
and Hendrik Hartog, *Man and Wife in America: A History* (Cambridge,
MA: Harvard University Press, 2000). On efforts to exclude women from
the professions, see Ellen Carol DuBois, "Taking the Law into Our Own
Hands: *Bradwell, Minor,* and Suffrage Militance, in the 1870s," in Ellen Carol
DuBois, ed., *Woman Suffrage and Women's Rights* (New York: New York
University Press, 1998), pp. 114–38.
   The literature on African American history is enormous. I could turn to it
only selectively. A useful general history was Ira Berlin, *The Making of African
America: Four Great Migrations* (New York: Viking, 2010). For Chapters 2
and 3, I consulted Sally E. Hadden, *Slave Patrols: Law and Violence in Virginia
and the Carolinas* (Cambridge, MA: Harvard University Press, 2001), and "The
Fragmented Laws of Slavery in the Colonial and Revolutionary Eras," *CHLA*,
vol. 1, pp. 253–87; and Gary B. Nash, *Red, White, and Black: The Peoples of
Early America* (Englewood Cliffs, NJ: Prentice Hall, 1974). For Chapters 3
and 4, I consulted Ira Berlin, *Slaves without Masters: The Free Negro in the
Antebellum South* (New York: New Press, 1974); Leon F. Litwack, *North*

*of Slavery: The Negro in the Free States, 1790–1860* (Chicago: University of Chicago Press, 1961); and P. J. Staudenraus, *The African Colonization Movement, 1816–1865* (New York: Columbia University Press, 1961). Berlin's and Litwack's wonderful books have been extremely influential in guiding my thinking about free blacks in antebellum America. The authoritative text on antebellum racial trials is Ariela J. Gross, *What Blood Won't Tell: A History of Race on Trial in America* (Cambridge, MA: Harvard University Press, 2009). Martha S. Jones, "*Hughes v. Jackson*: Race and Rights Beyond *Dred Scott*," *North Carolina Law Review* 91 (2013): 1757–84, is an excellent and detailed examination of the complexities of black citizenship during the antebellum period. On the career of the American Colonization Society after the Civil War (Chapter 5), I relied on Erwin S. Redkey, *Black Exodus: Black Nationalist and Back-to-Africa Movements, 1890–1910* (New Haven, CT: Yale University Press, 1969). For the late nineteenth and twentieth centuries more generally (Chapters 5 and 6), I consulted Kevin K. Gaines, *Uplifting the Race: Black Leadership, Politics, and Culture in the Twentieth Century* (Chapel Hill: University of North Carolina Press, 1996); James R. Grossman, *Land of Hope: Chicago, Black Southerners, and the Great Migration* (Chicago: University of Chicago Press, 1989); and Leon F. Litwack, *Been in the Storm So Long: The Aftermath of Slavery* (New York: Knopf, 1979) and *Trouble in Mind: Black Southerners in the Age of Jim Crow* (New York: Knopf, 1998). On racially restrictive covenants, I also consulted Michael Jones-Correa, "The Origins and Diffusion of Racial Restrictive Covenants," *Political Science Quarterly* 115 (2000–2001): 541–68. For the civil rights era (Chapter 7), I consulted William H. Chafe, *Civilities and Civil Rights: Greensboro, North Carolina and the Black Struggle for Freedom* (New York: Oxford University Press, 1980); Kevin M. Kruse, *White Flight: Atlanta and the Making of Modern Conservatism* (Princeton, NJ: Princeton University Press, 2005); and Thomas J. Sugrue, *The Origins of the Urban Crisis: Race and Inequality in Postwar Detroit* (Princeton, NJ: Princeton University Press, 1996). Kruse's brilliant and detailed discussion of the desegregation of Atlanta informs my discussion in Chapter 7.

On the dispossession of Native Americans, I consulted Stuart Banner, *How the Indians Lost Their Land: Law and Power on the Frontier* (Cambridge, MA: Belknap Press of Harvard University Press, 2005). For Chapter 2, I relied especially on Yasuhide Kawashima, *Puritan Justice and the Indian: White Man's Law in Massachusetts, 1630–1763* (Middletown, CT: Wesleyan University Press, 1986), and Nash, *Red, White, and Black*. For the revolutionary period and the early Republic (Chapter 3), I relied on Francis Paul Prucha, *American Indian Policy in the Formative Years: The Indian Trade and Intercourse Acts, 1790–1834* (Cambridge, MA: Harvard University Press, 1962). On removal in the Jacksonian era, see Daniel Walker Howe, *What Hath God Wrought: The Transformation of America, 1815–1848* (New York: Oxford University Press, 2007); Ronald N. Satz, *American Indian Policy in the Jacksonian Era* (Lincoln: University of Nebraska Press, 1975); and Tim Allen Garrison, *The Legal Ideology of Removal: The Southern*

*Judiciary and the Sovereignty of Native American Nations* (Athens: University of Georgia Press, 2003). Satz was especially useful to me in Chapter 4. On the era of the Dawes Act and allotment, I read David A. Chang, *The Color of the Land: Race, Nation, and the Politics of Landownership in Oklahoma, 1866–1929* (Chapel Hill: University of North Carolina Press, 2010); Frederick E. Hoxie, *A Final Promise: The Campaign to Assimilate the Indians, 1880–1920* (Lincoln: University of Nebraska Press, 1984); and Janet A. McDowell, *The Dispossession of the American Indian, 1887–1934* (Bloomington: Indiana University Press, 1991). I relied most on Hoxie. Absolutely central to my analysis of "plenary power" as extended to Native Americans in the late nineteenth century was Sarah Cleveland's exhaustive and indispensable article, "Powers Inherent in Sovereignty: Indians, Aliens, Territories, and the Nineteenth-Century Origins of Plenary Power over Foreign Relations," *Texas Law Review* 81(2002): 1–284. For the second half of the twentieth century, see Aleinikoff's treatment of Native American issues in *Semblances of Sovereignty* and Frank Pommersheim, *Broken Landscape: Indians, Indian Tribes, and the Constitution* (New York: Oxford University Press, 2009).

On Mexican Americans, in addition to the literature on immigration and borderlands already discussed, I consulted Rodolfo F. Acuña, *Occupied America: A History of Chicanos* (New York: Harper & Row, 1981) (2d ed.); Francisco E. Balderrama, *Decade of Betrayal: Mexican Repatriation in the 1930s* (Albuquerque: University of New Mexico Press, 1995); David G. Gutiérrez, *Walls and Mirrors: Mexican Americans, Mexican Immigrants, and the Politics of Ethnicity* (Berkeley: University of California Press, 1995); Ian F. Haney-López, *Racism on Trial: The Chicano Fight for Justice* (Cambridge, MA: Harvard University Press, 2003); Arnaldo de León, *They Called Them Greasers: Anglo Attitudes Towards Mexicans in Texas, 1821–1900* (Austin: University of Texas Press, 1983); Laura E. Gómez, *Manifest Destinies: The Making of the Mexican American Race* (New York: New York University Press, 2007); Maria E. Montoya, *Translating Property: The Maxwell Land Grant and the Conflict over Land in the American West, 1840–1900* (Berkeley: University of California Press, 2002); and George G. Sánchez, *Becoming Mexican American: Ethnicity, Culture, and Identity in Chicano Los Angeles, 1900–1945* (New York: Oxford University Press, 1995). On Puerto Rico, see Christina Duffy Burnett and Burke Marshall, eds., *Foreign in a Domestic Sense: Puerto Rico, American Expansion, and the Constitution* (Durham, NC: Duke University Press, 2001), and Samuel Erman, "Meanings of Citizenship in the U.S. Empire: Puerto Rico, Isabel Gonzalez, and the Supreme Court, 1898–1905," *Journal of American Ethnic History* 27 (2008): 5–33.

Historians of Asian Americans have given us highly detailed accounts of the legal experiences of gendered and racialized Asian immigrants in the late nineteenth and early twentieth centuries. In Chapters 5 and 6, in addition to the general literature on immigration and citizenship law cited earlier, I relied on Kerry Abrams, "Polygamy, Prostitution, and the Federalization of Immigration Law," *Columbia Law Review* 105 (2005): 641–716; Sucheng

Chan, *Entry Denied: Exclusion and the Chinese Community, 1882–1943* (Philadelphia: Temple University Press, 1994); Roger Daniels, *The Politics of Prejudice, the Anti-Japanese Movement in California, and the Struggle for Japanese Exclusion* (Berkeley: University of California Press, 1962); *Concentration Camps USA: Japanese Americans and World War II* (New York: Holt, Rinehart & Winston, 1972); *Not Like Us: Immigrants and Minorities in America, 1890–1924* (Chicago: Ivan R. Dee, 1997); and *Debating American Immigration, 1882–Present* (Lanham, MD: Rowman & Littlefield, 2001); Madeline Y. Hsu, *Dreaming of Gold, Dreaming of Home: Transnationalism and Migration Between the United States and South China, 1882–1943* (Stanford, CA: Stanford University Press, 2000); Erika Lee, *At America's Gates: Chinese Americans During the Exclusion Era, 1882–1943* (Chapel Hill: University of North Carolina Press, 2004); Charles J. McClain, *Chinese Immigrants and American Law* (New York: Garland, 1994); *Japanese Immigrants and American Law: The Alien Land Laws and Other Issues* (New York: Garland, 1994); *Asian Indians, Filipinos, Other Asian Communities and the Law* (New York: Garland, 1994); Mae Ngai, *The Lucky Ones: One Family and the Extraordinary Invention of Chinese America* (Boston: Houghton Mifflin Harcourt, 2010); Gary Y. Okihiro, *Margins and Mainstreams: Asians in American History and Culture* (Seattle: University of Washington Press, 1994); Nayan Shah, *Contagious Divides: Epidemics and Race in San Francisco's Chinatown* (Berkeley: University of California Press, 2001); and Ronald Takaki, *Strangers from a Different Shore: A History of Asian Americans* (Boston: Little, Brown, 1989).

# Index

CPSIA information can be obtained
at www.ICGtesting.com
Printed in the USA
LVOW13s0240120118
562823LV00027B/1403/P